SOUNDS FROM THE OTHER SIDE

SOUNDS FROM THE OTHER SIDE

AFRO–SOUTH ASIAN COLLABORATIONS IN BLACK POPULAR MUSIC

Elliott H. Powell

UNIVERSITY OF MINNESOTA PRESS

MINNEAPOLIS • LONDON

This book is freely available in an open access edition thanks to TOME
(Toward an Open Monograph Ecosystem)—a collaboration of the Association of
American Universities, the Association of University Presses, and the Association
of Research Libraries—and the generous support of the College of Liberal Arts
at the University of Minnesota, Twin Cities. Learn more at the TOME website,
available at: openmonographs.org.

The University of Minnesota Press gratefully acknowledges the financial assistance
provided for the publication of this book by the AMS 75 PAYS Endowment of the
American Musicological Society, supported in part by the National Endowment for
the Humanities and the Andrew W. Mellon Foundation.

The publication of this book was supported by an Imagine Fund grant for the
arts, design, and humanities, an annual award from the
University of Minnesota's Provost Office.

Portions of chapter 2 were originally published as "Coalitional Auralities:
Notes on a Soundtrack to Punks, Bulldaggers, and Welfare Queens," *GLQ* 25,
no. 1 (2019): 188–93; copyright 2019 Duke University Press; all rights reserved;
reprinted by permission. Portions of chapter 4 were originally published as "Addict(ive)
Sex: Toward an Intersectional Approach to Truth Hurts' 'Addictive' and Afro–South
Asian Hip Hop and R&B," in *Popular Music and the Politics of Hope: Queer and Feminist
Interventions,* ed. Susan Fast and Craig Jennex (New York: Routledge, 2019), 173–86;
reprinted by permission of Taylor and Francis Group.

Published by the University of Minnesota Press
111 Third Avenue South, Suite 290
Minneapolis, MN 55401-2520
http://www.upress.umn.edu

ISBN 978-1-5179-1003-7 (hc)
ISBN 978-1-5179-1004-4 (pb)
DOI: https://doi.org/10.5749/9781452965963

A Cataloging-in-Publication record for this book is available from the
Library of Congress.

To the power of Black music

Contents

Introduction

The stakes for identifying new comparative models are immensely high.
—Grace K. Hong and Roderick A. Ferguson, *Strange Affinities*

Side One: Introducing the Other Side

Let's start with a story. A couple of years ago, I was on a nighttime flight headed to a conference at which I was scheduled to present, and, like most academics, I had yet to finish my paper—which I was supposed to give the following morning—and was frantically trying to complete it. The passenger seated next to me perhaps failed to pick up on any of the clues that I could not be bothered, and decided to tap me on my shoulder and ask me what I was writing. I quickly informed him that it was a presentation based on a book that I was working on (and which you're now reading). My seatmate then followed with a "So what's the book about?" response. I was frankly frustrated at this point, but since this kind question is common and tied to our professions as academics, I politely told him that it was about African American musicians' interest in and collaborations with South Asian and South Asian American music and artists in the United States. To my dismay, however, the passenger was puzzled by my response and proceeded to further probe: "Hmmm . . . African American musicians . . . like who?" Looking to end the conversation, I promptly listed John Coltrane's well-known embrace of Indian culture and Missy Elliott's Indian-inspired hit song "Get Ur Freak On" as exemplary case studies with which my book is concerned. But, still not satisfied with my response (and clearly not picking up on my growing frustration with the conversation and him), my fellow passenger paused and asked, "But what about Madonna and the Beatles? Weren't they also doing the same thing?" To which I then exasperatedly excused myself, plugged my headphone jack into my laptop, put on my headphones, and tried to imagine that this conversation never occurred.

This story is both real, in the sense that it actually happened, and representative (sans my negative affect), in the sense that it is a recurring experience for me outside of as well as within the academy. Over the past several years that I have been working on and discussing this book, I have encountered some variation of the above conversational exchange. When I talk about my book's focus on Black and South Asian (American) artists and music with colleagues, family members, friends, or just random people (like my seatmate) interested in striking up a conversation, they invariably and inevitably bring up Madonna and/or the Beatles. These references to the Beatles are most likely tied to George Harrison's well-publicized studies of Indian music and spirituality as well as the Beatles' popular participation in the 1960s and 1970s "raga rock" trend; and the allusions to Madonna presumably originate from her storied partnership with English musician William Orbit for her 1998 Indophilic album *Ray of Light*, and Madonna's own set of highly circulated Orientalist visual performances that accompanied and promoted the record.[1] But while Madonna and the Beatles created music that drew from South Asian culture, neither Madonna nor the Beatles are Black or South Asian—the two racialized groups and cultures that sit at the heart of my book. Therefore, these conversational invocations of Madonna and the Beatles, for me, are as misguided as they are misplaced. By bringing up Madonna and the Beatles, these responses to my work move a conversation initially (and centrally) about Black and South Asian artists and sounds to one now about white and South Asian music and musicians—the focus shifts from an exploration of the kinds of relationalities between two marginalized communities in the United States to a centering of the white–nonwhite binary.

Importantly, while such an anecdote is certainly indicative of the place of the Beatles and Madonna, and their South Asian influences, within in the U.S. popular imaginary, it also overlaps with, and by extension speaks to, a similar and dominant outlook within academic literature on this subject. In an effort to contextualize African American musicians' interest in and incorporation of South Asian (American) culture, popular music studies scholarship often places such Afro–South Asian cross-cultural activities within the broader place of South Asian sounds in twentieth- and twenty-first-century Western popular music. Specifically, this scholarship situates U.S.-based Afro–South Asian musical practices within the 1960s and 1970s white counterculture psychedelia of acts like the Beatles and/or the late-capitalist "Indo-chic" trend of the 1990s and early 2000s of artists like Madonna.[2] Yet, much like my recurring and representative conversations about my book, these aims in popular music studies to broaden the field (inadvertently) work to whiten it. They place Black artists in relation to white artists, and they entangle and implicate African Americans with Western appropriative practices. This is a potentially problematic rendering as the West has been (and continues to be) upheld through anti-Blackness. Such scholarship, thus, obfuscates the particularities of cross-cultural musical making practices between racially marginalized musicians, shores up whiteness and the West through the privileging and (re)centering of a white–nonwhite binary, and makes whiteness and white Western modes of engagement the origin of such intercultural musical innovation. And so it's here, at the anecdotal and academic papering over of Afro–South Asian intercultural music making endeavors, that I ask: What happens when we consider Black musicians' South Asian sonic explorations as distinct from those of their white Western counterparts? What happens if and when we consider the other side of things, the music and sounds from the other side?

Sounds from the Other Side: Afro–South Asian Collaborations in Black Popular Music is a possible answer to these questions. It is a reimagining of African American musical collaborative endeavors with South Asian and South Asian American artists and sounds. By collaborative endeavors, I am not solely talking about interactions that manifest within the realm of the interpersonal, but also music making activities that occur between and among sounds themselves. I read the meetings, blendings, and entanglements of sounds in a recording or performance as key cultural sites and encounters that are just as central to the construction and meaning of Afro–South Asian music as are the Black and South Asian (American) subjects who produce them.[3] The intersections of the face-to-face and sound-to-sound within these Black and South Asian collaborations are indicative of what T. Carlis Roberts calls "Afro Asian performance," or the "physical and/or sonic spaces in which blackness and Asianness coincide, through the juxtaposition of musical traditions, visual representations, and the identities of the artists that perform them."[4] Using Carlis's conception of Afro Asian performance to bear on African American and South Asian musical collectivities, I survey Black popular musics like jazz, funk, and hip-hop from the 1960s to the present, and look to Black artists like John Coltrane, Miles

Davis, Rick James, André 3000, Truth Hurts, Missy Elliott, Timbaland, and Beyoncé in order to reveal, trace, and produce a particular narrative about the rich and robust musical histories of African American interest in and engagements with South Asian (American) music and musicians—what we might call an Afro–South Asian genealogy of sound. My use of genealogy here is deliberate and draws on and aligns with Michel Foucault's theorization of the term: as an attempt and as a tactic to "desubjugate historical knowledges, to set them free, or in other words to enable them to oppose and struggle against the coercion of a unitary, formal, and scientific theoretical discourse."[5] The kinds of Afro–South Asian cross-racial musics that I'm interested in, then, are those that are rendered minor, inconsequential, and tangential— those that are situated on and relegated to the other side—under the dominant logics of white–South Asian musical practices. It is thus through an excavation of an Afro–South Asian genealogy of sound that I illustrate how Afro–South Asian performances produce their own knowledge, how they proffer new ways of being and knowing, in Black popular music. Indeed, if, as Stuart Hall argues, Black popular culture, and especially Black popular music, enables "the surfacing . . . of elements of a discourse that is different— other forms of life, other traditions of representation," then what I am concerned with in this book is interrogating what these other forms and traditions look and sound like when they articulate with (to borrow from Hall again) South Asian cultural production.[6] I'm interested in developing lenses that will help scholars grapple with and underscore the alternative epistemologies and possibilities that are expressed, enacted, and imagined through Black and South Asian relationalities through and as sound.

I call such a lens and the alternative epistemological and imaginative space that it explicates "the other side of things." The other side of things is an analytical framework that describes and renders legible the sociopolitical and sociocultural import of Afro–South Asian collaborative performances and recordings in and for Black popular music. The other side of things is less about why certain African American musicians incorporate South Asian music in their work or why they work with South Asian and South Asian American artists. Rather, the other side of things names and interprets this musical work and its broader implications—it helps us to see and hear what these cross-cultural musics do and what they produce. In particular, the other side of things examines what these Afro–South Asian collaborative music making practices mean for Black popular music, Blackness, and the politics of Black social life. It attempts to make sense of and articulate how the work by African American musicians who draw on and embrace South Asian musicians and music foster new and exciting epistemologies of Black life, Black politics, and Black cultural production. In chapter 2 of this book, for example, I explore Miles Davis's 1972 album *On the Corner*, and illustrate how the centrality of South Asian music and musicians on the album expressed Davis's belief that South Asian culture and people were key to new formations of Black music and to Black political struggle and freedom, especially for those living and working on the street corner. In this sense, the other side of things is akin to the long twentieth-century Black "radical imagination" that Robin D. G. Kelley calls "freedom dreams."[7] Notably, Kelley identifies his mother, a Black woman who he explains has made Indian spiritualities a central part of her life (changing her name to Ananda and adopting beliefs of reincarnation), as informing his conception of freedom dreams because "she wanted us to visualize a more expansive, fluid, 'cosmos-politan' definition of blackness, to teach us that we are not merely inheritors of a culture but its makers."[8] The Black artists and Afro–South Asian performances featured in *Sounds from the Other Side* are key social actors and actions of such a remaking and reimagining of Black freedom dreams. They develop, delineate, and desire something different. For these artists and musics, to pursue the other side of things means to create music that hones in on the political importance of Black and South Asian relationalities, and how they might help us imagine and create other possible worlds of and for Black music, politics, and peoples.

Side Two: Queering the Other Side

Several years ago, I attended and presented at a music conference (not the one mentioned in the previous section) that comprised scholars, journalists, and music industry personnel. My presentation centered on Miles Davis's *On the Corner* (the album alluded to above and discussed in further detail in chapter 2). I argued that the album's expression of Black radical politics was not simply inextricable from South Asianness, but that, via the album's artwork and Davis's own personal life, it—the album—and they—South Asianness and Blackness—articulated with Black queer aesthetics and sociality. During the Q&A and following my presentation, I was struck by the number of people who told me that *On the Corner* was one of their favorite Miles

Davis albums, that they had always heard the South Asian aspects of the album, but disclosed (sometimes in a hushed tone) that they had never seen or realized its queer expressions until my talk. Like my first story about the failures of reading U.S.-based Afro–South Asian sonic connections in Black popular music as its own distinct formation and genealogy without associating it with and anchoring it to whiteness, this second story about the failures to read race and sexuality together is both a real and recurring conversation I've had with others (scholars and non-scholars) about this book. But more to the point, and again much like the first story, this second story is indicative of a much larger problematic in certain scholarly fields.

Indeed, and in particular, this problem with thinking about and taking seriously analyses that center the constitutive relationships of race, gender, and sexuality is one that is especially present in Afro-Asian studies, arguably the field with which this book most explicitly resonates. Afro-Asian studies emerged in the early 2000s as a specific iteration of comparative race and ethnic studies, and it sought to detail the long historical bonds between Africa and Asia and their respective diasporas.[9] Central to these emergent and still dominant writings in Afro-Asian studies are two interrelated ideas. First, the constitutive global violences of white supremacy, capitalism, and U.S. and/or Western European imperialism brought African and Asian (diasporic) people and politics in close proximity and relationality. These shared (but still distinct) forms and experiences of oppression produced transnational and cross-racial, anti-imperial, anti-racist, and anti-capitalist solidarity, and thereby created the conditions for Afro-Asian coalitional politics. Consider, for example, the 1955 Bandung Conference that set the stage for Afro-Asian nonalignment during the Cold War, or Lala Lajpat Rai and W. E. B. Du Bois's friendship that entailed a commitment to shared struggle against anti-Black racism in the United States and Indian independence from Britain.[10] Second, Afro-Asian studies scholarship contends that in part due to, but also exceeding and preceding, these shared experiences of capitalist, white supremacist, and imperial oppressions, African and Asian (diasporic) histories and social identities are not bounded and discrete but rather "polycultural." Borrowing from Robin D. G. Kelley's initial coining of the term, Afro-Asian scholars, particularly Vijay Prashad, use polyculturalism to highlight the ways in which the boundaries of African American and Asian American are always already porous and subject to "constant interpenetration."[11] We might consider the African and Indian roots of Rastafarianism and the overlapping African and Asian diasporic aesthetics in hip-hop as historical examples of polyculturalism. The polycultural wing of Afro-Asian studies, thus, illustrates how African and Asian America are not, and should not be, antagonistic and oppositional—as the model minority myth attests— but instead projects and formations of collectivity. And it's here that the two dominant schools of thought in Afro-Asian studies—political solidarity and polyculturalism—demand an understanding of African and Asian (diasporic) comparative racialization as a site of kinship and anti-imperial, anti-capitalist, and anti-racist alliances.

And yet, as scholars like Vanita Reddy, Anantha Sudhakar, and others have compellingly explained, Afro-Asian studies' tendency to focus on empire, capitalism, and racism as critical rubrics informing African and Asian (diasporic) encounters and exchanges renders unmarked (and by extension unremarkable) gender and sexuality as attendant and constitutive categories of analysis.[12] This unmarking naturalizes norms of gender and sexuality, and it ultimately positions hetero-masculinity (e.g., the relationships between Martin Luther King Jr. and Mahatma Gandhi) and heterosexuality (e.g., the marriage and radical politics of James and Grace Lee Boggs) as necessary and central conditions of Afro-Asian solidarity and liberation. Such a privileging of the heteronormative and the heteropatriarchal demands, as Reddy and Sudhakar argue, a "calling for queer and feminist approaches to comparative racialization" that is a "counterdiscourse that challenges not only racism, imperialism, and class disparities, but also heteropatriarchy and sexism."[13]

As we will see throughout this book, the other side of things, as an analytic and imaginative praxis that is invested in alternative formations of comparative racializations, is one such counterdiscourse that attends to the gender and sexual dimensions of Afro-Asian studies. It acts as a mode of critique that contends with how Afro–South Asian collaborative music and sounds are gendered and sexualized affairs. The other side of things, in part, draws on Kimberlé Crenshaw's framework of intersectionality and Mari Matsuda's concept of "asking the other question" to develop a women of color feminist approach to the comparative formations of Afro–South Asian musical performances.[14] Crenshaw uses the juridical inability of the law to recognize racism and sexism as interlocking oppressions of Black women as way to name, via intersectionality, the interlocked ways that people experience and institutions exercise oppression and privilege. Matsuda's idea of asking the other question builds on this work of intersectionality to mine the coalitional stakes of such a structural web of oppression. For Matsuda, asking the other question involves a continual interrogation of seemingly discrete social formations such that their discreteness becomes understood as relational and interdependent: "When I see something that looks racist, I ask, 'Where is the patriarchy in this?' When I see something that looks sexist, I ask, 'Where is the heterosexism in this?' When I see something that looks homophobic, I ask, 'Where are the class interests in this?' Working in coalition forces us to look for both the obvious and non-obvious relationships of domination, helping us to realize that no form of subordination ever stands alone."[15] Following and bridging intersectionality and asking the other question, the other side of things acknowledges the cross-racial alliances and comparative racialization of Afro–South Asian performances while also pursuing what such ethnoracial relationalities tell us about gender and sexuality. For example, in chapter 4, I examine the 2002 hit song "Addictive" by African American female singer Truth Hurts and its sampling of a Bollywood film song sung by Lata Mangeshkar. I look at both songs' dealings with S/M sex to consider what they might teach us about an Afro–South Asian feminist politics of sex that troubles the policing and surveillance of women of color's sexual desires and practices, and that imagines a new and transformative collective women of color experience of pleasure.

And as Grace K. Hong and Roderick A. Ferguson remind us, because "lesbian practice and identity were central to many of the most foundational women of color feminists," women of color feminism directly informs the mode of analysis about and the coalitional oppositional politics against the state regulation of "racialized nonnormative gender and sexual formations" that Ferguson calls queer of color critique.[16] As such, the other side of things, importantly, is a lens that illustrates Afro–South Asian collaborative performances as sites of queer of color formation and possibility. To be clear, and in full disclosure, the majority of the cultural producers in this book identify as cisgender men and/or heterosexual men and women, and so it might seem odd for me to find queerness and queer of color critique to be apt analytics. And yet, by queer here I am not simply talking about queer subjects as defined by sexual identities, pleasures, and desires (though I will be talking about that in this book, too). Rather, I am more interested in following Cathy Cohen's pathbreaking conception of queer as defined by "one's relation to power, and not some homogenized identity . . . [as] those who stand on the outside of the dominant constructed norm of state-sanctioned white middle- and upper-class heterosexuality."[17] Routing and rooting queerness in this way allows for people "who may fit into the category of heterosexual, but whose sexual choices are not perceived as normal, moral, or worthy of state support."[18] Cohen's reading of queer thus advances a much more expansive and broad-base political framework that can facilitate alliances across race, gender, class, and nation—like those Afro–South Asian relationalities that I seek to explicate with the other side of things. Indeed, deploying queerness in the Cohen sense of the term brings into sharp focus a shared (but still distinct) history of Black and South Asian (American) gender and sexual nonnormativity in the United States. From the ungendered enslaved African to the "biologically impossible body" of the Chinese and Indian coolie, from the Moynihan Report pathologizing Black women–led households as perversions of the nuclear family to juridical and media institutions' production of the sodomizing and miscegenating South Asian immigrant bachelor, from the police murders of Michael Brown and Rekia Boyd through which those victims served "as targets of racial normalizing projects intent on pathologizing them" to the post-9/11 production of the Muslim and South Asian "monster–terrorist–fag," racialized gender and sexuality nonnormativity in the United States has created "strange affinities" (to borrow again from Hong and Ferguson) between Black and South Asian (American) peoples and histories.[19]

The other side of things is, thus, an attempt to sound such strange affinities. I continue the work of articulating the braided (yet, again, distinct) histories of South Asian and African American relationalities by situating this cultural history within larger global and domestic sociohistorical junctures that link African American and South Asian diasporic communities in the United States—the feminist, queer, civil rights and Black Power, and Third World social movements of the 1960s and 1970s; Reaganomics and the AIDS crisis of the 1980s; the 1980s and 1990s narratives of the (South) Asian American "model minority" as a "solution" to the African American–monitored minority; and the racial and sexual politics of post-9/11 U.S. culture. In so doing, I illuminate how minoritarian artists' Afro–South Asian performances and recordings are as much about the musical as they are about the extramusical, how they are about music and sound as well as the racial, gendered, and sexualized politics and histories that produce such collaborative music and sound. Simply put, these Afro–South Asian musical crossings are catalytic sites where aesthetics and politics meet. To that end, the other side of things is a three-pronged approach to studying Afro–South Asian music in Black popular music: (1) it is an intellectual intervention, one that demands that we see African American interest and collaborations with South Asian music(ians) as separate from and a disruption to the white-nonwhite binary; (2) it is an insistence on accounting for how such comparative ethnoracial cultural practices inform and shape the contours of Blackness and Black cultural production; and (3) it is a women of color and queer of color hermeneutic of music and sound that contextualizes these Afro–South Asian musical crossings within the strictures and structures of race, gender, sexuality and excavates their racialized queer relationalities. In the end, the other side of things outlines the ways this Afro–South Asian genealogy of sound in Black popular music is a dynamic, complex, and contradictory cultural site where comparative racialization, transformative gender and queer politics, and coalitional politics intertwine.

Side Three: (In)Appropriating the Other Side

While I was in the final stages of completing revisions for this book, a friend texted "they comin for your work lol," and then followed this message with a link to what I would later find out was a viral tweet. At nearly five thousand retweets and eighteen thousand likes at the time of this writing, the tweet was a clip of the music video for Truth Hurts's "Addictive," a song that is the subject of chapter 4 of this book, as mentioned above. The author of the tweet, @tomorrowmanx, captioned it with the message "Listen . . . when all the Black producers started infusing Bollywood samples in everything . . . you wanna talk about a fuggin ERA in hip hop/R&B??"[20] I was excited to see this tweet for two main reasons. One, it let me know that nearly two decades after its release, "Addictive" still resonated with people. Second, the Twitter user's use of the word "fuggin," a euphemism for "fucking," spoke to some of the main impulses of this book and what I'm calling the other side of things. Fuggin/fucking is deployed to emphasize the ubiquity and greatness of Afro–South Asian rap and R&B during this moment. But it also signals the sexual politics, the literal fucking, that I argue informs much of this music—that sex and sexuality articulate with these cross-racial Afro–South Asian musical performances.[21]

I soon noticed that the viral tweet was the first in a longer thread, and decided to scroll through and read it. The user gave a standard narrative of the song, including its sampling background and the controversy surrounding it (this is a narrative that I complicate in chapter 4). And then the user finished the thread by stating, "And just in case it's not spelled out, yes: This would fall under cultural appropriation, and it is indeed problematic. Not cool, but we still love the song," and then used a GIF of actor Steven Yeun shrugging to caption the tweet.[22] Like the first tweet of the thread, I was struck by this closing statement for two reasons. First, similar to the previous two stories in this introduction, the topic of cultural appropriation was increasingly coming up in academic and nonacademic circles when I discussed this book. And second, despite the user claiming that "Addictive" is a clear and problematic product of cultural appropriation, the Yeun shrugging GIF literally and figuratively signals uncertainty about such a claim.

And it's this notion and affective position of uncertainty that I believe best captures the complicated terrain of cultural appropriation with respect to Afro–(South) Asian exchanges. Black popular music and culture has historically and contemporaneously (and rightly) sat at the center of discussions about cultural appropriation, especially when it concerns the interrelated formations of power, property, and whiteness.[23] To be clear, I am not suggesting that Afro-Asian studies has not broached or cannot broach the topic of cultural appropriation. For example, Sunaina Maira famously discussed how South Asian American male youth appropriate hip-hop as a way to consume and mark a Black masculine cool.[24] And Nitasha Sharma has also argued for an "appropriation as identification" versus "appropriation as othering" model that reads Afro-Asian exchanges as either (1) offering social critique on issues like imperialism, militarization, racism, and oppression; or (2) espousing a form of "American nationalism aligned with Western imperial projects," respectively.[25] But as a book about African American–directed engagements with South Asian music and musicians, Maira's work doesn't necessarily resonate. And because Sharma's binary approach to appropriation seemingly relies on a politics of intentionality, it does not fully address the ways in which my conception of the other side of things is more about the how than the why. As Homi Bhabha explains, intentionality is not the best rubric for describing appropriation because "we can never quite control these acts and their signification. They exceed intention."[26]

Thus, a question still remains as to how can we make sense of appropriation when it deals with dually and differentially marginalized communities like African Americans and South Asians and South Asian Americans?

Indeed, as the works of Claire Jean Kim and Helen Jun compellingly explain, African Americans and Asian Americans are positioned in a constantly shifting racial triangulation that unevenly and contingently confers power and privilege along the lines of race, class, and citizenship status.[27] Moreover, because polyculturalism, one of the defining frameworks of Afro-Asian studies, demands a cultural dynamism and relationality, it complicates facile markers of ownership that are central to the ways in which, citing Bhabha again, "appropriation assumes a proprietorial sense: Who owns what? In what sense do I own my history, or you own your art?"[28]

It is for these reasons that I do not find appropriation to be the most adequate, appropriate, and uniform framework to describe and analyze the music making activities that African American musicians in this book take on when incorporating South Asian sound or collaborating with South Asians and South Asian Americans. I don't believe that these are zero-sum engagements. I don't see them as either being totally invested in cultural appropriation or totally devoid of such actions. Instead, I contend that they resemble more of what Deborah Wong sees as the "need to rethink the politics of appropriation in ways that will allow for combustion as well as colonization," and also allow for the potential for Afro-Asian cross-cultural musics to be "pedagogical rather than appropriating, [where] we can see anger, interrogation, coalition, action, revolution, in motion."[29] *Sounds from the Other Side,* then, wades into the entanglements of appropriation. If, as Stuart Hall famously argued, the terrain of popular culture is a battlefield stuck in the double movement between containment and resistance, then this book remains attuned to such shifting terrain, exploring what Black and South Asian musical and sonic collaborations might reveal about the place of power, privilege, and belonging within such musical relationalities.[30]

Side Four: Narrating the Other Side

In order to excavate and narrate this women of color feminist and queer of color Afro–South Asian genealogy of sound that I'm calling the other side of things, I rely on what Jack Halberstam and Gayatri Gopinath have separately referred to as a "scavenger methodology": a queer approach that "uses different methods to collect and produce information on subjects who have been deliberately or accidentally excluded from traditional studies of human behavior."[31] Alternative epistemologies—proffering a new narrative of African American artists' interest in and collaborations with South Asian music(ians)—require attendant methodological reimaginings, those that disrupt the boundedness of traditional disciplinary approach. And to that end, I use personal interviews, archival materials, music analysis, and close readings to make sense of periodicals, recorded interviews, recorded music, and album covers as well as my own interviews with visual artists, sound engineers, producers, managers, and recording executives. Bringing these methodologies together allows this project to highlight the historical and contemporary issues that this research raises. It allows the book to chart a specific arc and genealogy. Further, the multitude of voices and sources used in my book present a textured account of African American musical engagements with South Asian musicians and sound that ultimately demonstrates how producers, studio musicians, and other social actors envision(ed) the musical, cultural, and political significance of South Asian (diasporic) culture and artists within Black popular music. And in so doing, I highlight the complexity and meaning-making practices of the artists and cultural products for and with whom and which there is deep political and personal resonance, affinity, and promise.

The first chapter begins the study of Afro–South Asian collaborative music and sound with one of its most prominent figures: jazz saxophonist John Coltrane. I refer to Coltrane as a leading figure for the ways in which jazz critics have remarked on Coltrane's excursions into South Asian music as innovative, and for how his musical approaches to South Asian sound frame and inform the kinds of cross-cultural engagements that will be explored for the remainder of the book. Coltrane's use of South Asian music held in tension the complex, dynamic, contradictory, and politically transformative meanings and imaginings within this alternative narrative of Afro–South Asian sound that I'm calling the other side of things. Key to grappling with Coltrane's Afro–South Asian political imaginings is to reframe how we typically understand Coltrane's forays into Indian culture and his general political impulse. Indeed, jazz and African American studies scholars frequently analyze Coltrane's interest in Indian culture as depoliticized endeavors, and instead contend that Coltrane developed a Malcolm X– or Martin Luther King–inspired political approach to song with his more explicit Afro-diasporic song choices (e.g., *Africa/Brass*, "Reverend King"). This chapter posits that we cannot disarticulate Coltrane's Indian and Afro-diasporic interests, and the political potential residing in both. As Coltrane began to incorporate Indian culture into his work, jazz critics began to refer to him as the "James Baldwin of horn sound." This chapter takes that nickname seriously to ask what happens when we route Coltrane's persona through the queer spiritual, musical, and transnational politics of James Baldwin? How might this open up ways not only to understand Coltrane's Indian and Afro-diasporic recordings as co-constitutive, but also to gesture toward a music-based vision of queer Black internationalism?

Moving from John Coltrane to one of his former mentors and band leaders, the second chapter examines the Afro–South Asian music of Miles Davis during the 1970s. Unlike Coltrane, Davis's use of Indian sound is less studied, and as a quick intervention, this chapter works to address this paucity in scholarship. Nevertheless, this chapter examines the place of queer Black masculinity and South Asian instrumentation in and on Davis's 1972 album *On the Corner*. Davis envisioned it as a record that would attract politically active African American youth. For Davis, the rise of R&B and funk in the 1960s as cultural signifiers of Black Power politics diminished jazz's popularity among young Black people in the United States, and severed jazz's previous ties to African American political ideologies. Unwilling to allow his music and politics to be relegated to the past, Davis mixed funk, R&B, and jazz on *On the Corner*. Yet, as stated above, South Asian performers and sounds also played a central role, as did representations of queer Black masculinity. Thus, this chapter asks: In an era where many Black teens are listening to the politically charged albums and songs by hetero-masculinist artists like James Brown ("Say It Loud—I'm Black and I'm Proud"), what does it mean for Miles Davis to use South Asian music and queer Black masculinity to reach these same teens and to tap into dominant Black Power ideologies? This chapter addresses this question by deploying a framework that I call "corner politics," which bridges queerness and South Asian culture as central formations that animate and organize Blackness in general and Black political consciousness in particular. Corner politics illumines how Davis's *On the Corner* album broadened dominant articulations of Black Power and Black identity to include queerness and South Asian culture as formations that inform and shape Black political identity.

The third chapter moves from Black jazz and jazz-fusion musicians' 1970s work with and interest in South Asian cultural production and producers to the realm of 1980s and 1990s funk and hip-hop. Popular music scholars generally contend that the 1980s and early to mid-1990s witnessed increased politically charged musical cross-currents between Black and South Asian sounds and musicians in the United Kingdom and the Caribbean, but not in the United States. Such an approach ignores the ways in which African American artists continued the history of Afro–South Asian musical crossing. In particular, such scholarship elides the work of Rick James and hiphop duo OutKast. This chapter examines Rick James's 1986 album *The Flag* and OutKast's 1996 album *ATLiens* to think through the place and political potential of South Asian music and culture in shaping these albums and artists. Further, such influence of South Asian culture on these artists and albums are also tied to their articulations of Blackness and masculinity. Rick James pushed the parameters of Black male masculinity and sexuality, and he continued such endeavors on his 1986 concept album, but with an explicit political charge: James's interest in Reaganomics and the Cold War. Much like Davis's *On the Corner*, *The Flag* owes a debt to South Asian instrumentation, utilizing sitars and tablas, and as a result foregrounds the complexities of Black politics and masculinity at a moment in the United States when South Asian immigrants were being hailed as a model minority, as a means of disciplining African Americans. Such a cultural and political intersection continued into the 1990s, as did the influence of James on hip-hop groups like the Atlanta-based duo OutKast. *ATLiens*, the group's second album, witnessed member André "André 3000" Benjamin donning an Indian turban, a move that popular music critics and rappers saw as a break from southern Black masculine forms of expression. Such sartorial choices dually aligned Benjamin with Indian customs as well as an older tradition in Black southern women's head-wrapping. These deviations from dominant forms of southern male Black masculinity provide an opportunity to think through the multiple "Souths" in a space like Georgia during the 1990s: the increased immigration of South Asians from the global South to the U.S. South. In all, this chapter examines how, despite efforts to distance African American and South Asian (diasporic) communities in the United States during the 1980s and 1990s, African American funk and rap artists maintained such bonds to create anti-imperial, anti-racist, and anti-masculinist Black politics.

For many popular music studies scholars, U.S.-based hip-hop's sampling of South Asian music at the turn of the twenty-first century represented a musical extension of post-9/11 U.S. imperialist endeavors and Orientalist fantasies. Scholars note the increasing popularity of South Asian music and mixing of South Asian– and Middle Eastern–style commodities in rap videos in

2002 and 2003, and subsequently label African American rap musicians engaging in such practices as cultural imperialists who dangerously reproduced the conflations of South Asia and the Middle East within the post-9/11 U.S. racial imaginary. These scholars further argued that such rap videos and songs were usually produced by men and relied on Orientalist tropes that musically and visually represented South Asia as feminine and sexually as objects made available to and consumed by the Western male heteronormative gaze. Yet, chapter 4 asks: What does it mean to argue that these African American musicians, who come from a historically marginalized group whose oppression was and is a necessity in order to fulfill U.S. nation-building and imperial interests, are complicit in U.S. empire? And further, how can this scholarship's reliance on male-centered musical examples account for African American women musicians whose work also drew on South Asian sound and culture at this time? This chapter addresses these questions through an examination of the 2002 hit song "Addictive" by African American R&B / hop-hop female singer Truth Hurts. Many scholars and journalists have studied "Addictive" since its release, but most of their analyses operate from a linear temporal logic that always already binds "Addictive" to post-9/11 U.S. empire and Orientalism and elides Truth Hurts's Black female subjectivity— "Addictive" is released after 9/11 and therefore must be Orientalist, imperial, and shore up norms of race, gender, and sexuality. This chapter resists such normative approaches, and instead draws specifically on the queer and feminist of color impulse of "Addictive." I use interviews, music analysis, and close-reading practices in order to illustrate how "Addictive" makes audible the other side of things. "Addictive" advances the kinds of alternative formations, relations, and political possibilities of post-9/11 Afro–South Asian hip-hop and R&B that are rendered unimaginable within dominant analyses. It makes possible those that are anti-Orientalist and anti-imperial, that are Black feminist and queer, and that are invested in Afro–South Asian political solidarity.

The final chapter addresses a particular issue within scholarly and journalist approaches to Afro–South Asian hip-hop in the United States. One school of thought reads African American hip-hop practitioners' encounters with South Asian culture and people solely as a site of commodification of South Asian culture. The other school of thought articulates how South Asian American participation in rap music has informed South Asian American identity formations, but this school of thought fails to adequately consider what such encounters mean to and for Black rap musicians. That is, both sides are stuck in a theoretical problematic of representation. Thus, this chapter asks: What happens when we move from the representational to the agential, to collaborations between African American and South Asian American artists in rap? Using the partnership between African American rap producer Timbaland and South Asian American singer Rajé Shwari, I explore how their collaborative work transgresses constructed boundaries of race, gender, and nation in order to cultivate feminist and transnational Afro–South Asian bonds. Timbaland and Shwari, as I argue in the chapter, think crossracial collaborations differently, reading it through the other side of things, in ways that imagine new expressions of transnational coalition building and of making audible the political struggles and possibilities of creating music and forming alliances between and across the margins.

1

A Desi Love Supreme

John Coltrane, James Baldwin, and the
Life Side of Afro–South Asian Music

I guess I was on my way in '57, when I started to get myself together
musically, although at the time I was working academically and technically.
It's just recently that I've tried to become even more aware of this other side—
the life side of music.

—John Coltrane, *Down Beat*

On September 1, 1962, journalist Louise Davis Stone reviewed John
Coltrane's *Coltrane Plays the Blues* album for the Black newspaper
the *Baltimore Afro-American*. A glowing review, Stone especially praises the
album's opening song "Blues to Elvin." Stone notes that the song's "stretched
tonality extensions, blues roots and Eastern minor shades" make it "an ex-
cellent expression of himself [i.e., Coltrane]."[1] This wasn't first time that
Stone read "Eastern" music as a particular expression of Coltrane's artistry.
A few months prior to her review of *Coltrane Plays the Blues*, Stone reviewed
his *My Favorite Things* album, and noted that the "Eastern sound" of the
titular song was "most compelling."[2] Stone's use of "Eastern" was most likely
code for "Indian." By the time he recorded *My Favorite Things*, it was already
widely known that Coltrane was deeply invested in studying Indian culture,
especially the work of *shenai* player Bismillah Khan.[3] Coltrane would even
later assert that "My Favorite Things" contained Indian elements that were
"more or less subconscious, unconscious."[4] Coincidentally, "My Favorite
Things" appears in Stone's review of *Coltrane Plays the Blues*, as she compares
"My Favorite Things" to the fourth song on the album, "Mr. Day," and underscores, in an Orientalist manner, their shared "hypnotic texture." For Stone,

19

such a blending of Black musical traditions like the blues with "Eastern" sounds of India is part of what makes *Coltrane Plays the Blues* an album that uniquely and most aptly provides a "tour of the Coltrane terrain," a "rarely frantic or obtuse" journey of the masterful saxophonist John Coltrane, or, as Stone lauds in her review, "the James Baldwin of horn sound."[5]

Stone's analogization of Coltrane to Baldwin is quite striking. Baldwin's love for and literary indebtedness to jazz in his life and work are well-known, and by the time of Stone's review in 1962, he used jazz as one of the central organizing thematics in some of his most famous works like *Go Tell It on the Mountain, The Amen Corner,* "Sonny's Blues," and *Another Country*.[6] And yet, scholars, journalists, artists, and activists generally read Coltrane's music (during his life and especially after his death) in relation to two other African American political leaders (both of whom were Baldwin's personal and political friends and contemporaries): Dr. Martin Luther King Jr. and Malcolm X. Coltrane's southern Black Christian church upbringing, affinity for gospel, and recordings like "Reverend King" draw obvious connections to King; and his songs like "Liberia" and punctuated horn screams in the *altissimo* register presented a militancy that, particularly for the Black Arts Movement, align with Malcolm X.[7] These comparisons of Coltrane to King or Malcolm X make use of the two most prominent political leaders of the 1960s in ways that give political meaning and urgency to an artist who generally shied away from formal political participation.[8] Moreover, and perhaps most important, such a likening of Coltrane with Malcolm X and King place Coltrane within what Erica Edwards calls the "black charisma" of the 1960s Black freedom struggles, a "cultural–political ideal that rests on a particular and persistent marking of normative masculinity as the most proper site of political expression."[9]

James Baldwin transgressed this normative masculinity of 1960s Black leadership. The James Baldwin referenced in Stone's review was the James Baldwin prior to the publication of *The Fire Next Time* (or the previously published articles that composed this monograph), which established him as one of the leading voices of the civil rights movement. This was instead a James Baldwin who had, by February 1961, made it a point to publicly write in *Harper's Magazine* that Martin Luther King Jr. "lost much moral credit" with young civil rights activists for giving into the homophobia of Adam Clayton Powell and forcing "the resignation of his [i.e., King's] extremely able organizer and lieutenant," the queer Black activist Bayard Rustin.[10] This was a James Baldwin who in April 1961, two months after the *Harper's* article, debated Malcolm X, critiqued his equation of effective anti-racist activism with violent masculinity, and concluded that the standards of masculinity "need to be revised."[11] This was a queer Black James Baldwin whom some civil rights activists privately and homophobically called "Martin Luther Queen." And this was a queer Black James Baldwin whose most famous literary works at the time of Stone's review sat at the intersection of race and dissident sexualities.[12] In essence, as Edwards articulates, Stone's Baldwin was someone "positioned as outside of, if not dangerous to, the images of Black leadership that circulated in mass culture," and whose "performance of leadership did not conform to the performative demands of Black charismatic leadership that had solidified in U.S. culture by the 1960s."[13] It is against this backdrop that I want to approach Stone's reference to Coltrane as the "James Baldwin of horn sound." I want to question its racialized gender and sexual stakes for Black queer masculinity, contend with its Black political significance, and think through how, if at all, Coltrane's blending of Afro-diasporic blues structure with an Indian-inflected "Eastern" sound, a music that was central to Stone's review, was also part of such superlative appellation.

This is to say that this chapter uses Stone's comparison of John Coltrane to James Baldwin as an opening into what I'm calling the other side of things, an alternative reading and meaning-making practice of African American musicians' engagements with South Asian sounds and artists in and across Black popular musics. Rather than trace the similarities between Coltrane and Baldwin, I am more interested in using their overlaps as a point of departure and provide new insight into Coltrane's music. Routing Coltrane's well-known interests in and embrace of Indian music and spirituality through Baldwin produces new ways of imagining and grappling with Coltrane's Afro–South Asian musical and extramusical crossings. Far too often, scholarly approaches to Coltrane songs like "India," albums like *Om*, and even his naming of his son after sitarist Ravi Shankar treat such acts solely as examples of Coltrane's *personal* investments in Indian music and spirituality that neither articulate with his interests in African American musical traditions nor carry Black political import. That is, this literature, when it concerns Coltrane's engagements with Indian expressive culture, disaggregates the Indian from the African American as well as the personal and the spiritual from the social and the political. This chapter resists such a disarticulation and argues instead that we cannot adequately address the relations between the political possibilities of Coltrane's Afro-diasporic-inflected music during the 1960s without concomitantly investigating their constitutive interactions with Indian music and spirituality. If we take seriously Coltrane as the "James Baldwin of horn sound," and if, as Lawrie Balfour contends, Baldwin's political impulse centers on his "unwillingness to disentangle political matters from discussion of spiritual or cultural or personal subjects," then we must demand interpretive channels—like the other sides of things—that necessitate the mutually constitutive and that illuminate the ways in which the political, the spiritual, the cultural, and their attendant Afro-diasporic and Indian manifestations as necessarily intertwined in the work and life of John Coltrane.[14]

The focus of this chapter is on a perhaps unlikely recording: Coltrane's 1965 four-part suite *A Love Supreme*. A deeply spiritual album, for sure, *A Love Supreme* is also a record that scholars generally do not read as tied to Indian spirituality and musical traditions—or certainly not in the way that one might read *Ascension, Meditations,* or *Om*. But this is precisely why I'm interested in *A Love Supreme*. If we solely examine Coltrane's engagements with Indian expressive culture as occurring on recordings that explicitly gesture toward Indian musical and spiritual traditions, then we undertheorize and subsequently overlook how deeply committed Coltrane was to Indian music and spirituality, how such a commitment is at the heart of much of his discography, and how such a commitment involves bridging Afro-diasporic and Indian expressive culture. This is the importance of the other side of things. It's an insistence to look beyond the evident in order to perceive what's obscured. And so to that end, just as analyses of *A Love Supreme* frequently elide Indian spirituality, the same is true for its political implications, a remainder of a far too frequent, but in no way unreasonable, reticence to tie Coltrane to political protest. As Lewis Porter and Ingrid Monson point out, unlike fellow jazz musicians like Max Roach and Abbey Lincoln, Coltrane seemed to lack participation in explicit engagements with domestic and international political actions.[15] While I agree that Coltrane was not overwhelmingly involved in formal politics, I posit that investigating Coltrane's music like *A Love Supreme* and placing it within its larger sociohistorical and political contexts actually allows us to glean the ways in which Coltrane engaged in politics in a different way, a politics that sits outside the realm of formal and conventional understandings of political engagement and that resonates with and expands James Scott's framework of "infrapolitics."[16]

If, as Gerald Horne, Nico Slate, Vijay Prashad, Sudarshan Kapur, and others have illustrated, Indian and African American activists during the long twentieth century forged collective bonds to combat anti-racist and anti-colonial practices in India and the United States as well as the "darker nations" around the world, then Coltrane's music—here, *A Love Supreme*—not only speaks to the larger Afro-Asian political actions taking place, but also the ways in which these new cultural expressions held the potential to extend these transnational, cross-cultural, and anti-imperial modes of political, spatial, and racial solidarity.[17]

Further, using Baldwin as a lens through which to listen to Coltrane sheds light on how Coltrane's expressions of the political and spiritual collectivity of Afro–South Asian sound must also contend with how such cross-cultural, political, and spiritual linkages articulate with Black queer masculinities. To be clear, Coltrane never identified as queer and I'm not attempting to impose such an identity on him. Rather, my aim is in part to take seriously Stone's analogization of Coltrane and Baldwin, and to treat it as an opening into Coltrane's sonic modalities of nonnormativity. As Gerald Early suggests, Coltrane was a different kind of jazzman:

> Coltrane was not, after all, an especially flamboyant jazz musician as Dizzy Gillespie or Illinois Jacquet or Art Blakey each was in his own way; Coltrane did not embody any sense of masculine cool or Hemingway bravado like Miles Davis; he was not mysterious and enigmatic like Thelonious Monk or Sun Ra; he was not as openly Afrocentric or Pan-Africanist in his religious inclination as Rashaan Roland Kirk or Yusef Lateef or Sun Ra; nor was he as overtly political with his music as Max Roach or Archie Shepp or Charles Mingus; he was not popular with the masses of working-class blacks as were "Cannonball" Adderley, Jimmy Smith, Les McCann, Horace Silver, or Bobby Timmons . . . and he was certainly not as accomplished in the range of what he could do musically or in the way he could exploit the talents of the musicians around him as Duke Ellington.[18]

Early is not simply comparing Coltrane to his jazz forbearers and contemporaries at the level of artistic creativity; he is also assessing Coltrane's relation to archetypes of Black jazzmen—the political jazzman, the masculine cool jazzman, the Afrocentric jazzman, the working-class jazzman. Coltrane fails to fit into these established scripts that render Black jazzmen legible and proper. Much like Baldwin's transgressions of normative Black male leadership, Coltrane sits outside the set aesthetic patterns that define Black jazzmen. Coltrane thus performs a "radical rescripting of the accepted performances of a heteronormative black masculinity" that is indicative of what Mark Anthony Neal calls "illegible masculinities."[19]

Indeed, the "James Baldwin of horn sound" moniker works as a nod to Coltrane's affinity for the soprano saxophone, the smaller and sonically lighter instrument that most jazz male musicians did not play, opting instead for the larger, sonically deeper, and thus coded as more masculine tenor iteration. Stone's title for Coltrane perhaps also signals Coltrane's acknowledgment of and collaborations with women who shaped his life and sound, disrupting the normative narratives of patrilineality that inform jazz male influences, collaborations, and historiography. Coltrane's second wife, Alice McLeod, who joined and played a pivotal role in Coltrane's mid to late 1960s band, is the more well-known example here. But his first wife Naima, to whom Coltrane was married at the time of Stone's review, is also noteworthy. She helped Coltrane get and stay sober, expanded his mind about other spiritual traditions, came up with the titles to some of his songs like "Equinox," and, along with her daughter Sayeeda, had other songs of Coltrane's named after her. But Stone's nickname for Coltrane potentially also speaks to his complicated relationship with religion and spirituality. Baldwin famously did not believe in, and at times critiqued, Christianity and Islam, but still centered religion in his work. Coltrane was similarly critical of religions. In 1958 he expressed to August Blume that he was "disappointed" with the multitude of, and in particular the apparent antagonisms between, various religions: "When I saw there were so many religions and kind of opposed somewhere to the next and so forth, you know, it screwed with my head. . . . I just couldn't believe that one guy could be right. 'Cause if he's right, somebody else got to be wrong, you know?"[20] Coltrane subsequently began to study multiple religions from across the world in the hopes of "bring[ing] them all together," and was most drawn to Indian spirituality, which failed to map on to—to return to Early—the "Afrocentric or Pan-Africanist . . . inclination as Rashaan Roland Kirk or Yusef Lateef or Sun Ra." In fact, it is Coltrane's embrace of Indian spirituality that is partly tied to his love of the soprano saxophone and his relationship with Naima. The soprano saxophone, as Peter Lavezzoli articulates, is "crisp and dry" and has "a bright nasal tone" that is reminiscent of the *shenai*; and Naima and Coltrane studied Indian spirituality together, and his song named after her, "Naima," uses rhythmic bass accompaniment common in North Indian classical music.[21] This is all to say that Coltrane's Baldwin sound, his queer sound of illegible masculinities, articulates with his use of Indian expressive culture. It is part and parcel of his nonnormative aesthetics that violate the sonic schema of Black jazzmen at the time.

We, thus, might call Coltrane "eccentric" in Francesca Royster's framing of the term. Royster defines an eccentric performer as "not only out of the ordinary or unconventional . . . but also those that are ambiguous, uncanny, or difficult to read . . . through acts of spectacular creativity, the eccentric joins forces with the 'queer,' 'freak,' and 'pervert' to see around corners, push the edges of the present to create a language not yet recognized: new sounds, new dances, new configurations of self—the makings of a black utopia."[22] The queer Black utopic space that Coltrane's eccentricity engenders, especially on a record like *A Love Supreme*, is one of political immediacy that articulates with Indian spirituality and sound. It is a Black utopia that sounds the other side of things. It purses and produces an imaginative space that challenges Early's jazzmen archetype through its formation of a political, spiritual, and Afro–South Asian collectivity.

I locate Coltrane's queer Afro–South Asian sound, his Baldwin sound, in 1957. It is in 1957 that Coltrane had what he would later describe as a "spiritual awakening." This spiritual awakening led Coltrane, with the help of his wife (Naima) and others, to quit drugs and alcohol, an addiction that had led to Coltrane's firing from Miles Davis's quintet in April of that year. Newly sober and looking to live a different life, Coltrane started to study and incorporate non-Western religious, philosophical, and musical traditions in his life and artistry. Admittedly, Coltrane started to stray from and question Black Christianity as a teenager, and he was "introduced to" Islam in his early twenties, which "shook" him because he "had never thought about" another religion outside of Christianity.[23] But it wasn't until the spiritual shift in his life in 1957 that Coltrane desired to "see what other people are [spiritually] thinking," and delve deep into African, Chinese, and especially Indian philosophies and spiritualities.[24]

It is also in 1957 that Coltrane's interest in Indian spirituality and philosophy dovetailed with his studies of Indian classical music. Ethnomusicologist Carl Clements, for example, argues that Coltrane started studying and using the concept of *vikriti*, an exploration of "the various permutations of limited sets of notes," in his work in 1957.[25] *Vikriti* shares much with Coltrane's famous "sheets of sounds" aesthetic that he popularized while recording and working with Thelonious Monk a year later, and thus might have served as a model for Coltrane's new sound. Moreover, and more broadly, Coltrane developed an interest in North Indian or Hindustani classical music in 1957, especially its melodic and rhythmic structure. Rather than a highly harmonic musical tradition, Hindustani music centers on a rag or raga, a collection of pitches and their attendant musical characteristics (the predominant pitch, its implied mood, the number of pitches, etc.), which a soloist explores through improvisation. Key to such performances is the use of a sustained drone (usually on a tamboura or harmonium), which allows the soloist to improvise for an unspecified duration. Coltrane's interest in Hindustani music converged with the emergence of modal jazz. Ingrid Monson outlines how modal jazz, much like Hindustani music, often includes, among other things, "(1) a lower density of chords . . . or whose harmonic frame is speci-fied in scales; (2) extended horizontally conceived solos that use scales and their segments to connect harmonies; (3) the use of vamps and pedal points to create open-ended frameworks for improvisation."[26] And so when Col-trane rejoined Miles Davis's band in 1958, the trumpeter's sound had moved more toward modal jazz (exemplified in Davis's 1959 track "So What?"), which allowed Coltrane to bridge modal jazz with Hindustani music. As Coltrane would later remark in a 1963 interview, he was initially drawn to Ravi Shankar's music because of the "modal aspect of his [Shankar's] art."[27]

The year 1957 is also important for the purposes of this chapter and Col-trane's Baldwin horn sound—his queer Afro–South Asian sound—because it is in 1957 that James Baldwin returned to the United States from his self-imposed exile in France, and did so in order to more directly participate in the civil rights movement. Oddly enough, John Coltrane's hometown Charlotte, North Carolina, was Baldwin's first stop back in the United States. It was then and there that Baldwin interviewed and wrote about the fight for school integration. While the overlaps between Baldwin and Coltrane in year (1957) and location (Charlotte) are certainly coincidences, my aim here is to follow Melani McAlister's call to "explain the coincidence that brings specific cultural products into conversation with specific political discourses."[28] It is thus at the 1957 convergences of Baldwin's political return home and Coltrane's sonic and spiritual trek abroad that we might locate and imagine the sociocultural and sociopolitical implications of Coltrane's expression of the other side of things. Thinking through the coincidences of Baldwin and Coltrane illuminates how Coltrane's Baldwin sound is domestic and transnational, spiritual and political, Black and South Asian.

It is because of 1957's centrality to Baldwin and Coltrane, and most fundamentally to Coltrane, that this chapter focuses on Coltrane's 1965 album *A Love Supreme*, and especially the "Acknowledgement" and "Psalm" movements. In his self-written liner notes, Coltrane begins with a reference to his 1957 spiritual awakening, and lauds it for bringing him closer to God (I will speak more about which kind of God below) as well as leading him to "a richer, fuller, more productive life."[29] Coltrane continues that *A Love Supreme* is his "humble offering" of thanks to God for his post–spiritual awakening life, and as such, I want to read the album as a commemoration of 1957 and the spiritual, musical, personal, and political events and stakes that are attached to and surround Coltrane at that time and the recording of *A Love Supreme*. The liner notes are again instructive here. Coltrane remarks that at the time of his spiritual awakening, he asked God to provide him with the "means and privilege to make others happy through music," an appeal that Coltrane believes God granted and a feeling that he believes his music now expresses. This request to "make others happy through music" is not individual but rather institutional, social instead of personal, transformative instead of reparative. It identified a deep desire for what Coltrane notes in his and Eric Dolphy's well-known 1962 *Down Beat* interview as the "other side—the life side of music."[30] Coltrane's iteration of the other side of things involves addressing life events of the present (e.g., sadness) and transforming them for a better future world (e.g., happiness). The transformative effect of music comes up again a year later in a 1963 French interview. As Coltrane explains, "I wish I could bring people something that looks like happiness. . . . If one of my friends were sick, I would play a certain tune and he would be healed; when he was broke, I would play another tune and he would immediately receive all the money he needed."[31] In highlighting health care (emotional and otherwise) and poverty as issues of the life side of music, Coltrane underscores the sociocultural and sociopolitical stakes of the other side of things, and the import of the music on *A Love Supreme*. As I show below, *A Love Supreme,* in particular "Acknowledgement" and "Psalm," evoke Coltrane's life side of music. It musically articulates the Black utopian longing or utopian ideal of Coltrane's queer sonic eccentricity. The sound that emits from Coltrane's saxophone, from Coltrane's Baldwinian bend of the horn, announces and binds the personal and the political, the spiritual and the social, and Afro-diasporic and Indian aesthetic formations.

A Desi Love Supreme

"Acknowledgement," the first movement of *A Love Supreme,* opens with John Coltrane on tenor saxophone playing an unmetered fanfare in E major, pianist McCoy Tyner supporting with a left-hand tremolo and right-hand group of triads, and drummer Elvin Jones striking a gong before moving to a cymbal roll. Once the fanfare subsides, bassist Jimmy Garrison starts to play a four-note ostinato, a repeated melodic/rhythmic phrasing, in F minor (with the first note being a pickup note). After four measures, Jones joins Garrison's four-note cell groove with a full drum kit in tow. Jones keeps the 4/4 meter with the cymbal, but helps establish a somewhat offbeat groove with accents on the one and three on the tom-tom, and an eighth note rim shot before the two and four. Following another four measures of Garrison and Jones, Tyner reappears playing "chords built of superimposed fourths, using notes from within the pentatonic scale."[32] The trio plays together for eight measures before Coltrane begins his 149-measure solo. During Coltrane's solo, Tyner maintains his quartal harmonies, Garrison drops the ostinato pattern to explore other melodic avenues, and Jones develops an Afro-Cuban rhythm while simultaneously retaining the rhythmic pulse of the vamp and keeping the quartet in a "loose interlocking groove."[33] Lewis Porter divides Coltrane's solo into three parts: "First, he intensifies the rhythm. . . . Secondly, he utilizes the range of his instrument, building up to the altissimo register for climaxes. . . . Third, Coltrane transposes the motive outside the scale."[34] Picking up from this final part, Coltrane musically states the "rhythm and shape of the bass ostinato" on all twelve keys, and eventually ends the solo by joining Garrison for eight measures in the cell's original key in F minor. As the solo concludes, Coltrane removes his saxophone from his mouth and begins to repeat, with his own overdubbed voice, the words "a love supreme" in unison with the bass ostinato. It appears that Coltrane is using the opening four-note riff on bass as a stringed reproduction of the vocal recitation— it alludes to both a harking back to and continuation of the bass-line riff. After twenty measures of repeating the vocal phrase in unison with Garrison, Coltrane exits the recording completely. Jones and Tyner soon follow suit, and Garrison closes the song alone. Garrison ends the performance with a bass line that "maintains the rhythmic pulse yet works toward a new melodic area" and that seamlessly flows into and anticipates the next song, "Resolution."[35]

Taken as a whole, "Acknowledgement" alludes to certain music making tendencies in sub-Saharan Africa and the African diaspora. Perhaps most explicitly, and it is an aspect of the composition that I will expound on later, Jimmy Garrison's bass ostinato underscores the influence of African music on Coltrane and the quartet in particular and Afro-diasporic genres like jazz in general. Olly Wilson famously explains that cyclical patterns in sub-Saharan Africa can produce spiritual effects, and that their central role within musical performances sustain a composition through its repetition as well as invite "communal activity."[36] We witness this call to collectivity as the motif starts in near silence, and then, one by one, Jones, Tyner, and Coltrane join the performance. As the open-ended organizing rubric of the composition, the ostinato sets up an interlocking collective engagement between Coltrane, Tyner, and Jones (and even Garrison) that create space for each artist's playing, but it does so while still remaining in dialogue with one another, what Wilson refers to as the "heterogenous sound ideal."[37] Ashley Kahn supports this point as he argues that while Tyner and Garrison imply a 4/4 rhythm with the bass-line and left-hand comps, Jones is "playing double-time, even triple-time patterns on the cymbals; fills on the snare rim and tom-toms simultaneously define a 6/8 meter with a slight Latin lilt."[38] Jones's Afro-Latin playing alone does not produce a polyrhythmic effect, but his interactions with Tyner and Garrison create a tense and intricate cross-rhythm that push and pull the listener, and accent and inform Coltrane's soloing.

And yet, just as Coltrane alludes to African and Afro-diasporic rhythms on "Acknowledgment," he also signals Indian spiritual and musical traditions. In particular, Coltrane's use of the ostinato figure gestures toward a musical overlap between North Indian classical and sub-Saharan African musical practices. Near the end of the piece, Coltrane reveals that the four-note cell anchoring "Acknowledgement" is a bass-line rendition of the phrase "a love supreme": Coltrane repeatedly sings in the same intonation as the bass line. Yet, the verb "sing" fails to accurately capture the meaning and power of Coltrane's vocal display. In a 1965 interview with Michiel de Ruyter about *A Love Supreme*, Coltrane remarks, "I had one part that I was singing on—not singing, *chanting*."[39] I want to sit with Coltrane's self-correction here. His reversal, his replacement of "singing" with "chanting," reorients our analyses of and listening to the phrasing of "a love supreme." It shifts our attention away from dominant understandings that treat the vocalized phrase on "Acknowledgement" as a simple recitation, and moves it more toward an approximation of what I believe qualifies as a Vedic chant. The Vedas are a collection of scriptures in Hinduism that contain, among other items, hymns and devotional poetry. I am not suggesting that Coltrane's use of the word "chant" to describe his vocal approach on "Acknowledgement" as solely signifying a connection to Indian spirituality and music; the fact that chants are used in many spiritual traditions, including those in sub-Saharan Africa, speaks to the multiple and collective spiritual frameworks with which Coltrane engages. Instead, I want to point out the ways in which Coltrane's chant taps into various thematic structures organizing Vedic chants. Vedic chanting is a syllabic recitation that engenders a harmonically limited vocal style and creates a rhythmic pulse in a performance.[40] Coltrane's chant performance of "a love supreme" dovetails with the structure of Vedic chants. The phrase comprises four syllables based on an equal four-note ostinato that harmonically suspends while also rhythmically animating "Acknowledgment."

Cultural studies scholar Moustafa Bayoumi uses Islam to further theorize the spiritual and South Asian connections to the "a love supreme" chant. Bayoumi compares the "a love supreme" chant to a Sufi *dhikr*, a devotional recitation, and notes that the chant sounds similar to and possibly slips into a rhythmic phrasing of "Allah supreme."[41] While there isn't any archival or oral history evidence to substantiate Bayoumi's claim, the microphone levels on Coltrane's voice, in addition to Coltrane's vocal overdubs, make it difficult for listeners to clearly discern Coltrane's enunciation of "a love supreme." The mixing of "Acknowledgment" opens up differing perceptions of the chant, like Bayoumi hearing "Allah supreme," and thus allow for a layered understanding of the chant that gestures toward multiplicity and collectivity. Bayoumi's alternative listening practice marks the elasticity of the chant, its ability to speak to and connect listeners from spiritual beliefs that include and sit outside of Christian-derived or Christian-centered notions of a Higher Power. In so doing, Bayoumi's reading complicates Lewis Porter and Scott Saul's approaches to Coltrane's saxophone and vocal sounding of the chant, which interpret Coltrane's twelve key transpositions of the four-note cell figure as signaling God's omnipresence—"telling us that God is everywhere"—and omnibenevolence—God "can bless even the most dissonant notes with the ability to sound as though they have their place"—respectively.[42] And so,

I read the importance of Bayoumi's hearing of "Allah supreme" as (re)ori-
enting the focus to a community-based approach that pushes us to consider
the chant, and by extension "Acknowledgment," as centering and creating
relationality, resonance, and forms of kinship. Its open-ended framework
refuses the singular and personal to allow for the multiple and the social.[43]

On this point of the chant's performance of relationality and resonance,
it's important to note that Bayoumi contextualizes his Islamic reading of the
chant within the history of African American interests in and conversions
to "Ahmadi-type Islam."[44] The Ahmadiyya movement began in India during
the late nineteenth century, but eventually spread to the United States during the early to mid-twentieth century with the help of one of its more
prominent followers, Mufti Muhammad Sadiq, who spoke to and converted
many African American men and women, including two of Coltrane's clos-
est friends and interlocutors, his mentor Yusef Lateef and his sideman
McCoy Tyner (both of whom are credited with getting Coltrane more deeply
interested in Indian music and spirituality).[45] For Bayoumi, African Americans gravitated toward the Ahmadiyya movement partly out of a shared
experience of institutional oppression via the British Raj and U.S. nation-
state, respectively. Ahmadi Islam offered African Americans a minoritarian
structure of belonging forged out of the political, social, cultural, psychic,
and affective weight of colonization that could help them navigate the strictures of U.S. forms of white supremacy as well as create and imagine Afro–
South Asian cross-cultural and transnational bonds. Through Islam within
the Ahmadiyya community, Bayoumi argues, "African Americans could
metaphorically travel beyond the confines of national identities. They could
become 'Asiatics' and remain Black, could be proud of their African heritage
and feel a sense of belonging to and participation with Asia."[46] In other
words, for African American converts, Ahmadi-type Islam animates a coalitional ideal that refuses a masking of difference in order to proffer an
Afro–South Asian collective. As such, in framing "Acknowledgment" and
the "a love supreme" chant within the Ahmadiyya movement, Bayoumi
lays the groundwork for us to consider the political import of the recording.
The slippage between "a love supreme" and "Allah supreme," then, is one
that indexes the Afro–South Asian history of Ahmadi Islam in the United
States as well as sonically expresses the future Black utopic possibilities of
such coalitional formations. What "Acknowledgement" does, then, through
linking Afro-diasporic and Indian spiritual traditions, musical structures,

and political histories, is introduce listeners to a world of *A Love Supreme*, an imaginative space where the spiritual and the political, and the Afro-diasporic and the Indian, necessarily co-articulate and intertwine. It is an entanglement that exists throughout the entire album, but is especially apparent in "Psalm," the final movement of the *A Love Supreme* suite.

A Love Psalm

"Psalm," the final movement of *A Love Supreme*, structurally seems to be somewhat of an outlier on the album. Tony Whyton notes that "Psalm" is dramatically different from the opening three movements, which "feed off active nouns, in that they relate to verb forms ('Acknowledgement,' 'Resolution,' 'Pursuance'), and are multilayered in meaning and also suggestive of forms of religious observance." Whyton continues that "Psalm" also lacks the "blues, Afro-Cuban, and swing feel of earlier sections."[47] But I want to argue here that "Psalm" isn't exactly an outlier, especially when compared to "Acknowledgement." I believe that there exists commonalities between "Psalm" and "Acknowledgement," and that their overlaps further the constellation of spiritual, political, and Afro–South Asian utopic imaginations that I refer to as the other side of things.

"Psalm" shares the unmetered opening of "Acknowledgement," with Tyner again playing triads and tremolos, Jones on the timpani, and Coltrane playing a transposed four-note bass line from "Acknowledgement." The act of transposing and gesturing back to the ostinato in the first section of *A Love Supreme* functions to mark "Psalm" as a continuation of "Acknowledgment." And yet, what appears to be simply the introduction of "Psalm" is actually the structure of the entire recording. "Psalm," as a recording, is a seven-minute, harmonically static, and unmetered improvisation. For the majority of the song, Coltrane solos at various tempos over Tyner's left-handed drone in C minor (and right-hand quartal harmonies), Jones's vacillations between timpani rolls and cymbal clashes, and Garrison's barely audible walking bass. Near the end of the solo, Coltrane quickly reaches intense altissimo registers, but soon descends into a slow-paced middle-register melodic wander. Coltrane concludes his solo with a tenor saxophone overdub, an "upper-register vibrato mix with his own low-end phrasing," (similar to the overdub in "Acknowledgment") and a recapitulation of the opening saxophone fanfare in E major from "Acknowledgement" (again, the conflation of the

beginning and the end, but this time in terms of the sections of the suite).
Following Coltrane's exit, "Psalm" closes with "Garrison's bow bouncing on
the bass strings," Jones delicately hitting the cymbal, and Tyner quietly replay-
ing the ostinato theme of "Acknowledgement."

The lack of structure for "Psalm" is directly tied to a poem in the liner
notes of *A Love Supreme*. Coltrane alludes to this relationship between the
poem and "Psalm" in the notes' track outline: "The fourth and last part is
a musical narration of the theme, 'A Love Supreme,' which is written in the
context; it is entitled 'PSALM.'"[48] The "A Love Supreme" that Coltrane references here is the title of a poem that Coltrane wrote exclusively for, and
features in, the album's liner notes. In "A Love Supreme" (the poem) Coltrane uses phrases like "God is. God Loves" and "ELATION—ELEGANCE—
EXALTATION—All from God" to articulate his unyielding devotion, love, and
gratitude to a Higher Power. In a compelling study, Lewis Porter argues that "a
comparison of the poem with Coltrane's improvisation reveals that his saxophone solo is a wordless 'recitation,' if you will, of the words of the poem,
beginning with the title, 'A Love Supreme.'"[49] Coltrane not only narrates the
phrases of the poem via his saxophone, but also each syllable. He also provides
various accents to certain words that produce an emotional effect on the
recording and for its listeners. Put simply, and in the words of former Coltrane
sideman Reggie Workman, "Psalm *is* a psalm"; it is a poetic song of praise.[50]

Using Coltrane's religious upbringing in the African Methodist Episcopal
Church and the rubato—ascending/descending play style—and solitary feel
of "Psalm" (the entire track is an improvisation), Porter and Saul argue that
Coltrane's playing mirrors the vocal performance of an African American
male pastor preaching a sermon.[51] Coltrane's ascending phrases that build to
intensity and descending phrases that effect an added stillness (remember,
the improvisation is held harmonically together by Tyner's left-hand drone
in C minor) mimic similar male-centered oratory devices within dominant
African American Christian churches. Moreover, Kahn and Porter contend
that Coltrane uses the phrase "Thank you, God," which appears several times
in the poem, in an increasingly punctuated way that suggests a Black preacher's emphatic "Oh, Lord" expression.[52]

These comparisons of Coltrane's playing on "Psalm" to African American
male ministers' sermon deliveries seemingly ring true. In 1964, Coltrane
released a song titled "Alabama," which is based on a 1963 Martin Luther
King Jr. speech, and marks the only other known example (previous, of

course, to the recording of "Psalm") of Coltrane employing the wordless recitation musical device.[53] King's speech was a eulogy at the funeral for three of the four young African American girls (Denise McNair, Cynthia Wesley, and Addie Mae Collins) killed in the anti-Black bombing of the 16th Street Baptist Church in Birmingham, Alabama.[54] According to McCoy Tyner, Coltrane was familiar with the bombing, read a transcript of the eulogy in a local newspaper, and "took the rhythmic patterns of his [King's] speech and came up with 'Alabama.'"[55]

"Alabama" shares many similarities with "Psalm." "Alabama" is predominantly an unmetered and harmonically static improvisation. There is a middle section where the performance moves into a more metered nature—there's a 4/4 swing—but the composition quickly moves back to its unmetered opening. During this unmetered opening and closing, Jones alternates between timpani rolls and cymbal clashes, Tyner vacillates between a low-register tremolo and a left-hand drone, and Garrison quietly plays around the tonal center. Coltrane in "Alabama," like his playing in "Psalm," plays an array of ascending and descending notes, with short and long phrases that seemingly mimic human speech. Lastly, the final piece of evidence that seems to suggest the connection between "Psalm" and "Alabama," and by extension Coltrane's approximation of an African American Christian minister, is that "Alabama" appears in Coltrane's preliminary notes for A Love Supreme. In 2005, Guernsey's Auctions in New York auctioned a few of Coltrane's personal and professional items. The outline for A Love Supreme was among the auction materials, and in it, Coltrane notes that he wants the last chord of "Acknowledgement," the suite's first movement, to "sound like the final chord of Alabama."[56] This note is important because if, as I am arguing, the cyclical—via Indian and African musical structures—opens up and frames new possibilities of imagining A Love Supreme and its embrace of multiplicity, and if "Acknowledgement" and "Psalm" are connected through their mutually constitutive allusions to each other, then the fact that Coltrane ends "Acknowledgement" with the final chord of "Alabama" suggests that "Psalm" is a new iteration of "Alabama." Put another way, Coltrane creates a sonically transitive and triangulated framework and experience that draws a cyclical and mutually constitutive relationship between "Alabama" and "Psalm," through "Acknowledgement." As such, "Psalm" and "Alabama," through its narration of King's eulogy, carry traces of African American Christian spiritualism and Black political ideological narratives—"Psalm" is tied to Black spirituality, but because of its link to "Alabama," it also shares a similar tone of political urgency. "Psalm," then, as an ultimate exaltation of spirituality, gestures toward spirituality as the path leading to and a necessary site of Black liberation.

And yet, this use of Black male preachers' oratory devices as a way to analyze "Psalm" is complicated by "Psalm" being a poem rather than a sermon/eulogy (vis-à-vis Martin Luther King Jr.). "Psalm," as a poem that is translated into and performed as a song, indexes the long history of the relationship between the literary and the musical in Black politics and culture.[57] I want to consider this relationship between music and literature in light of Coltrane's nickname as the "James Baldwin of horn sound." Although Baldwin is, of course, known more for his prose, he did write poetry, especially poetry that held a musical bent. It's where, according to Nikky Finney, Baldwin saw himself as "more poet than anything else."[58] Regardless of Baldwin's identification as a poet, I am more drawn to what Fred Moten sees as part of the power of Baldwin's writing within the Black radical tradition. For Moten, the political meaning of Baldwin's connection to Black music and sound lies in how "the nonexclusion of sound, the nonreduction of nonmeaning, is tied to another understanding of literary resistance, one that moves within and without the black tradition, activating the sound in a way that opens the possibility of a nonexclusion of sexual difference whose exclusion has otherwise marked that tradition and that has been an inescapable part of that tradition's own scopophilia. His writing is pierced with screams and songs and prayers and cries and groans, their materiality, their maternity, and that's important."[59] Coltrane's play with higher and lower registers on "Psalm," his performance of Black minister–punctuated cadence, seems to mirror the characteristics that Moten describes concerning Baldwin's writing. It makes room for Black queerness within Coltrane's performance. Indeed, how might Coltrane's overlap with Baldwin, through Coltrane's musical narration of a poem, produce a Black queerness that is rendered illegible and ineligible from the scene of the pulpit? That is to say, if the pulpit (but not the church) has been a site of Black queer antagonism, then Coltrane's Baldwinian refusal to disentangle the literary from the musical on "Psalm" (via poetry) coupled with a mimicking of Black male preacher performance operates as a disidentifcatory practice (in José Muñoz's framing of the term) that opens up "Psalm" to Black queerness, an "otherwise possibility" in the words of Ashon Crawley.[60] Coltrane's blending of poetry, music, and Black male Christian oration disarticulates "Psalm" from being solely tied to the potential queerphobia of Black male preacher performances. It instead positions and proffers "Psalm" as an alternative space, one that can account for Black queerness as well as other social formations, sonic modalities, and political possibilities.

And it's this opening up to other possibilities that also connects "Psalm" to Indian music and spirituality. "Psalm" mirrors the *alap* portion of a Hindustani raga performance. An *alap* is the opening unmetered and harmonically static section of a raga. The featured improviser abstractly develops the various features of a raga (its mood, scale type, etc.), and primarily utilizes a drone as the tonal center from which to explore the melodic phrases and high and low registers of a particular raga.[61] Thus, these rhythmic/metric and melodic characteristics of an *alap* converge with the structural markers of "Psalm." Moreover, the resonances between the two also reside within the way they produce the feel of a solo performance. While a tamboura and tabla player might perform alongside a sitarist or sarodist, the *alap* section is meant to highlight the sitar/sarod. Likewise, as stated above, despite the contributions from the rest of the quartet, "Psalm" feels isolating. Ashley Kahn describes Coltrane's performance on "Psalm" as a "one-to-one conversation."[62] His use of the term "conversation" to depict "Psalm" is especially fascinating, as it points to another North Indian overlap with "Psalm": *alap* literally translates into English as "conversation."[63] These convergences inform and illustrate the kinds of collectivities that this chapter aims to explicate and that Coltrane's music assembles.

Indeed, the place of the drone in an *alap* is central to "Psalm" as well as Coltrane's 1957 spiritual awakening that engendered *A Love Supreme*. In an interview with Coltrane biographer Cuthbert Simpkins, Coltrane's first wife, Naima Grubbs, recounts a night in 1957 where Coltrane had a musical vision. Coltrane excitedly informed Grubbs that "I had a dream. . . . It was this beautiful droning sound, it was so beautiful."[64] Unable to describe to Naima the sound of this presumed powerful and inspiring drone, Coltrane attempted to re-create it *on the piano*. I emphasize the fact that Coltrane reproduced the drone on the piano as a way to signal its relation to Tyner's droning on "Psalm." And as such, I want to proffer a much larger claim that McCoy Tyner's drone in "Psalm" was an allusion to the drone in Coltrane's 1957 musical (and, quite frankly, spiritual) revelation. This is to say, the drone in "Psalm" indexes the 1957 dream and enacts a spiritual belief system that does not reside within one religious tradition. Instead, the spiritual awakening points to a belief in a Higher Power that allows for an abstract exploration of and connection to spirituality. Placing Hindustani music within the narrative of "Psalm" produces a collectivity joined through a continued, multiple, and communal relationship with and infinite adoration of a Higher Power, a true Love Supreme.

I do not highlight the place and influence of North Indian classical music and spirituality in "Psalm" as a way to disregard readings of the track as an exercise in African American spirituality and politics. Rather, my aim is to trouble either/or arguments that analyze songs like "Psalm" through only one framework (African American male gospel and politics, or Indian classical music and spirituality). I argue that these African American and Indian spiritual and musical allusions work in tandem. We cannot view "Psalm" as solely a reproduction of an Indian *alap* or exclusively as an African American male Christian preacher's sermon. We must instead see them as mutually constitutive interests and formations ("Psalm" looks back to 1963/"Alabama" and his 1957 dream), and we must think about the cultural and sociopolitical possibilities that arise out of these overlapping and coterminous relations. Taking such concomitant analyses seriously allows us to underscore the ways "Psalm" dovetails with and expands on the place of, for example, Gandhian principles of nonviolence in King's spiritually informed political ideology during the early to mid-1960s. It aligns with the well-known influence of Gandhi's tenets of nonviolent activism on King and the larger nonviolent civil rights struggle in the United States. "Psalm" expounds on this commonly known history by complicating how, as Ingrid Monson explains, African American newspapers and activists underscored the resonances between Gandhi's teachings and biblical scriptures concerning passive resistance, and consequently positioned Gandhi within the Christian terrain and even, at times, compared him to Jesus Christ, thereby detaching him from Hinduism.[65] Recasting such a reading, "Psalm" highlights the overlap between African American and Indian spiritual and political engagements without making one cultural formation the center from which the other emanates. "Psalm" musically articulates collectivity through difference—jazz with a difference.

Placing "Psalm" in conversation with "Acknowledgment," a performance that, because of the cyclicality of *A Love Supreme*, always already informs and shapes "Psalm," opens up a way for us to broaden the parameters of the attachment of "Psalm" to African American and Indian musical, spiritual, and political overlaps. As "Acknowledgement" centers on the phrase "a love supreme," which is the name of the poem that "Psalm" narrates, it reorients the focus of "Psalm" on African American / Indian relations to include Afro-Latinidad (via Tyner's Afro-Latin rhythm), sub-Saharan Africa (via the composition's allusion to Olly Wilson's principles of African and Afro-diasporic music making), the transnational and political meanings of Ahmadiyya Islam, and Black queerness (via the entanglement of the literary and the musical). In so doing, *A Love Supreme* gestures toward an Afro–South Asian utopic space. This is a utopic political future that cultivates connections without eschewing differences between regions, ethnoracial backgrounds, spiritualities, and sexualities. It is a way of thinking about the interlocking systems of Black freedom and third world liberation; black religiosity and transnational spirituality; African and Afro-diasporic music and Indian music; and Black queer futures. It critiques (without transcending) national, ethnoracial, spiritual, and sexual borders. It enacts political possibilities and structures of belonging that demand and critically engage the promise of difference. It imagines and announces the other side of things.

Love on the Life Side of Things

In his 1962 article "Letter from a Region in my Mind," which would later form half of his classic *The Fire Next Time,* James Baldwin writes, "Love takes off the masks that we fear we cannot live without and know we cannot live within. I use the word 'love' here not merely in the personal sense but as a state of being, or a state of grace—not in the infantile American sense of being made happy but in the tough and universal sense of quest and daring and growth."[66] If Baldwin sees love as that which resists the personal and the limits of the nation-state to pursue something more transformative, then this chapter has attempted to theorize the kind of love that John Coltrane, as the "James Baldwin of horn sound," imagines with *A Love Supreme.* For Coltrane, this is a love that informs and is informed by his pursuit of the life side of things. It is a love that sets the groundwork for a Black queer utopian musical vision that is personal and political, spiritual and social, Afro-diasporic and South Asian; and thus, that challenges previous dominant framings of Coltrane that treat such formations as disparate. It is a love that engenders new possibilities of music making and world making. A love that is never satisfied with the present but constantly looks toward and beyond the future—and hence the power of modal jazz in general, and its working in *A Love Supreme* in particular, in allowing Coltrane to endlessly improvise. It is a love that, much like Muñoz's conception of queerness, is always on the horizon.[67] This is perhaps why Coltrane's later albums are titled *Ascension, Sun Ship, Cosmic Music, Stellar Regions,* and *Interstellar Space*—he was searching for a love whose social and political transformative reach knew no bounds. And it's Coltrane's tireless transgression of boundaries that potentially marks his work as queer, or at least queer in relation to Baldwin. His collaborative work with his wife, Alice Coltrane, his enlisting of her to work as his pianist in his band, broke gendered norms within jazz, a legacy that Alice Coltrane continued after her husband's death.[68] For both Alice and John Coltrane, the love they practiced and played, the love that we hear on *A Love Supreme,* is a love that is multiple and collective. It is a love that engaged Afro–South Asian music in such a way that it became a cultural site of political struggles and possibilities. And it was a political struggle that Coltrane's friend and mentor Miles Davis would continue seven years later.

2

Corner Politics

The Queer and South Asian Coalitional
Black Politics of Miles Davis

The corner was our time when time stood still. . . . The corner was our magic,
our music, our politics. . . . The corner was our Rock of Gibraltar, our
Stonehenge, our Taj Mahal, our monument, our testimonial to freedom, to
peace, and to love.

—The Last Poets, "The Corner"

Do you know why he's off to the side [on *On the Corner*]? Because that's
where we push gay people.

—Cortez "Corky" McCoy, interview

His manager called it an "experiment."[1] Miles Davis had offered to curate
and headline the December 12, 1969, reopening of the jazz venue at
the legendary New York City entertainment nightclub the Village Gate (aka
the Gate). A generally trendy and lucrative establishment since its opening
in 1958, the Gate's jazz space experienced such a severe drop in attendance
that it temporarily ceased operations in November 1969.[2] And so Davis, a
fixture at the Gate, devised a plan—an experiment, as his manager called
it—to attract a new wave of patrons and restore the jazz club to its previous
prominence. He organized a two-weekend, three-set performance series
that included his own working group, African American comedian Richard
Pryor, and an unnamed South Asian sitar player.[3] The word "experiment"
not only adequately describes the demographic makeup of the performance
itself—Davis, a renowned, older, African American jazz musician; Pryor, a
fairly new comedian; and an unannounced sitarist—but also captures the

41

essence of Davis and Pryor's respective acts. By December of 1969, Davis had finished recording *Bitches Brew,* started to play new music with a revamped working band that featured South Asian artists, and was working on ideas for what would later be his early 1970 African American–themed albums *Black Beauty* and *Jack Johnson.* Pryor, following a mental breakdown a year prior, had begun to test out edgier material in 1969 that dealt more with, as he later recounted in his autobiography, "the black man's struggle to make it in a white world." Pryor believed that the Gate's reopening was an appropriate site from which to express this new material centered on racial critique and anti-Black racism in the United States.[4] While neither Miles Davis nor Richard Pryor publicly discussed what happened on stage during that weekend, Pryor did share a behind-the-scenes anecdote in his autobiography. This joke suggested that another kind of experiment, an erotic experiment if you will, also took place that weekend: "When I entered [Davis's dressing room] he was kissing Dizzy Gillespie, with tongue and shit, which made me wonder what kind of shit he had planned for me."[5]

Over the next two years, Davis continued to intermittently experiment with South Asian musicians and music in his live sets, but it wasn't until his 1972 record *On the Corner* that he recorded his first and only studio album to include South Asian artists and instrumentation as well as, coincidentally (if not also unwittingly), engage the kinds of ethnoracial (Afro–South Asian) topical (centered on Black politics), and sexual (queer) valences that described his performance at the Gate. Davis's career was at a crossroads with Black audiences. Jazz purists (Black and non-Black) decried his new electric sound and forays into fusion like *Bitches Brew.* Jeremy Smith also argues that Columbia Records, Davis's parent label, brought his electric jazz sound under its national marketing strategy in an attempt to tap into the emergent white "college-aged middle-class" counterculture generation in the United States.[6] It was at this moment that Davis grew increasingly frustrated with this alienation from Black audiences, especially Black youth, telling music critic Stephen Davis, "They [Columbia] don't even try to go into the black neighborhoods and sell records. They tell me, 'We want to introduce you to a new audience,' but that audience is always white! Sheeit!"[7] Enter *On the Corner,* Davis's first and only studio album attempt to explicitly capture "black life" and "be heard by young black people."[8] Davis was especially interested in tapping into the Black Power generation. Musically, *On the Corner* draws on the funk-inspired rhythms of James Brown, Sly Stone, and the Last Poets, all cultural icons of the late 1960s / early 1970s Black Power movements. Visually, the cover dovetails with the political valences of the album's sound, and depicts Afro-donned characters in red, black, and green outfits as well as in black berets and leather jackets—symbols of pan-Africanism and the Black Panther Party, respectively.

And yet, despite *On the Corner's* musical and visual gestures to 1970s Black (cultural) politics, there are two aspects of the album that seemingly run antithetical to dominant articulations of the 1970s Black Power generation that Davis desired to attract with the album, but that also recall his experiment at the Gate: queerness and South Asianness. In addition to the Black male characters in pan-African and Black Panther–inspired garb, the *On the Corner* cover also depicts Black women sex workers and a Black man (and possible sex worker) whose gender presentation does not map onto the sartorial styles of the other men on the cover. They are queer in the Cathy Cohen sense, as I explained in this book's introduction, due to their gendered and sexual expression of a "radical politics of deviance" that is "often portrayed as directly in conflict with the normative assumptions of heterosexism and the nuclear family . . . [and] also often live under the constant surveillance of the state through regulatory agencies."[9] These queer characters complicate the ways in which, as Phillip Brian Harper and Tracye Matthews compellingly argue, dominant ideologies of Black cultural nationalism and the Black Panthers were routinely (but in no way universally) contingent on masculinist and heteronormative logics that often excluded, marginalized, and rendered illegible Black queer men and women.[10]

As the *On the Corner* album cover's queer representations complicate gender and sexual norms of late 1960s and early 1970s Black Power, the music on the album itself expresses deviations from such dominant framings with respect to race and ethnicity. In particular, *On the Corner* features South Asian musicians and music. Davis hired Bangladeshi tabla player Badal Roy and sitarist Khalil Balakrishna to play on all the songs for *On the Corner*. This move to make South Asian culture and subjects central to an album meant to be about "Black life" and articulate with African American politics at the time counters the ways the early to mid-twentieth-century influence and involvement of South Asian political activists on African American activism had waned by the late 1960s. While the late 1960s witnessed a number of coalitions between Asian American and African American political activists, these Afro-Asian crossings predominantly concerned Japanese,

Chinese, and Korean Americans. This elision of South Asian Americans was not only due to the smaller population of South Asians in the United States at the time, but also, as many scholars have pointed out, South Asians' historical and ongoing experience of belonging to and apart from Asian America.[11]

What I'd like to do in this chapter is think through how, and argue that, the place of queerness and South Asianness in *On the Corner* challenges mainstream articulations of Black political thought at the time, and that it offers us a different way of understanding and engaging Black transformative and radical politics. In particular, I'm interested in how *On the Corner* is emblematic of the other side of things, how it presents an alternative imaginary of what I'd like to call "corner politics." I define corner politics as a progressive political framework that employs the multiple and multidirectional meanings of the term "corner" in order to enact an expansive and broad-based leftist political movement that is intersectional, comparative, and transnational. Corner politics is a politics that animates and amplifies. It simultaneously pushes forward and expands in order to draw together, without flattening out, communities who have been pushed to the margins, to the corners of society, under the weight of, and in an allusion to bell hooks, global imperialist white supremacist capitalist heteropatriarchy.[12] And it develops such a vision by thinking through the corner in three interrelated and layered ways. The first uses the corner to address how we typically frame the corner: as a particular space of the urban ghetto—the street corner—that is the product of postwar racial capitalism, and that was the political site of Black liberation politics among the Black Power generation. The corner was, as Nikhil Singh points out, a zone filled with the deemed "denizens" of society who "were cast as potential heroes and liberators" of Black radical politics during the late 1960s and early 1970s.[13]

The second layered meaning of the corner in corner politics takes the fact that corners are literally formed at the intersections to imagine the corner as a site of interlocking systems of power, privilege, and oppression. While the first, typical definition of the corner generally frames it through the lens of race and class, the second definition holds the first accountable by demanding a politics that can also address gender, sexuality, and other vectors of power, difference, and belonging. This second definition rejects the corner (and publicness in general) as always already framed as hetero-masculinist—as a space of and for straight Black men—and considers the corner in relation to, for example, sex work and the queerness of sex work. It considers the labor of the corner that is gendered and sexualized.

Lastly, through the conception of the corner as a site that anchors and facilitates mobility and interaction, the third rubric of corner politics seeks transnational and comparative coalition building as a liberatory goal. It is at the corner, at the intersection, where various people, goods, and ideas are constantly moving, overlapping, and interacting. It is this dynamism of the corner that destabilizes a kind of coalitional vision trapped within the assumed discreteness of identity categories. This final iteration and tier of corner politics consequently pursues a more progressive political vision of transnational and comparative work, and one that creates the possibilities for the kinds of Afro–South Asian work of *On the Corner*.

Corner politics thus is in conversation with but also complicates what Marlon Bailey and Rashad Shabazz call "around the corner."[14] Rooted in the theories of Michel Foucault's "heterotopias" and Katherine McKittrick and Clyde Woods's "black geographies," Bailey and Shabazz use "around the corner" as a concept through which to name the placeless geographies that render visible and invisible Black "so-called deviant subjects, [and] the sexual labor they perform."[15] For Bailey and Shabazz, the corner is a site where Black queer desire is pursued and articulated. However, since such expressions and desires can only occur as tucked away and "around the corner," the corner also names the space of Black queer marginalization. "Corner politics" shares with "around the corner" a focus on the intersections of Blackness, queerness, and labor, but it does so by also considering how such intersections work relationally with other ethnoracial groups (e.g., South Asians). Corner politics seeks to understand how comparative racialization shapes and articulates with around the corner. And in so doing, corner politics names the corner as a cross-racial and queer coalitional site of struggle and possibility.

To be clear, corner politics in general, and its particular manifestation with Davis's *On the Corner*, is not an entirely easy, uncomplicated, or clean liberatory project. Miles Davis, after all, has a long history of misogyny and violence against women (by his own admission), and so it is perhaps somewhat awkward to explore and exalt Davis's pursuit of the other side of things and his engagements with the progressive imaginary of corner politics in *On the Corner*.[16] But it is precisely Davis's violent sexism and misogyny in relation to the transformative work of corner politics and *On the Corner* that interests me. It is emblematic of the struggle of what Cathy Cohen terms "principled coalition work" because it requires us to uncomfortably confront "the relative power and privilege" of our positionalities that "challenge dichotomies such as . . . enemy/comrade."[17] *On the Corner,* then, is a cultural work that visually and sonically represents the process, and not the product, of corner politics. It offers a way for how we might see and sound the kinds of complicated possibilities that corner politics, as an iteration of the other side of things, can express and imagine.

On the Way to the Corner

By the time Miles Davis began recording *On the Corner,* his sound was less strictly attached to the modal and free jazz idioms of the early to mid-1960s, and more in tune with the popular, and often political, genres of rock, soul, R&B, and funk. This is not to say that jazz was no longer political—Joe McPhee's Amiri Baraka–inspired live album *Nation Time,* Pharoah Sanders's *Black Unity,* and the work of the Art Ensemble of Chicago are some of the more explicit examples. Rather, I am saying that by the late 1960s, the forms of popular music, and especially Black popular music, that gained more traction with younger people, and again particularly African American youth, were those aligned with the racialized aesthetics and politics of artists like Sly and the Family Stone, Curtis Mayfield and the Impressions, Aretha Franklin, Vicki Anderson, and James Brown.[18] And so for Davis, the writing was on the wall. He wanted his music to be more timely, topical, and immediate. He wasn't, as he noted in his autobiography, "prepared to be a memory yet."[19]

It was at this moment of Miles Davis's pursuit of resonance in and with the present (to not be a memory yet) that the forty-one-year-old Davis met twenty-two-year-old model and singer-songwriter Betty Mabry. The two connected at the Village Gate in 1967, following one of his performances, and soon began dating. They married a year later, but eventually divorced in 1969. Despite the short-lived relationship, Betty Davis greatly influenced Miles Davis's musical career. Maureen Mahon posits that Betty Davis "was the guiding force behind the sharp musical turn that Miles Davis took at the end of the 1960s" that would come to frame albums like *On the Corner.* It was through Betty Davis that Miles Davis listened to and learned from (and met) Jimi Hendrix, Sly Stone, Aretha Franklin, and James Brown. As Betty Davis helped broaden Miles Davis's musical vision, he started to use more electric instruments in his bands and adopt more rhythmic patterns in line with funk, R&B, and rock. These shifts in Davis's sound marked the beginning of his controversial "electric" turn that can be heard on albums like *Filles de Kilimanjaro*—where Betty Davis appears on the cover; and which contains the song "Mademoiselle Mabry (Miss Mabry)," named after Betty Davis, "a reworking of Hendrix's 'The Wind Cries Mary'"—and *Bitches Brew*—an album name that Betty Davis helped craft and one that popularized the "jazz fusion" subgenre.

Kevin Fellezs writes that fusion is a "broken middle," a permanently un-stable and "liminal space between genres" that tested the limits of rock, funk, and jazz during the late 1960s and early 1970s, and, drawing on Fabian Holt, produced "new social collectivities" that crossed racial and generational borders of young and old, Black and white.[20] As stated at the outset of this chapter, the rock-inspired *Bitches Brew*, with the assistance of the Columbia Records marketing team, attracted a new cohort of college-aged listeners to Davis and his music. But this was a predominantly white audience and one that still eluded his desired Black youth of the Black Power generation. It is perhaps no surprise then that Davis's subsequent studio album, a sound-track to the 1971 documentary film *Jack Johnson*, dabbled in the world of funk: the songs "Right Off" and "Yesternow" contain replayed and reinter-preted elements from Sly and the Family Stone's "Sing a Simple Song" and James Brown's "Say It Loud—I'm Black and I'm Proud," respectively. Fellezs argues that funk "was a musical genre created by, marketed to, and popular within an urban African American audience, sounding out the social reali-ties brought by urban 'renewal' white flight to the suburbs, and the political sensibilities that emerged in an increasingly pessimistic post–civil rights era."[21] By 1971, the year of the release of *Jack Johnson*, Sly Stone was delving into a darker political world with *There's a Riot Goin' On*, James Brown traded in his signature perm for an Afro and was recording songs like "Soul Power," and a newly "soul styled" (in an allusion to Tanisha Ford) Aretha Franklin was publicly supporting and organizing fund-raising events to free Black Power activist Angela Davis.[22] Miles Davis's use of Stone and espe-cially Brown on *Jack Johnson* provided an added musical texture that height-ened the political urgency of a documentary about the historical Black male political figure. With *Jack Johnson*, Miles Davis began to experiment with his own take on a musical album that addressed Black politics of the time. *Jack Johnson* spoke to these politics because the use of funk for a soundtrack

about a Black boxer who challenged the U.S. racial logics of whiteness, masculinity, and civilization tapped into the heteropatriarchal norms of Black
Power; and it was an album that was experimental because Davis's use of
Brown and Stone were hidden and gestural rather than explicit and direct.
But with *On the Corner,* Davis made explicit his forays into a musical aesthetics of Black Power politics, and did so in ways that dramatically reimagined dominant strains of the movement. It was an album that remade the
corner to be a cross-cultural, queer, and coalitional site. It was with *On the
Corner* that Miles Davis advanced the other side of things of Black radical
politics.

Hearing the Corner

On the Corner was recorded over three separate days in the summer of 1972.
The album contains four songs—"On the Corner / New York Girl / Thinkin'
of One Thing and Doin' Another / Vote For Miles" (I have shortened this
title to "On the Corner"), "Black Satin," "One and One," and "Helen Butte /
Mr. Freedom X" (I will refer to this song as "Mr. Freedom X"). "On the
Corner" was laid down on the first day of recording, the remainder of the
album was recorded during the second recording session, and the third session involved overdubbing the tracks recorded during the second session.
Similar to "Yesternow," *On the Corner* features heavily edited material from
the recording sessions. Engineer Teo Macero extracted various parts of the
material from each day of recording, and used a number of postproduction
recording techniques to manipulate each song. Upon the album's release, the
liner notes did not contain the names of the musicians playing on the album,
aside from Miles Davis. Despite Columbia's, Davis's, and other musicians'
attempts over the years to correctly identify the album's personnel, an official
list of Davis's studio bands featured on *On the Corner* remains incomplete.[23]
As a result, I will only refer to certain artists by name if it has been established (through various accounts) that a particular musician played on *On
the Corner.*[24] Regardless of the confusion of personnel, *On the Corner* offers
listeners material that lasts nearly an hour and that constantly incorporates
and shifts between jazz, rock, and funk aesthetics as well as West African,
Afro-diasporic, and South Asian musical practices and idioms.

"On the Corner" starts mid-track (a point in the recording session that
is neither the beginning nor the end) with Michael Henderson, a funk and

R&B bass guitarist who'd been a part of Davis's band for two years, and jazz-fusion drummers/percussionists Billy Hart and Jack DeJohnette, who collaboratively establish a recursive bass and drum groove. Henderson's bass-line riff consists of two sixteenth notes on the downbeat, and Hart and DeJohnette play a sixteenth-note rhythm on the hi-hat. "On the Corner" does not feature a melody or harmonic progression, and leaves the groove to anchor the entire song. The rest of the band indiscriminately plays around this groove, in an almost free improvisational manner. The majority of "On the Corner" involves looped (endlessly repeated) conga and tabla percussive patterns, organ riffs, and guitar and sitar stabs. Jazz-fusion and funk pianist Herbie Hancock plays a synthesizer melody. Davis, jazz-rock fusion guitarist John McLaughlin, jazz-fusion saxophonist David Liebman, and jazz-fusion and funk organist Harold "Ivory" Williams perform solos, but they are lost in the fray of the track's density. The track ends with all the instruments fading out except the percussion elements, which have established a 4/4 pattern, and a looped sitar drone.

"Black Satin" begins where "On the Corner" ends. Tabla player Badal Roy engages a sitarist, but this interplay abruptly ends thirty seconds into the song. Again, like "On the Corner," a mid-track groove is inserted into "Black Satin," featuring another Henderson bass line playing atop a two-bar drum pattern that, as musicologist Jesse Stewart accurately points out, is eerily reminiscent of James Brown's 1967 song "Cold Sweat."[25] Four measures into the "Cold Sweat" groove, Davis and a collective ensemble establish a melody using overdubs of whistling and a wah-wah trumpet. A series of looped handclaps and bells join in the overdubbing, and someone plays a series of synthesizer arpeggios. Davis solos, but is, again, washed out by and engulfed within the rhythmic and melodic complexity and density of the track. James Mtume enhances the rhythmic complexity of "Black Satin" by playing what sounds like a West African *djidundun* (a water drum) in conversation with Roy on the tabla. "Black Satin" concludes with a reintroduction of the tabla/sitar looped opening.

"One and One" and "Mr. Freedom X" are essentially variations of "Black Satin." They both work on the "Cold Sweat" groove by adding a fuller bass line. Moreover, Roy and Mtume continue to play dueling and interlocking percussion patterns on both tracks. "One and One" does not feature any handclaps or whistles, but it does reuse the bells and shakers from "Black Satin." Instead of a Davis solo, multi-reedists Bennie Maupin and Carlos

Garnett perform looped solos on bass clarinet and soprano saxophone, respectively. "One and One" ends with a thunderous hi-hat that coincidently starts "Mr. Freedom X." If one were simply to start with "Mr. Freedom X" without having heard "One and One," one would have imagined the start of "Mr. Freedom X" to feature another mid-track opening. Perhaps a result of how Macero mixed "Mr. Freedom X," Mtume and Roy's percussion appear at the center of the basic drum groove rather than sitting on the periphery like on "One and One" and "Black Satin." That is to say, rather than playing in response to the groove, Roy and Mtume are incorporated into the groove; they are the groove. This sonic layering continues with Hancock and organist Chick Corea playing frequent offbeat chordal voicings. Davis, Garnett, and fusion guitarist David Creamer provide solos that, consistent with the entire album, seem to play at the center rather than the foreground of the recording. Oddly, "Mr. Freedom X" ends just as the band's playing intensifies and the tempo speeds up.

On the Corner constantly weaves in and out of the musical aesthetics of jazz, rock, and funk. The multitude of instrument play and improvisational style signal practices in free jazz, the album's amplified sounds and use of musicians like David Creamer and John McLaughlin gesture toward rock, and its interpolation of James Brown's "Cold Sweat" squarely situates On the Corner in funk. Yet it is precisely Davis's use of these singular elements of funk, rock, and jazz as a musical constellation that transgress the normative divides of these genres.[26] Upon the album's release, music critics as well as the musicians involved in the making of On the Corner had difficulty labeling the work.[27] It was perhaps in light of On the Corner's ambiguity, disruption, and multiplicity of approaches that Miles Davis proclaimed that the record "had no label," and rejected allegiance to a particular genre.[28] The most important thing for Davis was that On the Corner adequately spoke to his vision of Blackness and African American street life.

To help fulfill this vision, Davis sought a sound and a band for On the Corner that could, as he would later explain, provide a "deep African thing, a deep African-American groove, with a lot of emphasis on drums and rhythm, and not on individual solos."[29] Davis's words and vision align with Olly Wilson's tenets of African and Afro-diasporic music making tendencies, which John Coltrane pursued with A Love Supreme. On the Corner's inclusion of multiple percussion instruments and emphasis on repetitious grooves, at the expense of harmonic progressions or melody, ties into the centrality of rhythm and cyclicality in West African music. Further, Davis's insistence on filling dead space with guitar stabs and synthesizer arpeggios underscores West African musicians' tendency to create dense music. *On the Corner*'s density is enacted through the employment of a large ensemble (a rough estimate is fourteen players) and varied musical instruments (tablas, sitars, electric guitar, bass guitar, congas, hi-hats, wah-wah-inflected trumpet, etc.) that speaks to what Wilson calls the "kaleidoscopic" basis of the heterogeneous sound ideal of African musical production. These are approaches that create a collective music making experience. Indeed, all the riffs, stabs, licks, and comps interlock with the overall makeup of each song. Teo Macero also plays with the EQ levels on the album, a technique that refuses a foregrounding of solos and pushes a blending of them with the rest of the studio working group. *On the Corner* thus makes audible the kind of participatory democracy that marks much of West African music—it marks an embrace of the collective and the communal.[30]

The adapted "Cold Sweat" groove throughout most of *On the Corner* also illuminates Davis's desire for an African and Afro-diasporic aesthetic. Olly Wilson is again useful here as he famously explained how James Brown's music during the 1960s and 1970s draws on musical practices of West Africa— its heterogenous sound ideal—and that it is this kind of adaptation that explicates Brown's popularity in West Africa and his role in the creation of Afrobeat.[31] Brown's music simultaneously represents the historical traces of and contemporary links to West African musical traditions. Davis's allusions to "Cold Sweat," then, dually mark an embrace of funk as well as a late 1960s / early 1970s pan-Africanist engagement with transnational forms of relatedness and belonging, illustrating a cultural and political commitment to domestic and transnational Black expression.

And yet, as Davis unites West African and Afro-diasporic musical aesthetics on *On the Corner*, and articulates a cultural and political ideology of Blackness, the presence of Badal Roy (and to a lesser extent Khalil Balakrishna) gesture to how such expressions of Blackness are contingent on, if not inextricably tied to, South Asian culture. Throughout *On the Corner*, Roy's tabla playing is in dialogue with a West African or Afro-diasporic instrument. Teo Macero uses stereo-switching to pan a conga or *djidundun* (depending on the recording session) and Roy's tabla to opposite outlet sides, and then loops each percussive phrasing after every measure. This technique produces an effect where both percussion instruments are involved in a duet. This is not call-and-response, but rather a different form of musical dialogue that, through looping each instrument at equal temporal sequences and units, approximates collective, interlocked, mutually constitutive, and simultaneous sonic conversations.

Additionally, just as Badal Roy's collaborative work with the entire *On the Corner* studio band underscores the linkages between South Asian, West African, and Afro-diasporic culture, Miles Davis's reasoning behind inviting Roy to play on the album highlights a much deeper cross-racial and transnational engagement. When I interviewed Roy and his wife, Geeta (a jazz tambourist in her own right), I asked him why Davis wanted him on the album. Roy responded, "He wanted to introduce the Indian sound. Miles really wanted to introduce the Indian sound."[32] Perhaps influenced by the increasing use of the electric sitar in R&B songs like Stevie Wonder's "Signed, Sealed, Delivered (I'm Yours)" or tracks by Philadelphia Soul artists like the Delfonics' "Didn't I (Blow Your Mind This Time)," Davis and his friends visited Indian restaurants in New York City to find and hire South Asian talent.[33] According to James Mtume, Davis frequented an Indian restaurant on 125th Street in Harlem to gather ideas "of using the electric sitar and tablas."[34] And Roy informed me that Teo Macero was the one who initially approached him about playing for Davis after hearing Roy perform at an Indian restaurant in the East Village. I soon asked Roy what the first recording session was like with Davis after he was hired to perform on the album. He told me, "I was sitting on the floor with my tabla, and all of these musicians were there. And before we started, he [Davis] comes to me and says, 'You start.' And then I didn't understand, but I started the groove anyway."[35] Roy did not have any formal training in jazz or in Indian classical music, and had a limited professional history playing with ensembles.[36] To that end, Roy was anxious about being the one who would start the first rehearsals and recording sessions for *On the Corner*. Roy informed me that he expressed his nervousness to Davis, who responded by saying, "Play like a nigga. Just play like a nigga."[37]

Roy told me that while he "did not understand what he [Davis] meant," Roy read Davis's remark as indicating a desire for Roy to "play from the heart." Understanding Roy's reading of this statement, I want to take a broader step back and consider what it means for a Black man who's developing an album about Black politics and geared toward Black youth to ask a South Asian man to "play like a nigga" in 1972. While there are certainly a number of ways to interpret Davis's response to Roy—race as a social construct, "nigger" versus "nigga," and affective structures of racial formation—I read Davis's remark as a request for Roy to commit what Vijay Prashad calls "model minority suicide."[38] For Prashad, "model minority" is a sociopolitical and sociohistorical category that frames Asian Americans (and particularly South Asian Americans and immigrants in the United States) as figurative weapons to be used against African Americans in order to maintain Black alterity and uphold white supremacy. As a result, to commit model minority suicide means to express and enact solidarity with African Americans and work together to subvert and dismantle white supremacy and other structures of inequality.

To be clear, the model minority category was not as firmly rooted in U.S. politics and culture in 1972 as it is today, but it still had a particular effect among South Asian American and South Asian immigrant groups. Susan Koshy notes that 1970 was the first and only time in U.S. history that the census officially counted South Asians as white.[39] As a result, by the time Roy became involved in *On the Corner*, the United States had created a path for South Asian immigration, and thereby a path for South Asian immigrants and South Asian Americans toward whiteness. The U.S. racialization of South Asians as white dates back to the early twentieth century. But as scholars like Mae Ngai and Ian Haney López explain, South Asian immigrants used this turn-of-the-century association with whiteness in order to subvert the racial and spatial exclusionary parameters of U.S. citizenship.[40] By contrast, this 1970s racialization of South Asians as white was state-led and state-sanctioned, and worked to distance and discipline African American subjects. Indeed, this census change worked in tandem with the class and sexually normative kinship–biased legislative provisions of the Immigration Act of 1965 that disproportionately increased the number of middle- and upper-class Asian immigrant nuclear families in the United States, and consequently created a political and cultural assimilative space and incentive through which South Asian immigrants like Roy could identify with whiteness, middle-classness, and normative housing formations through and against the criminalized, policed, and often deemed sexually nonnormative Black working-class communities.[41] To "play like a nigga," then, serves as an invitation to sever ties with whiteness and be in solidarity with Black people, Black life, Blackness, and Black music. It is an insistence on Roy to align with rather than stand against Black working-class quotidian life that the legal and political regimes of the U.S. nation-state and mainstream culture actively and violently sought to curtail. It is a call to reject the hailing

of white-middle class normativity—"model minority suicide"—in order to
form alliances with Black communities against such race, gender, class, and
sexual normative systems of oppression. It is an insistence to live and play
within the other side of things.

We can hear these kinds of Afro–South Asian alliances, these coalitional
auralities, on *On the Corner*. Roy and Mtume participate in rhythmic duets
and interlock the percussive sounds of a tabla and Afro-diasporic drumming
(Figures 1a and 1b). Macero's manipulation of the recording sessions and
play with the structures of both Roy and Mtume present percussive patterns
that refuse the sonic norms governing their instruments' traditional (and
masculinist) histories, and instead allow for a collective playing against one
another. They perform what Afro–South Asian solidarity might sound like
when a South Asian immigrant and/or American commits model minority
suicide and resists the racial, gender, and sexual normativity that such a category demands. This is the kind of (queer?) approach to recording that Roy
and Mtume share in the same aural space on *On the Corner*. They develop
an overlapping, homosocial, and Afro–South Asian sonic collective—their
playing enacts a sonic manifestation of corner politics.

Seeing the Corner

The complex Black, queer, and coalitional politics within the music of *On
the Corner* extends to the album's cover. Miles Davis's friend and personal
photographer Cortez "Corky" McCoy illustrated (with the assistance of
McCoy's wife, Sandra McCoy) the cover for *On the Corner*. Using a cartoon aesthetic, the front cover (Figure 2a) is set against a yellow background,
with the word "ON" atop the cover, and features eight African American
characters—seven men and one woman. There are two men with Afros
engaged in a "low five" hand greeting. Both men are wearing red, black, and
green sweaters, and one of the men has the phrase "VOTE MILES" written on
the sweater in red and green lettering. The sole woman on the front cover is
wearing a form-fitting outfit that ends at her butt. She is involved in a conversation with a man wearing a business suit, and he has pulled out his
empty pockets to signify to her that he does not have any money—an act
that suggests that the woman is a sex worker. This speculation is seemingly
confirmed as a man in a bright pink suit, and even brighter yellow hat, is
pointing his finger in the woman's direction while speaking to another man,

a

Figure 1. (a) James Mtume
(congas), Miles Davis
(trumpet), and Badal Roy
(tabla), circa January 1973.
James Baker Free Spirit Press
Collection. Reproduced with
permission from the
Department of Special
Collections and University
Archives, W. E. B. Du Bois
Library, University of
Massachusetts Amherst.
(b) Miles Davis (trumpet),
Badal Roy (tabla), Khalil
Balakrishna (electric sitar),
circa January 1973. James
Baker Free Spirit Press
Collection. Reproduced with
permission from the
Department of Special
Collections and University
Archives, W. E. B. Du Bois
Library, University of
Massachusetts Amherst.

b

which suggests that the flamboyantly dressed man in pink is a pimp and the man next to him is a prospective client.[42] Near the bottom of the front cover, a middle-aged man wearing a black leather jacket, black beret, and a button that reads "FREE ME" is positioned in a way such that he is looking at the viewer. Each character is engaged with someone else (two youths, pimp and his prospective client, the man who does not have money to hire the sex worker, and the older man and the viewer), except one character. Off to the distance, there is a young man in a yellow sweater with his arms crossed, lips pursed, and pinky-finger pointed upward, and he is looking at the entire scene on the corner with a raised eyebrow.

The *On the Corner* back cover (Figure 2b) is similar but distinct from the front. This back cover has the word "OFF" written at the top as opposed to the front cover's use of the word "ON." Rather than eight, the back cover features seven characters; and instead of one woman, there are two. The sex worker and her would-be business-suited client are again engaged in conversation, but this time, he is holding a stack of books. The Black male youth in the "VOTE MILES" sweater is without his friend, but is still seen simultaneously raising his fist in the air while smiling at a woman wearing a crop top and miniskirt. The pimp is seen smiling at both the woman and this young man, implying that either she is also a sex worker or that the pimp wants her to work for him. Moreover, instead of looking at the viewer, the middle-aged man is holding on to an electrical plug for his trumpet and is wearing a button that reads "SOUL" on his leather jacket. Finally, the young Black man who was on the side of the corner and wearing a yellow sweater on the front cover is now wearing a midriff variation of this sweater, exposing his six-pack abs. Similar to the front cover, his lips are pursed and his pinky finger is extended on his left hand.

Taken as a whole, the front and back cover art of *On the Corner* aimed to depict the social climate and political possibilities of African American working-class people living in urban ghettos during the early 1970s. As the work of many postwar African American historians illustrates, many Black Power groupings saw the urban space of the ghetto in general, and the corner in particular, as a central site of Black liberation. From the 1940s through the 1970s various state-sanctioned economic and spatial policies and processes produced, to quote Arnold Hirsch, a "second ghetto" that segregated and confined working-class and working-poor African Americans to underdeveloped, economically strained, and heavily policed urban areas.[43] Black Power

Figure 2. (a) *On the Corner*, by Miles Davis, Columbia Records, album cover (front), 1972. Artwork by Cortez McCoy. (b) *On the Corner*, by Miles Davis, Columbia Records, album cover (back), 1972. Artwork by Cortez McCoy.

organizations, and in particular the Black Panthers, posited that the ghetto
constituted a U.S. internal colony, and therefore Black liberation struggles
demanded new approaches that challenged the United States as an empire
and not simply a nation. Moreover, the Panthers, drawing on Frantz Fanon,
argued that because the ghetto represented a U.S. colony, its residents were a
lumpenproletariat that comprises "the pimps, the hooligans, the unemployed
and the petty criminals" of "street corner society," and could be mobilized as
a political unit to address racial and economic structural inequalities.[44]
These colonized subjects' racialized and classed status provided them with
the consciousness of marginalization, and the Panthers sought to tap into
this consciousness to forge new collectivities as a way to combat and dismantle structural oppression.

The *On the Corner* album cover (back and front) thus illustrates a scene
of the Black ghetto present, with the two pan-African men representing
active members in Black liberation struggles, the pimp and prospective sex
worker clients as subjects to be mobilized in the movement, and the middle-
aged man in pseudo–Black Panther garb (he's missing a gun) as a presumed
leader of such political movements. I want to briefly draw attention to this
latter character because he not only is the sole figure staring at the viewer,
but also because he seems to symbolize Miles Davis. The back cover shows
this character playing the trumpet attached to an electronic device, which
recalls Davis's frequent use of the wah-wah pedal during the fusion period
of the recording. Moreover, his "SOUL" button speaks generally to the soul
style of the 1970s and its ties to Black politics, and it gestures specifically to
James Brown, known as the "Godfather of Soul." Brown had released "Soul
Power," a record that extended the rhetorical and cultural self-affirmation
"Black Power" just a year prior to *On the Corner* and, as noted above, Miles
Davis riffs off his song "Cold Sweat" for most of *On the Corner*.[45]

Brown and Davis are also known for their misogyny and abuse of women,
and there is perhaps evidence of this in the *On the Corner* album cover. For
example, the "FREE ME" button that the cartoon figure representing Miles
Davis wears signals the late 1960s imprisonment of Black Panther Minister
of Defense Huey Newton and the "Free Huey" slogans that responded to
and expressed solidarity with his incarceration. At the same time, however,
by having a man wear the "FREE ME" button, the illustration masks Angela
Davis's incarceration, which was more recent than Newton's. Further, the
male character wearing the "VOTE MILES" sweater alludes to the upcoming

1972 presidential election, but it does so in ways that paper over Shirley Chisholm's historic presidential run and reorients it toward that of a Black man. Lastly, Davis notes in his autobiography that he wanted Corky McCoy to depict "black women . . . wearing them real tight dresses that had their big butts sticking way out in the back . . . women trying to hide them big bad asses, trying to tuck them in."[46] In essence, Davis wanted McCoy to represent Black women in such a way that male consumers would be able to capture, fix, and gaze at the Black female body and the assumed already-present sexual availability of such bodies.

Yet, what Miles Davis imagined is not exactly what McCoy ended up illustrating. Corky and Sandra McCoy are known for their erotic representations of Black women. In particular, the McCoys worked for the Black pornography outlet *Players*, a magazine where, during McCoy's stint with them, poet Wanda Coleman served as the editor and sought cultural work whose nonnormativity was "wholly unaccounted for in the black arts movement or the womanist movement."[47] The depictions of sex workers on the *On the Corner* album cover speak to these kinds of representations that sit outside the heteronormativity of mainstream formations of the Black Arts Movement and the sex negativity of dominant strains of the womanist movement. More to the point, Sandra McCoy explained to me that while the drawings might feature "scantily clad women," these women also "respond to" the Black men with whom they engaged.[48] We see this on the front cover of *On the Corner* where the woman sex worker is taller than her prospective client, the client is noticeably embarrassed that he doesn't have any money, and the sex worker performs a hands-on-the-hip gesture of disapproval. These depictions work to illustrate and recast the corner as not simply a race- and class-based space of Black working-class and working-poor life, but also a site of sexual labor and desire, especially for Black women for whom sexuality is historically tied to violence and/or silence.

McCoy extends such sexual valences and gendered gestures of disapproval to the male character posing on the outskirts of the street corner of the front and back *On the Corner* covers. He is a character that I read as queer because his gender expression is vastly different from the other men on the cover, and because his pursed lips, exposed midriff, extended pinky, and devasting side-eye all point to the kinds of "communicative physical gestures" that José Muñoz refers to as the ephemeral evidence of queerness.[49] During my interview with Corky McCoy, I asked him about the character, and he told me, "Do you know why he's off to the side? Because that's where we push gay people. That's the answer. . . . This country is a great marginalizer."[50] McCoy would go on to tell me that Davis's out gay brother Vernon as well as Davis's generally unknown close friendship with James Baldwin inspired the illustration of the queer Black man on the cover.[51] McCoy's acknowledgment that Baldwin and Vernon Davis served as models for the queer Black man on the *On the Corner* cover speak to the kinds of queer antagonism that I described in the previous chapter that Baldwin faced—queerphobia that only exacerbated in the late 1960s and early 1970s, especially with activists like Eldridge Cleaver (who would eventually become Minister of Information for the Black Panthers)—and Vernon's frustration with McCoy for eliding queer people in his artwork. As McCoy explained to me, "Miles's brother would always say to me 'You do all these pictures, but you never draw any gay people.'"[52] The *On the Corner* cover thus makes visible as well as critiques the marginalization of Black queer men in mainstream articulations and representations of Black politics and everyday life in the early 1970s. McCoy's drawing of a Black queer male character works as a political statement that exposes rather than extends the sidelining of Black queer men. It is not a liberal assimilative representation of inclusion. It is a depiction that underscores Black gay men's marginality. We might thus read the character's ability to ignore (as we see on the back cover) or side-eye (as we see on the front cover) the other characters on the street corner as an acknowledgment of how he is erased under dominant Black Power ideologies, a displeasure at such an erasure, and a critical refusal to be incorporated within such an ideology that demands a further erasure of queerness.[53]

It is this marginality that positions the Black queer man and the Black women sex workers in relation to one another on the *On the Corner* album cover. The cover gestures toward nonnormative marginality as the basis through which to organize a leftist-inspired street corner political vision. Instead of fleeing the corner into the arms of a white mainstream gay politics or second-wave feminism (and thus muting their Blackness) or hiding from the corner (an act that pleases dominant Black Power ideologies), the characters remain firmly rooted in and on the corner. Marginality and nonnormativity, as Cathy Cohen argues, form "the basis for progressive transformative coalitional work," and so it is the corner that anchors and animates their political vision.[54] Thus, when paired with the Afro–South Asian sonics of the album, *On the Corner* provides an audiovisual guide of how to imagine transformative and radical politics differently, how to see and hear an iteration of the other side of things that I call corner politics.

Playing on the Corner

On September 29, 1972, almost two weeks before *On the Corner*'s release, Miles Davis and several members of the studio band held a live concert at the Philharmonic Hall in New York. The band performed all songs with a mix of West African, Afro-diasporic, and South Asian instrumentation and sound. The show was recorded and released as an album titled *In Concert*. Similar to *On the Corner*, Corky McCoy illustrated the record (Figure 3).

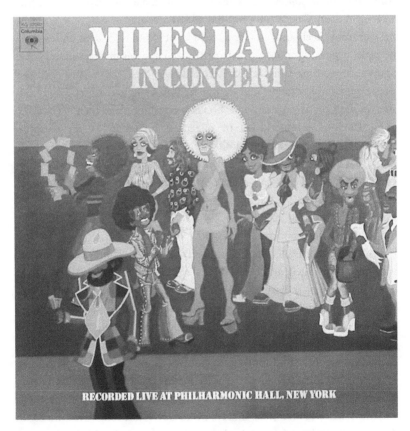

Figure 3. *In Concert*, by Miles Davis, Columbia Records, album cover, 1973. Artwork by Cortez McCoy.

McCoy again employed the medium of cartoon drawings to depict the demographic of the concert's audience. The cover features white hippie figures, which signified the fans Davis gained through *Bitches Brew*, and features the same cartoon characters from *On the Corner* to signal the return of Davis's imagined African American attendees and political and cultural community. Each Black character on the cover holds a ticket, which are absent from the hands of the white characters. This is a significant difference in the illustration, as it indexed Davis's 1971 concert at the Philharmonic where he provided free tickets to African American men and women who could not otherwise afford to attend the event.[55]

Perhaps surprisingly, the Black queer male from *On the Corner* is on the front cover of *In Concert*. He is again the only male with exposed skin (he's wearing a deep V-neck top), but has added a couple of new accessories to his wardrobe: heels and a suede purse. I want to focus for a bit on his purse because, beginning in 1970, Davis patronized a queer underground leather and suede clothing store called Hernando's in New York's West Village.[56] Many queer tourist guides during the early 1970s, like the 1971 *Timely Gay Bar Guide,* listed Hernando's as a shop of interest for queer men in the city.[57] While Davis never remarked on the queerness of Hernando's, he did express in his autobiography that the clothes sold there articulated "blackness, you know, the black consciousness movement."[58] In line with Davis's expansive expression of Blackness on *On the Corner,* Davis's ideal fashioning of Black consciousness from Hernando's included "a lot of African and Indian fabrics. . . . African dashikis and robes and looser clothes plus a lot of Indian tops."[59] Badal Roy confirmed Davis's love of Indian clothing to me. He also informed me that Davis would frequently ask Roy for kurtas: "He told me what color he wanted, and I gave several shirts to him."[60]

I conclude with a discussion of *In Concert* and Hernando's because they illustrate the interplay between Blackness, South Asianness, Black queerness, and Black politics within Miles Davis's music in 1972. I am not arguing that such a constitutive relationship was a necessary link for Davis throughout his career and life. Instead, I want to suggest that there was something in those 1972 recordings that provided a window into how Davis understood, or perhaps how he wanted us to see and hear, the political and cultural meanings and importance of Blackness. Indeed, Miles Davis's last song to feature South Asian artists and music was also his last song that dealt with Black queerness: "Billy Preston," a tribute to the legendary Black queer rock and funk musician of the same name. Thus, with *On the Corner* and his other 1972 recordings, Miles Davis expanded and reframed the then-present visions of Black political thought. He offered a different way of understanding and engaging Blackness that crosscut and included communities across the lines of race and sexuality. It was a politically framed articulation of Blackness that publicly embraced Black queerness and South Asian expressive culture as central formations through which to envision transformative politics, a corner politics, that would help us see and hear the other side of things. The kinds of collective playing heard on *On the Corner* (facilitated by Teo Macero's splicing of various recording sessions) would come to influence many artists in funk and rap. And, as we will see in the next chapter, it was an influence that also included queer Afro–South Asian musical and visual aesthetics and that shaped the work and artistry of musicians like Rick James, OutKast, and Missy Elliott.

3

Punks, Freaks, OutKasts, and ATLiens

The Afro–South Asian Imaginings of Rick James and André 3000

Strange! The gossip is so tragic / They call me a faggot / And me and all my women laugh at it.

—Rick James, "Pass the J"

Then the question is "Big Boi what's up with André? / Is he in a cult? Is he on drugs? Is he gay?"

—OutKast, "Return of the G"

In 1986 Rick James released *The Flag* (Figure 4), his final solo album under Motown Records. The album was a dramatic departure for James. Instead of the party-filled and drug-laden records that most listeners associated with him, James wanted *The Flag* to be a more serious take on his life and politics. James was purportedly now sober (after decades of drug abuse), he had briefly moved to Sint Maarten to record the album and maintain his sobriety, and he was increasingly upset with the nuclear crisis of the Cold War and what he called the "hypocrisy of the American empire" under President Ronald Reagan.[1] *The Flag* was James's response to these personal and political issues. He criticizes Reagan and Soviet Union General Secretary Mikhail Gorbachev on songs like "Funk in America / Silly Little Man"; and he discusses his struggles with sobriety on "Free to Be Me." When it came time to shoot the album cover, James did away with his standard long wigs and glittered body, and opted instead for a natural hair look and fully clothed all-black leather jumpsuit. Additionally, the cover finds James standing in front of and holding a red, black, and green flag, which James dubbed the "freak flag," an allusion to his erotic 1981 hit song "Super Freak." More than that, the colors of the flag and subject matter of the album signified an Afro-diasporic and pan-African political aesthetic that we saw in the previous chapter on Miles Davis's *On the Corner* album. And in addition to, and in conversation with, *The Flag*'s gestures to Black freedom struggles, James also saw this album as a symbol of "freedom, truth, a conviction of love for our brothers and sisters on the planet Earth."[2]

A decade later, southern hip-hop duo OutKast, comprising Antwan "Big Boi" Patton and André "André 3000" Benjamin, released their sophomore

Figure 4. *The Flag*, by Rick James, Gordy/Motown Records, album cover (front), 1986. Photographed by Chris Callis.

album, *ATLiens* (Figure 5). Like Rick James with *The Flag*, OutKast broke new creative ground with *ATLiens*. It came at a time of transitions for Big Boi, André, and OutKast as a whole. Big Boi was trying to make sense of the gift and the grief of his daughter's birth, on the one hand, and the death of his parental guardian, on the other. André was newly single and, following a trip to Jamaica, newly sober, vegetarian, and spiritual. Finally, as a group, OutKast was reeling from the controversy of unexpectedly winning Best New Rap Group at the 1995 Source Awards (at the time *The Source* was a leading hip-hop magazine in the United States) and then immediately contending with the mostly bicoastal audience publicly booing them as they accepted the award. While Big Boi tried to ignore the jeers by placating the

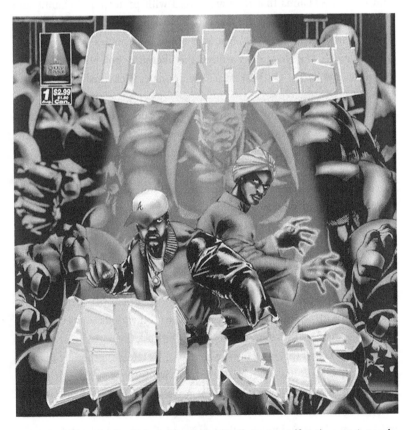

Figure 5. *ATLiens,* by OutKast, LaFace Records, album cover (front), 1996. Artwork by Frank Gomez.

audience with praises to New York, André responded with the now often-quoted, impassioned statement, "The South's got somethin' to say." It is within this personal and professional whirlwind that *ATLiens* embodies and Out-Kast articulates what exactly the South had to say. Musically, *ATLiens* draws on sparse, industrial, and minor dark tones in order to narrate the particular struggles of poverty, fame, relationships (romantic and platonic), and death and mourning in the Black South. Visually, *ATLiens* remakes OutKast into superhero aliens. Both the liner notes of the album, which took the form of a twenty-four-page comic book, and the album's accompanying music videos, present Big Boi and André as Afro-futuristic aliens who originated in an ancient, North Africa–like place called ATLantis on "new Earth." And it is in ATLantis that they are tasked with protecting ATLantis and "positive music" from an evil force called Nosamulli and, as the "Elevators (Me & You)" music video outlines, lead oppressed peoples from bondage.[3] If Rick James's *The Flag* rallies around the liberatory potential of the freak flag on "planet Earth," OutKast on *ATLiens* pursues such freedom dreams on "new Earth."[4]

In this chapter, I want place these albums and artists in conversation because I believe that, in addition to and constitutive of their similarities out-lined above, they exemplify 1980s and 1990s iterations of what I'm calling throughout this book the other side of things: those queer imaginative spaces that are expressed and enacted through sonic and cultural Black and South Asian relationalities. What I find most striking about both Rick James and *The Flag* in 1986 and OutKast and *ATLiens* in 1996 is that their respective Afro-diasporic (as both were influenced through travels in the Black Carib-bean) and Afrocentric (via ties to pre- and postcolonial Africa) political ide-ologies rely on South Asian aesthetics. *The Flag* is not simply Rick James's first and only explicitly political solo album; it is also his first and only solo album with South Asian instrumentation—on various songs contained therein James plays the sitar and tabla. For OutKast, the period surrounding the album *ATLiens* (prior to, during, and after its release) generally marks a moment in André's life when he started wearing turbans and South Asian–inspired clothing. While most likely a response to André's Jamaican spiritual awakening (similar to that of John Coltrane's outlined in chapter 1), the liner notes / comic book and music videos cast André's new sartorial style as indi-cative of his new alien life form Bin Hamin (a take on an Arabic and Muslim reworking of Benjamin, André's real-life surname) who couples a turban with an Indian *sherwani* or *kurta* or, in a possible nod to blending African and South Asian aesthetics, a dashiki.[5] Rick James and André 3000, thus, engage and adopt South Asian culture as essential elements in and extensions of their musical pursuits. They become central to their imaginings of a different kind of transnational, and for André otherworldly, Black aesthetics and politics—in other words, they become expressions of James and André's performance of the other side of things.

If the previous chapter explored Miles Davis's *On the Corner* to illustrate how the corner helps us imagine a political site and movement from which to articulate an intersectional and coalitional Afro–South Asian politics in the 1970s, this chapter locates Rick James's "freak" in *The Flag* and OutKast's "alien" in *ATLiens* as cultural figures who express a similar kind of queer and comparative political alliance in and for the 1980s and 1990s, respectively. Freaks and aliens are not neutral social formations. They are historically situated and are produced through race, class, gender, sexuality, ability, and other modes of power, difference, and belonging. To be a freak and/or an alien is to be a racial, gendered, and sexualized other. It is to be an assemblage of difference that is simultaneously separate(d) from and subject(ed) to norms of cultural and legal citizenship. As African Americans and South Asian Americans are routinely racialized as non-Americans whose outsider racialization is dependent on and conditioned by gender and sexual nonnormativity, the figure of the alien and freak holds particular resonance for both communities.[6] The freak and the alien are avatars of strangeness whose racial, gendered, and sexualized transgressions mark them as threats to the state as well as the norms governing "proper" racial identities (here, Black and brown identity). Indeed, the lyrics quoted in this chapter's epigraph are responses to the rumored queerness of James and André 3000 that Black funk and rap musicians fueled in the 1980s and 1990s for those figures' embrace of freak and alien aesthetics. And so when we consider how the 1980s and 1990s witnessed an increased rigidity and anxiety around social and geographical borders that came with the rise in the middle-class norms of respectability of African Americans and South Asian Americans as well as hysteria around public health (via HIV/AIDS) and immigration (via threats of communist infiltration, NAFTA, and H1-B visas), it not only makes it that much more important that we think through the linkages of queerness and Afro–South Asian cultural production in works like *The Flag* and *ATLiens*. It also underscores the political stakes of Rick James and André 3000 adopting the positionalities of aliens and freaks at this moment in time.

This chapter considers how Rick James and André 3000 cultivated new Black sonic and political possibilities through using freaks and aliens, respectively, as Afro–South Asian intercultural queer aesthetic formations. I argue that James and André's incorporations of South Asian culture were not anomalies in the sense of negligible encounters. Rather, they were anomalies in that they were crucial to and articulated with the outsider positionalities of aliens and freaks. South Asian style and sound in *ATLiens* and *The Flag* were necessary aberrations in the Black queer political performance of the alien and freak. James and André's engagements with South Asian culture helped them create new imaginative ground of Black identity, music, politics, and performance. I explicate these points, first, with Rick James's *The Flag* to think through what it means to build a cross-racial and queer coalition around a "freak flag" during the 1980s Cold War and AIDS crisis. I then move to Out-Kast and *ATLiens* to explore how André 3000 and Big Boi (although primarily André) use aliens in order to stage an Afro–South Asian futurist new South. Finally, I will close by briefly exploring Missy Elliott and her 2001 hit song "Get Ur Freak On." It is with "Get Ur Freak On" that I read how she continues the legacy, the Afro–South Asian genealogy of sound, of James and André's freak and alien, respectively, by bringing them into the twenty-first century.

Punk Funk and Desi Superfreaks

According to his autobiographies as well as published interviews, Rick James developed an appreciation of South Asian life and culture when he traveled to India in the late 1960s and early 1970s, prior to the start of his solo career. James claims that he and his then girlfriend Kelly were broke, and that a friend suggested that they try their hand at selling drugs in order to make some quick cash. This friend was a purported drug-dealing middleman between India and Toronto, where Kelly and James were living at the time, and co-ordinated the drug pickup. James and Kelly soon flew to New Delhi to pick up the shipment, which they would later sell in Canada as well as the United States, and it was in New Delhi that they met a relative of famed sitarist Ravi Shankar.[7] The meeting proved fruitful as James remarked that Shankar's relative "sold me a sitar and gave me lessons. I loved the axe."[8] After a few lessons, James returned to Toronto with weed, money, and his sitar in tow.

In order to get more insight into James's relationship to South Asian culture, I interviewed, separately, Rick James's brother and former manager LeRoi Johnson as well as Motown's former creative director Johnny Lee. For Johnson, he informed me that his brother "loved Indian culture. He even had a room in his home that he called the 'India room' that contained all kinds of Indian instruments."[9] Lee echoed Johnson's remarks, and noted that the "India room" was a space that "nobody got to go in to except Rick. . . . He wouldn't even let me see it when he was giving me the tour of his house! But he actually said to me, specifically, 'Nobody goes in to this room except me.'"[10] I continued my line of questioning with Johnson, and decided to bring up the drug-deal proposition that supposedly led to James's introduction to the sitar and Indian culture:

> EHP: I read in his autobiography as well as Peter's [Peter Benjaminson's] biography that Rick learned how to play the sitar during his time as a drug dealer when he traveled to India. What can you tell me about that?
>
> LJ: Well [long pause] I think you also have to consider that Rick was living in Toronto. He'd dodged the draft and a lot of draft dodgers were there. The counterculture and hippies were there, you know? That's where he started his first band with Neil Young and—
>
> EHP: The Mynah Birds, yeah.
>
> LJ: Yeah! And so you have the counterculture there. And there were also a lot of Indian people in Toronto, too. So that's where you have to start. London too.[11]

I want to focus a bit on Johnson's sidestepping of my question concerning James's drug dealing in India. I do so not because I think Johnson dismisses James's accounts in India, or because he might not be familiar with his brother's time in India or drug-dealing background, or even because he does not want to further tether his brother to drug culture. Rather, I'm interested in Johnson's reluctance to speak about Rick James's time in India, and instead digress to Toronto and London, because this move speaks to what Alexandra Vazquez theorizes as the power of "asides."[12] For Vazquez, following the work of Barbara Johnson, an aside "is a compelling example of what broadening the terms of the musical can make possible. It enables us to read and hear music as that which goes beyond songs and/or praxis. It is a thread of performance—if and when it is picked up—that allows for movement into critical and creative places often lost."[13] Johnson's aside, then, works as a reframing of my question. It is a directive to me to "consider" and to "start" elsewhere, an elsewhere that looks to relocate my intellectual inquiry and reorient a narrative. In particular, I read Johnson's aside as an opening into a different genealogy of James's artistry, one that places his interest in South Asian music (1) as an African *and* South Asian diasporic formation; and, relatedly, (2) in conversation with the other cultural and political developments that would come to shape James's signature "punk funk" sound and its attendant relation to the figure of the (super)freak.

By most accounts, Rick James's years outside the United States, and especially those in Toronto, were the most formative in his career. It was in Toronto that James became part of his first professional band, an R&B-forward rock group called the Mynah Birds (initially named the Sailor Boys) that he fronted and that included soon-to-be-famous rock artists Neil Young, Bruce Palmer, Nick St. Nicholas, and Goldy McJohn.[14] It was in Toronto that Motown Records signed the Mynah Birds, giving James his first record contract and initiating his professional relationship with the label. And it was in Toronto that James went AWOL due to his opposition to the Vietnam War and subsequently changed his name from James Johnson to Rick James. In essence, it was outside the United States that Rick James, literally and figuratively, became Rick James.

But LeRoi Johnson's interview with me complicates this standard narrative and the Black and white terms in which it is frequently framed. This general account places James, an African American man, in a predominantly white band, living in the predominantly white city (or imagined as such) of Toronto, and signed to a Black label (Motown).[15] But locating James's introduction to South Asian culture in Toronto (and later in London) and not in India, leads us to consider the ways South Asian diasporic culture was a part of these formative years as well. For Johnson, South Asian diasporic culture was a part of James's everyday life in the early 1960s, and not something he encountered later in his career. Moreover, Johnson's allusions to hippies and counterculture in Toronto and London serve as reminders of the place of Indophilia in psychedelic culture (e.g., yoga) and the music of bands like the Beatles that I outlined in this book's introduction. But since the Mynah Birds were an R&B band with a Black lead singer, these South Asian influences are routed through and in conversation with Black music. In his autobiography, James notes that he and his white bandmates shared music, with his bandmates introducing him to folk artists like Bob Dylan and James sharing the music of jazz musicians like Pharoah Sanders. While Dylan never dabbled in South Asian–appropriative practices, Sanders was a student of John Coltrane (and later played with Badal Roy) and adopted Coltrane's South Asian–inspired spirituality, politics, and sound. In this way, we might speculate that the influence of Indophilic psychedelia on James and the Mynah Birds—if any, because most of their recordings with Motown are lost—came as a comple-ment to the already-established Afro–South Asian linkages in jazz I dis-cussed in the previous two chapters.

Such Afro–South Asian connections that James listened to and through with musicians like Sanders were also present in the cities of London and Toronto during James's time there in the 1960s and 1970s. LeRoi Johnson's remark that "there were also a lot of Indian people" in Toronto and London highlights the postwar immigration patterns of Indians from the Caribbean and East Africa to Toronto and London. It also, though unstated, is a re-minder of the parallel patterns of Black Caribbean and West African immi-grants in those same cities who lived in the same or similar working-class neighborhoods as the South Asian immigrants. While, as many ethnomusi-cologists and popular music studies scholars note, the cross-cultural music that these immigrant communities collectively formed would not emerge until the 1980s and 1990s, we should not diminish how living among Black and brown people shaped James—Johnson's aside forces us to consider that possibility.[16] And when we think through, as I explained in the prior chap-ter on Miles Davis, that the late 1960s and early 1970s marked a period in the United States where South Asian and African diasporic solidarity and political possibility waned (via white supremacist legislation of the census and the 1965 Immigration Act), then we must wonder what it means for an African American individual like James to move to Toronto and London during this same period and to experience those collectivities intact. John-son's words caution us not to treat James's forays into South Asian music as experiences in exoticism. Rather they engage cultural practices that, in the context of the cultural and political disentanglements of Blackness and brownness in the United States at the time, held deep political significance and that are central to (if not always audibly present in) the formation of his solo music career.

Rick James defined the music of his solo career as "punk funk." For James, punk funk is a particular brand of funk that shares the working-class and anti-establishment "riotous spirit" that came to be associated with London-based punk of bands like the Sex Pistols, and whose antecedents (but in no way derivations) are located within the antiwar ethos of 1960s counterculture that James encountered in Toronto and London.[17] Punk funk deviates and it was deviant, breaking the traditional boundaries of funk as well as punk. And in suturing punk to funk, James's new sound offers an alternative formation of punk rooted in Blackness rather than whiteness. Jayna Brown, Patrick Deer, and Tavia Nyong'o note in their introduction to their special issue on punk for *Social Text* that the subculture and genre's attention to queer people, women, and people of color (and those at the intersections) is less about a liberal politics of inclusion and more about showing that "punk never was a bastion of straight, white masculinity."[18] In a similar vein, punk funk also offers a different kind of genealogy of punk, one situated within the Black radical tradition as it makes rebellion central to Black aesthetics.

But punk funk does not just recast the dominant tenets of funk. It also opens up new imaginings of and for funk. Punk funk does not have the interstellar thematics of Parliament or George Clinton; it is not clean and romantic like the music of the Isley Brothers or Earth, Wind & Fire; and it refuses the precise and tight style of James Brown. Punk funk is instead—again thinking about the working-class neighborhoods in Toronto and James's hometown of Buffalo, New York, where he honed his craft—a Black street aesthetic of the everyday. It is direct and transgressive, it is raunchy and rough, it is wild and loose. Punk funk's disruptions of Black sonic norms make it a queer Black aesthetic. Punk, after all, and as Tavia Nyong'o has powerfully articulated time and again, has a particular resonance in African American culture.[19] Punk is Black slang for a gay man, a "faggot," an always already assumed bottom. James's penchant for wigs, glitter, lip gloss, heels, and revealing clothing confounds norms of Black masculinity. He and his band developed a performance of Black nonconformity that further fueled James's punk subjectivity—that he was indeed a faggot.

Consider, for example, the now-infamous back cover of James's 1981 hit album *Street Songs* (Figure 6), in which a white police officer pats down a red leather, thigh-high-booted James and a Black woman sex worker in animal print, with both James and the sex worker lifting their asses in the air. James's hooker boots and ass-tooting emphasize his sex worker status and punkness, and the corner on which the scene is set underscores the street aesthetic of punk funk. But the image also does much more. By featuring a woman alongside James, the photograph troubles the Black vernacular logic that attaches punk to men. And her booty-tooch, to borrow from Tyra Banks, produces what Jennifer Christine Nash defines as "black anality," an analytic that describes "how black pleasures are imagined to be peculiarly and particularly oriented toward the anus."[20] Here, James and the female sex worker, much like the figures on the cover of Miles Davis's *On the Corner,* envelope a queerness in the Cathy Cohen sense of the framework I discussed in the introduction to this book as well as Cohen's related framing of queerness as "deviance." Cohen pushes us to think through deviance, especially when it concerns Black communities, as a broad concept that is about the pathologizing discourses of LGBT peoples as well as defining those like single Black mothers whose "intimate relationships and sexual behavior are often portrayed as directly in conflict with the normative assumptions of heterosexism and the nuclear family . . . [and] also often live under the constant surveillance of the state through regulatory agencies."[21] The power of such re-conception of queerness as deviance for Cohen resides in its ability to reframe "the reification of the nuclear family, the conformity to institutionally prescribed and informally regulated gender roles and intimate sexual relations."[22] On the *Street Songs* back cover, then, James's and the female sex worker's status as sex workers and their sexual behavior as sodomites represent—they literally depict—those Black subjects whose sexual behaviors, in labor (sex work) and leisure (noncommercial Black analities), were deemed deviant and therefore assumed to be deserving of surveillance, policing, and criminalization. James is not simply, or perhaps no longer, a punk. He and his fellow sex worker are and have transformed into, as the breakout single from *Street Songs* alludes, deviant freaks and super freaks.

In invoking freaks, I do not intend to set punks and freaks in opposition. My goal here is to instead illuminate the ways in which the freak, as a subject position and analytic, offers a more capacious framing to imagine differently otherness (erotic and otherwise) in the Black queer aesthetic of punk funk. Which is to say, if punk in Black vernacular is always already tethered to men and male-derived masculinity, then the freak presents a broader Black cultural lens from which to engage racial, gendered, and sexualized otherness. Take, for example, the fact that the super freak in James's biggest hit isn't a man, but a kinky, orgy-loving, female sex worker—she is, as the lyrics

Figure 6. *Street Songs,* by Rick James, Gordy/Motown Records, album cover (back), 1981. Photographed by Ron Slenzak.

outline, "a very kinky girl / the kind you don't take home to mother / she will never let your spirits down / once you get her off the streets." "Super Freak" was not the first time that James created music about the deviance of the freak. In his 1979 hit "Love Gun," James speaks about his love for a woman to penetrate him with her "love gun," a euphemism that critics rightly argue connotes a penis but wrongly posit that it is James's penis. James's imagined sexual partner appears to be a trans woman with an uncircumcised penis— "put your finger on the trigger / when you pull it back I'll figure"—and someone who James wishes would ejaculate inside of him—"give me a shot of your love gun / fire me up girl and we'll have big fun." James's investment, then, in the freak's resistance to heteropatriarchal and cisgender norms is, in part, why L. H. Stallings argues that the freak is a key cultural producer of funk who shares and informs funk's erotic, sensorial, and androgynous pos-sibilities. For Stallings, Rick James is an icon "of funk and superfreak extra-ordinaire" who performs and "personifies an ecstatic androgyny that could coalesce Black men and women into perversely playing with anti-bourgeois performances of gender and sexuality."[23]

But we must remember that such an anti-bourgeois stance of the freak for James is dually informed by and in conversation with a working-class street upbringing in Buffalo as well as his AWOL status in Toronto in which he participated in counterculture activities and, as his brother posits, was sur-rounded by South Asian immigrant and diasporic people and culture. If, as I described above, South Asian (diasporic) culture was a part of James's early professional life in Toronto and London, which was central in the produc-tion of punk funk, then we must also consider its place within its production of the punk's transformation into the freak. As I described in the introduc-tion, in addition to "freak" having a particular resonance in Black and queer cultural spaces, South Asian American and immigrant history in the Ameri-cas is also historically tied to representations of deviant freakiness. Scholars like Janet M. Davis, Nayan Shah, Jasbir Puar, and Susan Koshy have all argued that the early twentieth-century freak-show and immigration legislative pro-visions produced South Asians as gendered and sexual others within the racial imaginaries of the Americas (especially Canada and the United States). And it was this otherness that created a racial and sexual taxonomy that buttressed South Asian diasporic discrimination in housing, employment, and immi-gration status and admission.[24]

It is perhaps then not surprising that we later find James explicitly incor-porating South Asian music into the music of his multiracial all-female freak band the Mary Jane Girls. The Mary Jane Girls included a genderqueer and/ or butch woman and a whip- and handcuff-wielding leather dominatrix, and James wrote, produced, and played the sitar on their 1983 and 1985 albums.[25] The deviant and freaky sartorial styles of the Mary Jane Girls as well as their erotic lyrics led them to become listed among the Tipper Gore–led Parents Music Resource Center's infamous "Filthy Fifteen," a list of fifteen songs that the PMRC argued evidenced the deviance of "porn rock" and that threat-ened the normative nuclear family.[26] James's sitar playing on the Mary Jane Girls' perverse and "filthy" albums underscores the freak's ability to allow for relational resonances between Blackness, South Asianness, and queerness—

James brings these three formations in close proximity and intimacy. James would continue this three-way of queerness, South Asianness, and Blackness on his 1986 album *The Flag*, a record dedicated to the "freak." On *The Flag* James plays the sitar as well as the tabla, and he delves into the sexual and geopolitical politics of the freak. It is thus with *The Flag* that James explicitly showcases and expands his South Asian musical abilities and makes plain the queer relations of Afro–South Asian collectivities and collaborative sounds.

Let Your Freak Flag Fly

As I noted at the outset of this chapter, *The Flag* is Rick James's first and only solo album with South Asian instrumentation, his first and only explicitly/ self-described political album, and his first and only album that sought to address and critique life in the 1980s under the Reagan administration. James had been critical of Ronald Reagan since at least 1983 when, in an effort to get the audience to clap along to his music, he instructed them to pretend that their left hand was the KKK *and* Reagan and to smack their left with their right "as *hard* as you can."[27] Visually, the cover of *The Flag* speaks to the record's political import. On the front cover, James stands alone, staring at the camera/viewer with arms folded, rocking a shorn haircut, and dressed in an all-black leather ensemble. The background of the photograph is what James would later describe as the freak flag (hence the album's title). The flag is divided into the colors of red, black, and green, with a diagonal line sepa-rating the flag into a red and black side, and with green lining the flag's perim-eter. The back cover (Figure 7) features James in the same outfit, against the same flag backdrop, but this time he has his left hand on his popped-out hip and he is holding a smaller version of the freak flag.[28]

The album cover of *The Flag* represents many of the political and cultural facets of Rick James and the formations that produced punk funk's iteration of the freak. While the red, black, and green suggest a pan-African tie to the freak flag, James remarks in *The Flag*'s liner notes that the colors also con-note love and bloodshed, the circle of life and the inclusivity of Blackness, and Earth and "Mother Nature," respectively.[29] In so doing, the colors meld the pan-Africanist and hippie counterculture political projects that circu-lated during the social movements of the 1960s and 1970s of James's time in Toronto and London. Moreover, the diagonal split of the flag between red and black coincidentally replicates the anarchist flag, further emphasizing

Figure 7. *The Flag,* by Rick James, Gordy/Motown Records, album cover (back), 1986. Photographed by Chris Callis.

the punk in James's punk funk music as well as punk's leftist politics. But James also signals a Black queer articulation with the punk on the album's back cover. His shift in bodily comportment—hand on the popped-out hip—as well as all black leather attire mark James as perhaps a queer leather queen ("Leather Queen" was incidentally a song he recorded for the Mary Jane Girls a year prior to the release of *The Flag*). And as James is pictured center stage on the cover, we might also read this as suggesting how such Black queerness becomes a central component to the rest of the cover's racial, capitalist, and nation-state allusions. Which is to say, the freak flag operates as an assemblage of anti-racist, anti-capitalist, and anti-queerphobic politics. The freak flag signals where and how these political imaginings overlap and intertwine.[30]

Musically, *The Flag* deepens such intersectional and coalitional projects. The album opens with James and his Black R&B female protégé Val Young singing in harmony on a song aptly titled "Freak Flag." They sing, "Wave your freak flag / wave your freak flag / rally 'round the red, black, and green." This collaboration between James and Young on "Freak Flag" is important because it underscores and sets the tone for the concept of the freak flag, and the freak aesthetic, as an embrace and expression of gender and sexual nonnormative collectivity. James's freak status, as I explained above, had already been established by the time of *The Flag*'s release, and Young, while a relatively new artist, had started to establish an image as a sexually desiring and desirable Black woman. James famously dubbed her the "Black Marilyn Monroe" as a means to mark and promote Young's beauty and vivacious erotics. Johnny Lee, creative director at Motown Records, shot the cover of Young's debut album *Seduction,* and when I asked him what he could share with me about Young and the photo, he replied, "I really like Val! She's no-holds-barred! If she was horny she'd tell you she's horny! [laughs]."[31] But while Lee appreciated the personal frankness of Young as a Black woman who took charge of her own sexuality, he did not believe that such an identity and personality should be attached to Young's professional image. He explained to me that when it came time to shoot the cover for *Seduction,* "I wanted to make her a little more acceptable. Rick and I fought a lot about that. I was not too happy with her first cover. It was too nasty."[32] Here Lee's desire to make Young "acceptable" speaks to the kinds of capitalist and Black middle-class normative logics of respectability and sexual silence that too often organize Black women's sexualities. Lee, it would seem, was not only concerned that Young, as an emerging artist, would get caught up in the conservatism and controversy of the PMRC, but also extend the racist and sexist stereotypes of Black women as sexually excessive. Nevertheless, James (and I'd argue Young) decided to connect Young's personal sexual politics to her professional erotic representation, as evidenced by the cover of *Seduction,* which finds Young sitting atop a satin bed; and by Young and James singing together on "Freak Flag." It's that song, as the opening track, that frames the remainder of the album. Indeed, "Freak Flag," and Young and James's attendant harmonizing lyrics on it, are repeated again as an interlude in the middle of the album as well as *The Flag*'s closing song.

And it's on this point of how the album ends, especially the final three songs, that I want to turn my attention. The antepenultimate song is titled

"Om Raga" (sometimes referred to as "Rick's Raga"), and it is a thirty-second instrumental of James playing the sitar and tabla.[33] "Om Raga" is an *alap* of sorts, referring to the introductory section of a North Indian classical music piece where a soloist (here James on sitar) explores the raga (or collection of pitches) of a performance. But rather than provide listeners with a full version of this performance, the song abruptly ends and transitions into the next one, titled "Painted Pictures." "Painted Pictures" is a sitar-driven funk ballad that examines the problems with erotic façades. Notably, James treats the sitar as a bass, and only uses it to amplify the sonic hallmark of funk music: the one. The one is, as many scholars and musicians have explained, "the first beat of the pattern and as such the focal point of the groove."[34] In essence, the one is what makes funk funk. And so in playing the sitar and the bass on the one, Rick James, much like Badal Roy during the recording sessions of *On the Corner* discussed in the last chapter, blends South Asian music—and specifically North Indian classical music, given that the preceding song is an *alap*—with Black music. James makes them central to and puts them in conversation with each other. And since the lyrics deal with erotic play, he underscores the ways such relationalities articulate with sex and sexuality. And it is probably for this reason that "Painted Pictures" is the final full song before James and Young reprise "Freak Flag" to conclude the album. That is, the Afro–South Asian coalitional erotics of "Painted Pictures" allow for a circling back to James and Young's sex-centered collaborations and imaginations of the freak flag. This transition and looping back brings listeners back to the beginning of the album and its purpose: for us to proudly proclaim and embrace our freakiness, to move from the hidden and enclosed erotics of "Painted Pictures" to the explicit publics of the freak. South Asian and African culture, then, in conjunction with the Afro-diasporic aesthetics of funk, leads us (back) to an uncompromising and unapologetic freakiness.

Freakin'/Freak in Politics

But what does it mean to center and be an unapologetic freak in 1986, at a time of increased AIDS-related deaths, the Reagan administration's disturbing silence around such a public health crisis, and the racist and queerphobic violence and hysteria that informed—and were informed by—such silences? In calling for listeners to rally around the freak and its pan-Africanist colors of red, black, and green, *The Flag* frames the freak as the primary subject from which to build a broad-based coalition. Similar to Cathy Cohen's notion of a radical queer politics that is defined by one's relation to power rather than a subject identity, *The Flag*'s organizing around the figure of the freak eschews the narrowness of bounded framings of identity for a radical and transformative vision, grounded in the politics of Black culture, that addresses multiple oppressions. The freak cuts across and binds various differences to speak to and sound ways in which power unevenly affects and marginalizes communities across the lines of race, class, gender, sexuality, and citizenship. *The Flag*'s centering of the freak jettisons single-identity frameworks in order to pursue a multi-issue platform. And it is one that builds solidarity between, among, and for those whose histories and lived realities are imbricated with production of the racialized gender and sexual nonnormative and outsider positionality of the freak.

To be clear, I am not arguing that *The Flag* or Rick James must be seen as leading figures in 1980s AIDS activism. But what I am saying is that historical context lays bare political import. And thus we cannot detach *The Flag* from the political terrain from which it emerges. Its music and visuality signal multiple and heterogeneous marginalized communities—African Americans, South Asians, anarchists, queers, (Black) women, and those at the intersections—affected by AIDS and involved in AIDS activism during the mid to late 1980s. From the Gay Men of African Descent, to the Women's AIDS Network, to the anarchist influences of ACT UP, to the Third World AIDS Advisory Task Force, the thematics of *The Flag* speak to these organizations and the HIV-affected communities for which they organized. *The Flag*'s privileging of the freak, then, resists the dominant image of white gay male AIDS activism to pursue something else, to create the sounds of and for coalition building. To go back to the album again, Rick James's harmonizing with Val Young on the opening and closing of *The Flag* and the South Asian instrumentation that leads to such a finale are important acts because they position Black women's voices and South Asian cultural formations as emblematic of the solidarity that resides in the potential of the freak.

Moreover, to continue this line of thought around situating *The Flag* within 1980s U.S. politics, while James's song "Free to Be Me," which addresses drug addiction (he discusses freebasing and smoking crack cocaine), is a tale of personal struggle, it must also be read alongside Reagan's war on drugs and its centrality in the mass incarceration of Black and brown people that increased the rates of new HIV infections. And when we couple this with the AIDS quarantine ballot in California in 1986 and the *Bowers v. Hardwick* case that eventually upheld anti-sodomy laws (the Supreme Court had yet to rule on the case by the time *The Flag* was released), then we are faced with an album like *The Flag* that culturally articulates with the fight against the criminalization of racialized, gendered, and sexually marginalized groups. *The Flag's* multiple resonances link HIV/AIDS activism with challenges to the carceral state, and consequently suggest that the politics of the freak are what we might call the politics of the punk, bulldagger, and welfare queen.

The Flag's use of the freak as an intersectional and coalitional framework isn't limited to the domestic; it's also international(ist) in its political scope and reach. Recall that Rick James recorded *The Flag* in part as a response to 1980s U.S. imperialism and Cold War politics. *The Flag*, then, returns James to his AWOL history and the counterculture antiwar working-class musical space in Toronto. The Vietnam War was obviously over by 1986, but the United States and the Soviet Union still waged war and occupied geopolitical spaces, doing so under the auspices of spreading/saving democracy or communism. James expresses his frustration with the United States and the Soviet Union on the song "Funk in America / Silly Little Man," where he ridicules Reagan and Gorbachev as "silly little boys," attacks the proliferation and genocidal implications of U.S. global nuclear arsenal, and laments that the Cold War is a "a shame and a pity."[35] Despite all of this, James remains hopeful for the future. He insists that "it's time to take other measures," which he qualifies as an alternative agenda focused on the practice of anti-militarism through nonalignment. The goal here for James is, as he and Val Young sing at the beginning and end of *The Flag*, to rally around the freak flag. James is not interested in finding space to critique U.S. imperialism while still remaining allegiant to it. Nor does his critique of U.S. empire move him to support Soviet-defined communism. He and Val Young are aligned with neither nation-state or empire and instead pledge allegiance to the freak and their own freakiness.

This move toward nonalignment recalls the Bandung conference of 1955 where newly sovereign African and Asian nations formed an alliance against U.S. and Soviet imperialism. This position expressed an outright refusal to participate in war (and a nuclear war at that) as well as an "us versus them" ideological hailing that sought to interpellate African and Asian nations and communities (and those tracing cultural/historical ties to these areas and peoples) as subjects loyal to the United States or the Soviet Union. The title of James's "Free to Be Me" song, while again about struggles with drug abuse, intimates a sense of self-determination that organized much of the political movements that led to the independence of these African and Asian nations and their orientation toward nonalignment. Moreover, and perhaps most important, James's sitar and tabla playing on *The Flag*, and his transition into "Freak Flag," make audible and present such Afro-Asian histories. To instrumentally close with South Asian sounds and vocally end with collective singing about organizing around "red, black, and green" produces an Afro–South Asian musical melding. It forms the literal culmination of *The Flag*, a sonic meeting between, to, and through the South Asian and the African diasporas. These Afro–South Asian sounds of solidarity, thus, index Bandung and bring its 1950s transnational politics into the then present, and helps listeners imagine what nonalignment might sound like in and for the 1980s.

But because this updated Bandung sound centers the queer (of color) subject of the freak, it is a sound that intertwines Afro–South Asian anti-imperialist/nonaligned formations with racialized nonnormative erotics. Indeed, as L. H. Stallings argues, the slippage of "funk" and "fuck" holds potential to produce "identity and subjectivity anew and alter political and artistic movements."[36] To that end, "Funk in America," which speaks out against the military–industrial complex and the imperial logics of Reagan's Cold War, simultaneously becomes "Fuck in America," thereby signaling Reagan's anti-queer policies. But the slippage continues. Because the phrase "Funk in America" appears by itself and not attached to the surrounding lyrics, "Fuck in America" can also read as "Fuck-in America," as a directive to beat-in to disrupt or rupture America, or as a sit-in style protest of public sex; we might also interpret it as an exasperated "Fuck, in America"; as an affective disappointment of "Fuckin' America"; or as a queering method where one is invested in "Fuckin' America." The point is not to discern which interpretation is the "correct" one, but rather to show how the multiple (mis) readings further underscore how organizing around the freak, as articulated in *The Flag*, allows for a political vision that powerfully addresses the entanglements of race, gender, sexuality, nation, and war in the 1980s. *The Flag*, thus, not only links AIDS activism with the prison–industrial complex, but also, by raising the specter of Bandung and Cold War nonalignment, it connects both formations to antiwar politics.

It's perhaps because of this that Johnny Lee compared Rick James's vision for *The Flag* as similar to his 1981 album *Street Songs*, and saw the former, visually and musically, as a concept album that is anchored by "an anthem."[37] Shana Redmond defines anthems as "world-altering collective visions" that "symbolize and call into being a system of sociopolitical ideas or positions . . . [and] that make the listening audience and political public merge."[38] "Freak Flag" is such an anthem. It is, of course, an anthem of *The Flag*, but more to the point, it is an anthem for those in 1986 facing multiple and overlapping oppressions of racism, sexism, imperialism, serosorting, queerphobia, and mass incarceration.[39] Like the corner was the site for collective action for Miles Davis in 1972, the freak was the figure through which Rick James offered an anthem of coalitional organizing.

In a way, then, *The Flag* is the culmination of Rick James's earlier career (at least as it was outlined in LeRoi Johnson's interview with me). His initial engagements with South Asian music came at a moment of outsiderness, a moment of exile (similar to but still separate from Baldwin and Coltrane's that I wrote about in chapter 1). He was AWOL, he was in Toronto, he traveled to London and India, and it was while in exile, while an outsider, that he encountered and participated in the drugs and antiwar politics of counterculture as well as South Asian music. These encounters in exile led James to the queer Black aesthetic sounds of punk funk and its central figure: the freak. *The Flag* was James's only album that was dedicated to the freak and that made plain how political organizing around the freak can lead to radical visions of intersectional, transnational, and coalitional politics, ones that James witnessed as an outsider, as a funky freaky punk.

Unfortunately for Rick James, *The Flag*'s anthem went unheard. It was a commercial and critical failure, and is a largely forgotten album. In fact, when I initially interviewed LeRoi Johnson, James's brother, about *The Flag*, he confused it with another low-performing Rick James album. James was on a commercial and creative downswing following the lack of interest in *The Flag*. Within five years of the album's release, he had relapsed, sued Motown Records, and was incarcerated. And although Rick James never resurrected the cultural and political possibilities of the queer racialized other of the freak, a rap duo from Atlanta called OutKast would embrace another kind of othered and othering subject that shared James's punk and freak. For OutKast, the subject was an outcast of sorts, and one that was literally and figuratively out of this world.

Outlawing OutKasts

My move to place OutKast, and André 3000 specifically, in conversation with Rick James might come as a surprise. André is often, and rightly, discussed in relation to Prince. The falsetto style, songwriting, quirky Black masculinity, and Black dandyism that we now associate with André are clear citational expressions of Prince's legacy. My interest in tracing the resonances between James and André is not to diminish Prince's influence, but rather, as I did in chapter 1 with James Baldwin and John Coltrane, to open up and allow for new meanings of their music. In particular, my aim is to highlight how OutKast deployed and embraced positionalities of otherness on their second album, *ATLiens,* and did so in ways that drew on South Asianness and that imagined Blackness, Black music, and Black politics differently.[40] For James the figure through which to imagine this alterative formation of Blackness was the freak, rooted in and routed through the punk. As we shall see for OutKast, such an alternative formation manifested in and through the alien via the outcast.

Imani Perry argues that OutKast is emblematic of the "outlaw" tradition in hip-hop. For Perry, the outlaw is a multifaceted archetype that rejects "norms that unfairly punish Black communities or discount the complexity of choices faced by those Black and poor in the United States."[41] OutKast occupies this racialized position of the outlaw in its own name. Spoken-word artist Ruben "Big Rube" Bailey, member of the Atlanta-based rap collective the Dungeon Family that includes OutKast, reveals on OutKast's 1994 song "True Dat" (from their debut album *Southernplayalisticadillacmuzik*) that OutKast is an acronym: "Operating Under The Krooked American System Too (Long)." The parenthetical usage is of my own doing. I do so in order to underscore how the acronym does and doesn't spell out OUTKAST, and to show how the (mis)applied acronym simultaneously signals the enduring history and presence of injustice and oppression in the United States (i.e., "too long") as well as building a community of marginalized folks experiencing such oppression (i.e., "too"). That is to say, the slippage and flexibility in Big Rube's explanation of the acronym is productive because it names the system that produces outcasts while at the same time inviting and constructing a collective of outcasts. Additionally, the use of "K" instead of "C" in "K/Crooked" emphasizes the social structures producing an outcast/OutKast, as it is a signifyin' method that has roots in Black Power ideologies

of the 1970s and the use of satirical misspellings to highlight white supremacy (e.g., the Ku Klux Klan) in the United States (e.g., "Amerikkka" instead
of "America"). The "K" in "Krooked" indexes such Black radical history, inextricably tying OutKast to the long history of Black liberation struggles,
and particularly those in the U.S. South.

Indeed, OutKast is a southern rap group whose southern Black political
identity extends and explicates their layered outcast position. At the time of
Southernplayalisticadillacmuzik's release, hip-hop was largely understood and
treated like a bicoastal affair. Rap markets overwhelmingly ignored southern
hip-hop, and only paid slight attention to southern rap acts if they adhered
to either West or East Coast visual, lyrical, and sonic standards. The logic
went as follows: if it was not from or conformed to the East Coast or West
Coast, then it was not hip-hop. The name OutKast, then, also signaled their
racial, geographical, and cultural positions as outcasts.

When OutKast released their debut album in 1994, they refused assimilation to the normative logics governing rap at the time. To again quote Perry,
OutKast's music and image relied on and spoke to "the position of Otherness as a site of privileged knowledge and potential."[42] *Southernplayalisticadillacmuzik* was decidedly Black, southern, and rap. The album features Big
Boi and André 3000 as southern Black teenage womanizing "playas" who do
not hide their southern drawls, who routinely use geographical references
that only those familiar with Atlanta will understand, who rap over live instrumentation (courtesy of southern production team Organized Noize)
that departs from the sample-based music of New York or Los Angeles, and
who rap about the ongoing effects of racial segregation and displacement
and anti-Black policing (which is always already anti-Black) in Atlanta. Out-
Kast's debut album, thus, speaks to and cultivates a community for those
pushed to the margins and for whom assimilation is not an option.

But while OutKast's position as outcasts in 1994 seems to have coalition-
building possibilities, Big Rube ended up undercutting such potentiality
on the same song that he articulates the meaning of OutKast's name. Rube
implores those on the margins, those who are outcasts/OutKasts, to "take
back your existence" or "die like a punk." Rube's use of the pejorative "punk,"
an epithet for Black queerness that I discussed above, sets up an opposition
between outcasts/OutKast as the heroes challenging oppression—taking back
their existence—and the queer punks whose betrayal undermines the struggle and are therefore better off dead. Situating Rube's words in 1994, and

especially his linking of death and punks / Black queers, raises the specter of the AIDS crisis and the significant number of Black men who sleep with men (MSMs) who had seroconverted or had died from AIDS. Perry, again, writes that one of the powers of the outlaw figure is that it "presents itself in the creation of alternative values, norms, and ideals in contrast to those embraced in American society."[43] For OutKast on *Southernplayalisticadillacmuzik*, Big Rube's words suggest that the outcast/OutKast failed to create new norms of sexuality and gender—those norms looked a lot like, if they were not exactly the same as, the old norms. But, it appeared, these gendered and sexual norms would shift by the time of OutKast's follow-up album in 1996. It was at that point that OutKast had figuratively left America as well as Earth, and had transformed from outcasts into ATLiens.

ATLien Fantasies

I want to start this conversation about *ATLiens* by first going back to the 1995 Source Awards. It is there that OutKast won Best New Rap Group and where the majority of the attendees booed them. The experience of simultaneous celebration and condemnation led Big Boi and André to consider, and address on their album, the double-edged sword of success and scrutiny. It led them to think through the multiple ways in which they're rendered alien and respond to such alien status. *ATLiens* is the album that addresses these issues. Lyrically, the record remains rooted in the quotidian experiences of Black men in Atlanta. As mentioned above, many of the songs specifically namecheck places and areas that only people from Atlanta, from Georgia, and at most the South, will recognize. In so doing, OutKast embraces the ways in which bicoastal rap reads southern hip-hop as foreign. Further, songs like "Elevators (Me & You)" and "Mainstream" consider whether OutKast's newfound fame has alienated them from their initial, local fan base. These songs explored the following question: If fame has made OutKast, a group from Atlanta, alien to the people of Atlanta, then are OutKast consequently alien within their own home? And lastly, sonically, OutKast's *ATLiens* is drastically different and distant from their previous album and mainstream hip-hop in general. The opening song, for example, starts with a woman reading a Portuguese poem, deterritorializing the listener. André 3000 and Big Boi also began producing on their own on *ATLiens*. The resulting sound is one that is dark and sparse. *ATLiens* especially makes central guttural sounds like grunts, laughter, and sighs, which were not so common in hip-hop at the time, but sounds that are, following Samuel Floyd, indicative of musical traditions of the broader African diaspora and enslaved Black people in the South.[44] As Regina Bradley notes, if the Best New Artist win marked Out-Kast as the future of hip-hop, then *ATLiens* shows listeners what this alien Black future sounds like.[45]

Ironically, in presenting their *ATLiens* sound and exploring what it means to be an alien (to their home of Atlanta, to the bicoastal rap market, etc.), Big Boi and André 3000 were increasingly becoming alien to each other. I interviewed Vince Robinson, the former art director at LaFace Records, which was OutKast's record label, about *ATLiens,* an album he worked on as the illustrator of the album's comic book liner notes. I asked him to describe how, if at all, he saw Big Boi and André change between *Southernplayalisti-cadillacmuzik* and *ATLiens.* He informed me that "Big Boi had that cool pimp and playa thing going on both albums. He was the same guy." But when I asked Robinson about André 3000, Robinson remarked, "He was wearing turbans and weird clothes. With all kinds of colors and patterns. . . . He was just one way one minute and then turned into something else the next, you know. I just thought he was creatively dynamic like that."[46] I asked Robinson if he ever asked André why he changed his style, and his response surprised me. Robinson told me that he had not asked André about his decision to change his style because he didn't want to make things "awkward with André." Nevertheless, Robinson eventually confessed to me that he and his friends at LaFace would sometimes talk about, and notably not to, André and his clothes and wonder "what that was all about."[47]

It is here that we get a glimpse of the queer politics and purchase, the kinds of illegible masculinities that I discussed in reference to Coltrane in chapter 1, of the turban for André 3000. The narrative that Robinson tells me is one familiar to many queer people: friends and family see something "different" or "creative" about your way of dress, talking among themselves about this "difference" and the potential concerns that it raises, but never confronting the subject of this difference out of fear of making things "awkward." Such a narrative is part of a set of practices like silence, rumors, euphemisms, and gossip that surround the (in)visibility of and, to quote C. Riley Snorton, the "popular panopticism that regulates" nonnormative genders and sexualities.[48] It is an attempt to question illegible sexualities and genders in order to make and mark them as legible and open to more vulnerability and/or surveillance.

The questioning of André 3000's gender and dress was made even more evident in a 2004 VH1 special on OutKast. In it, they devote a small segment to André's turban and change in style during the *ATLiens* era. The segment features two Atlanta-based artists who are close to OutKast—producer and friend of Big Boi, Nsilo Reddick; and rapper and member of the Dungeon Family, Big Reese—and whose discussion of André's turban look echo and extend Robinson's comments to me:

> Nsilo Reddick: I still remember [pause] like one day he was in jeans and a T-shirt and a fresh, fresh pair of sneakers on. And then BAM! He's in a turban!
>
> Big Reese: It was actually a hat that you get from the beauty supply store. You know them little grandmama hats that they wear in church [laughs].
>
> NR: Dré walks out with a turban on and everybody's looking like [Reddick performs inquisitive side-eye for the camera] "Man, what in the hell is Dré doing? What does he have on?" The next second you go out to the mall and everybody got on turbans![49]

While the segment ends with a gesture toward André's influence on other men in Atlanta—"everybody got on turbans"—and thus a sign of André's successful entry into normative Black masculinity (the proceeding segment is about André's courtship of and child with Erykah Badu), Reddick and Big Reese's testimony also articulate an initial puzzlement with André's improper performance of masculinity. Big Reese's association of André's turban with those worn by Black southern grandmothers marks André as a cross-dresser of sorts whose gender transgressions are tied to his transgressions of temporality. For Big Reese, André participates in a queer, backward-looking aesthetic practice of crossing gender—man to woman—and time—young to elderly— that, as Reddick's statement notes, confound and render suspicious the norms of present-day Black masculinity. André 3000 would, as this chapter's epigraph attests, go on to recognize the heightened visibility and questioning of his sartorial choices as well as such surveillance's implications of dissident sexualities. And he addressed it on the song "Return of the G" from *Aquemini*, the album proceeding *ATLiens*. He raps, "Then the question is 'Big Boi what's up with André? / Is he in a cult? Is he on drugs? Is he gay?'"

Oddly enough, VH1 chose to use two South Asian–inspired rap songs to accompany Big Reese and Nsilo Reddick's commentary on André's turban.

As they spoke, listeners hear the *tumbi*-driven song "Ugly" by Georgia-based rapper Bubba Sparxxx as well as "Indian Flute" by Virginia-based African American rapper and producer Timbaland and his South Asian American protégé Rajé Shwari. Timbaland produced both songs, and I will discuss him at great length later in this chapter and especially in chapter 5. But for now, it is important to note that the choice to use South Asian music and South Asian American artists as background to André's initially perceived cross-dressing turban attire highlight the intersections and entanglements of Blackness, South Asianness, and queerness in Black popular music that I seek to grapple with throughout this book and especially this chapter.

To be clear, turbans are not exclusive to South Asia. Turbans exist across Asia and Africa, as part of various religions, and, as Big Reese explained to VH1, in southern African American women's style politics. But the turban, at least prior to 9/11, has often represented a marker of South Asianness within the broader U.S. racial imaginary. During the early twentieth century, political cartoons, film, and other media frequently depicted Indians as wearing turbans. And as Indian immigration—irrespective of religion—increased during this period, nativists came to fear what they saw as the rising "tide of the turbans."[50] The legacy of such a conflation between South Asianness and the turban emerged when I first mentioned to Vince Robinson that I was interested in talking with him about the *ATLiens* album, André 3000, and Black musicians donning turbans. Upon hearing my interest, Robinson told me, "Unless they are practicing Sikhism, I don't know what they are attempting to get across."[51] Here, Robinson, like Rick James's brother LeRoi Johnson, exercises an aside that reveals a perceived connection between a Punjabi-originated religion of Sikhism and the turban. That is, similar to Johnson's aside pushing me to consider Rick James's interest in South Asian culture through his encounters with South Asian immigrants and diasporic peoples in Toronto and London, Robinson's aside further signaled to me the need to pursue the South Asian—via Sikh—connections between André 3000 and his turban aesthetics.

And in so doing, I discovered that André 3000 is part of a longer history of African American men wearing turbans to signify South Asianness, especially in the segregated U.S. South. As Vivek Bald explains, donning a turban and posing as South Asian became one of the many ways that southern Black men sought to "cross the color line and temporarily, contingently, outwit the racial apartheid of Jim Crow."[52] This was such a "recurring and prominent theme" that two of the leading Black publications, *Ebony* and *Jet*, wrote about it.[53] *Ebony* referred to the practice as "do-it-yourself-segregation," and *Jet* wrote that "some of the race's best folk tales are tied up in turbans and a half dozen other ways dark negroes 'pass' down south."[54] Rather than pass as white, as is the often-told narrative of racial passing in African American history, these Black men passed as exotic and often wealthy South Asian men, and used Orientalist fantasies due to the ways white people in the South frequently (but in no ways exclusively) "treated them [South Asians] differently, afforded them greater privileges of movement, or even sought them out of the goods they sold, the 'wisdom' they bore, or the 'magic' they performed."[55] Historian Paul Kramer extends Bald's narrative by exploring African American male musicians' attempts to pass as South Asian. For example, Kramer tells the story of a late 1940s St. Louis–born Black artist named John Roland Redd who became the first Black man to own his own television show when he moved to Los Angeles, changed his name and identity to the turbaned Indian organist and spiritual personality Korla Pandit, and starred in the hit program Koral Pandit's Adventures in Music.[56] And while there were other Black male artists during the 1940s and 1950s who donned turbans and were not explicitly engaged in evading anti-Black racism, many Black male musicians like Babs Gonzales, Dizzy Gillespie, and the Reverend Jesse Routté found turbans to be cultural objects that offered relatively temporary and limited relief while touring in the U.S. South.[57]

André 3000's wearing of turbans during the *ATLiens* period revisits and revises this history. As a Black man from and living in the South, and as a Black man rapping about anti-Black racism in the South, André's turban acts as an homage to those African Americans (artists and nonartists alike) who saw the turban as a tactic and tool for navigating the Jim Crow South. And yet, and as we will see, while some African American men of the early and mid-twentieth century used the turban to temporarily mask their Blackness and adopt an ethnoracial positionality—South Asian—outside the strict Black–white binary, André's turban amplifies and rescripts his Blackness. The turban becomes part of André's alternative and Afro-futurist Black expression. It is an imagining that, via the turban, queerly resonates with South Asianness in order to express Black masculinity differently. As Jasbir Puar argues, the turbaned South Asian male subject is historically attached to "hypermasculinity, perverse heterosexuality . . . and warrior militancy" within the U.S. racial imaginary, and as such, it overlaps with the long history of representations of Black masculinity as a racialized site of immanent gendered and sexualized excess.[58] But the turban, as well as the South Asian subject, is also a marker of foreignness, of exoticness, of alienness. And so it is at this nexus of the turban's Afro-South Asianness and alienness that we locate André 3000's turbaned performance as a site of alternative and futuristic Black masculinities.

The *ATLiens* comic book is instructive here. To refresh, the comic book follows two alien superheroes from an outer space city called ATLantis as they fight to save music and ATLantis from an evil entity named Nosamulli. Big Boi's alien name is Daddy Fat Sax (also stylized Dad-Efat-Sax), a doubly hetero-masculinist name that signals the phallic and stereotypically masculine saxophone as well as the "sax" as a slang for testicles—(ball)sack—and therefore a sign of masculine virility. Moreover, Big Boi's superpower is the ability to summon a black panther. The overlaps of Black masculinity and the black panther not only draw parallels between the *ATLiens* comic book and the Afro-futurism of the *Black Panther* superhero comic, but more to the point, it also draws connections to a more conventional framing of the Black Panther Party as heteropatriarchal. As Regina Bradley notes, the comic situates Big Boi's alien character within larger Black freedom struggles, but it does so in ways that shore up norms of gender and sexuality.[59] Big Boi converges with the kinds of Black Panther aesthetics and politics that were a part of Miles Davis's political vision in 1972, as I discussed in chapter 2. But, importantly, in developing an alien character that espouses and summons Black gender and sexual normative superpowers, Big Boi deviates from Davis's positioning of queerness as central to the Black Panther Party and Black Power aesthetics.

André 3000, conversely, becomes the alien superhero Bin Hamin (sometimes written as Bin-Hamin) in the *ATLiens* comic. The name signals Arabic as well as Islam, and Robinson drew André (as Bin Hamin) as a turbaned fighter who works with Daddy Fat Sax in battling Nosamulli. While Daddy Fat Sax has an animal as a superpower—the black panther—Bin Hamin's superpower is the spiritual and intellectual gift of discernment, a third eye that allows him to "see through bulls#!t."[60]

There are four things I want to note about Bin Hamin's biography as narrated in the comic book. First, the use of a third eye as a superpower further illustrates the ways in which South Asian culture informs André 3000's superhero character, if not his rapper persona as well. Here, I'm reminded again of

Robin D. G. Kelley, whom I mentioned in this book's introduction, and the ways in which his Afro-diasporic mother and her beliefs in South Asian spiritualities informed the Black utopic praxis that Kelley calls "freedom dreams." For Kelley, his mother pushed his family to "live through our third eyes, to see life as possibility."[61] And it is this kind of third-eye training, grounded in, as Kelley explicates, the Black radical tradition, that Bin Hamin uses in helping to render life possible on ATLantis and new Earth.

Second, by featuring a superhero with an Arabic- and/or Muslim-inspired name like Bin Hamin, the comic book disentangles the turban from a strictly Sikh formation to one that signals the various regionalities and religious traditions in which turbans are worn. In so doing, it makes room for us to read the *ATLiens* iteration of André, via Bin Hamin, as participating in a broader legacy of Islam in rap music as well as indexing the history of turbaned Black men passing as South Asian in the U.S. South. This is not an either/or scenario, but an and/both, especially since Islam exists in South Asia. Nevertheless, as Sohail Daulatzai articulates, U.S.-based rap has increasingly focused on the "relationship between Blackness and Islam" since the mid-1980s with artists like Rakim, Lupe Fiasco, Ice Cube, and Jay Electronica.[62] But whereas Daulatzai reads Malcolm X as an explicit and central figure in these Black Islam recordings, we find no similar reference for Bin Hamin / André. Instead, I would argue, Sun Ra is perhaps the more appropriate historical reference for Bin Hamin, as his turbaned, third-eye, alien life-form interpellates Bin Hamin into a similar Afro-futurist trajectory.

Third, and related to Sun Ra, Bin Hamin expresses as queer racialized gender performance, an illegible alien masculinity (to extend Mark Anthony Neal's conception of illegible masculinities to its most futuristic possibilities). Whereas, as Francesca Royster illustrates, Sun Ra's "eccentric queerness" partly manifests in his "campy, outlandish, and gender-bending aesthetic," Bin Hamin's Black queer alien masculinity is more apparent in comparison to the phallocentrism of Daddy Fat Sax.[63] Moreover, in the two pictures that act as a preface to the *ATLiens* comic book / liner notes, André and Big Boi are photographed separately sitting in a wicker chair reminiscent of the one in the iconic 1967 photograph of Black Panther Party Minster of Defense Huey Newton (Figures 8a and 8b). Big Boi / Daddy Fat Sax is sitting upright with his daughter; and André / Bin Hamin is pictured childless, wearing what looks like a Chinese martial arts uniform, and slouching in his chair. André's failure to sit upright, his failure to sit *straight*, like his partner Big

Figure 8. (a) *ATLiens,* by OutKast, LaFace Records, album cover (inside), 1996. Photographed by John Halpern. (b) *ATLiens,* by OutKast, LaFace Records, album cover (inside), 1996. Photographed by John Halpern.

Boi, works as a queer bodily comportment. Because Daddy Fat Sax's super-power is the ability to summon animals like a black panther, then it makes sense for him to sit up straight in the Black Panther–like chair—he's align-ing himself with the Party. Bin Hamin, on the other hand, does not have a superpower that is explicitly tied to the Black Panther Party and so instead sits askew, in a pose that, when coupled with his childless anti-reproductive futurity and the Chinese martial arts sartorial style, renders and registers a queer embodied practice.

And so, fourth, and nevertheless, Bin Hamin and Daddy Fat Sax work together in the struggle for justice in ATLantis. They present readers with an Afro–(South) Asian alliance, a coalition that is literally otherworldly. It is a kind of Afro-futuristic practice of Afro–(South) Asian solidarity that bridges Alondra Nelson's "past–future visions" with Ramzi Fawaz's "popular fantasy" in order to "resist a variety of repressive social norms but also to facilitate the ground from which new kinds of choices about political affilia-tion and personal identification could be pursued."[64]

ATLiens Moving On Up Out of This World

It is with the *ATLiens* comic book's gesture toward Afro-Asian solidarity that I want to now turn, and think through the music video for "Elevators (Me and You)," the first single from the *ATLiens* album. Here we see Bin Hamin and Daddy Fat Sax lead a group of white and Black men and women through a jungle. Viewers do not realize until the end of the video that the group is headed toward, and successfully finds, the utopic space of ATLantis. What I find interesting about this video is that the first character to have a solo scene, or any scene of any significant length, is not André or Big Boi, but an Asian American male teenager reading the comic book chronicles of Bin Hamin and Daddy Fat Sax's journey to ATLantis (Figure 9). Asian Americans are both historically and currently racialized as perpetual foreigners within the U.S. popular imaginary. Legally, such alterity is the result of a series of laws that dramatically shaped Asian American immigration patterns in the United States. These include, but are not limited to: the 1875 Page law that outlawed Chinese women from immigrating to the United States; the 1882 Chinese Exclusion Act that barred Chinese men from entering the country; the period between 1913 and 1917 when Congress used the language of "aliens ineligible for citizenship" as code for Asian immigrants; the construction of

Figure 9. "Elevators (Me and You)" music video, by OutKast, La Face Records, 1996. Directed by Michael Martin.

the "Asiatic barred zone" as a way to geographically mark and exclude all Asians from entering the United States until 1965; and Japanese incarceration during World War II. In essence, these and other U.S. immigration laws helped create a culture whereby Asian Americans were rendered perpetual aliens. And it this racialized positionality that is represented in the "Elevators (Me and You)" music video, and that establishes a fantastical meeting between the forever alien of the Asian American and the ATLien of Big Boi and André 3000.

Importantly, temporality does a lot of work in mediating this kind of encounter between the Asian American male teenager reading a comic book in the present about a southern alien superhero duo of the future. Khyati Joshi and Jigna Desai posit that Asian Americans and the South have unique and oppositional relationships with time. The South is frequently depicted as belated and backwards while Asian Americans, as I articulated above, are often perceived to be foreign and by extension new immigrants. Such a relegation of the South to the past and the Asian American to the forever present "renders the two—the Asian American and the South—[as] allegedly mutually exclusive and incongruous."[65] As such, the *ATLiens* comic book and the act of the Asian American male teenager reading it makes the Asian American and the South congruous and constitutive because the future becomes a site of possibility. For the Asian American teenager, reading the *ATLiens* comic book helps him break free from the strictures of the present because it allows him to imagine life in the future. And for André / Bin Hamin and Big Boi / Daddy Fat Sax, living in the future resists the kinds of temporal attachments of the South and the past. That is, the "Elevators (Me and You)" music video illustrates the future as a space where cross-cultural coalitions can occur. It offers a kind of cross-racial identification that charts the resonances without flattening out the differences between African Americans and Asian Americans. And as the "model minority" category was in full swing by this time in 1996, the video refuses the pitting of Asian Americans against African Americans. It chooses instead to develop alternative temporalities that can render anew the dual alienations of Asian Americans and African Americans in the United States. The video makes room for Afro-Asian collectivities in the form of the Asian American male teenager and the characters of Bin Hamin and Daddy Fat Sax.

But this is also a kind of alliance that restricts the Asian American male teenager from solely using the scripts of Black heteropatriarchy to construct alternative identities, temporalities, and worlds. This character is privy to the hetero-masculinist Daddy Fat Sax as well as the queer male character in Bin Hamin, the latter of whom the teenager seems to identify as the scene in the music video and the panel in the comic book he's reading immediately segues into a scene with Bin Hamin. Which is to say, the video gives the Asian American male teenaged reader the space to develop cross-cultural and cross-racial queer imaginings, and imaginings that productively move beyond the confines of the nation-state as well as the world. To quote Fawaz again, the Asian American male teenager reading the *ATLiens* comic is a subject who is "witnessing impossible phenomena or experiencing life-worlds that have no everyday corollary."[66] As a music video, then, "Elevators (Me and You)" is a demand to imagine otherwise and to imagine the other-worldly, and is to do so in ways that are nonnormative and coalitional. It is to pursue and produce the other side of things.

And yet, this is not an entirely emancipatory vision within the world of ATLantis. Women are largely marginalized, and despite Bin Hamin's queer masculinity, his and André's personae on the album (and in the comic book) are still expressed through patriarchal narratives and practices. In the album's last single and music video, titled "Jazzy Belle," André 3000 engages in sex-negative slut-shaming of men and women in order to espouse a politics of romanticism centered on respectability. Jazzy Belle is a play on words that blends the African American female stereotype of the hypersexual jezebel with the southern womanhood archetype of the belle. Jazzy Belle, then, for OutKast is a southern form of a jezebel. In the song and music video for "Jazzy Belle," Black women are the props that work to further center André and Big Boi. In various scenes, André 3000 is in what looks like a club, perhaps even a strip club, with Big Boi, who is giddily flirting with and cruising for women. André looks disgusted at the display of sex work, and looks down on the women. For André / Bin Hamin, these female characters are perpetuating stereotypes of Black women as always already excessive. And so André's position on "Jazzy Belle" illustrates the need to remain attuned to how queer Afro–South Asian aesthetics are deployed, and the ways they might be liberatory for some and limiting to others along the lines of gender.

Soon after the release of "Jazzy Belle," André stopped wearing and performing in turbans and moved to other sartorial forms of expression. Furthermore, as Vince Robinson explained to me, while there were plans to develop a real-life OutKast/ATLiens comic book, LaFace Records quickly scrapped that idea. And with that, Bin Hamin and Daddy Fat Sax (at least in the new Earth iteration) were no more. But five years after the release of *ATLiens*, a Black woman rapper from the South—Virginia to be specific—would record and release a song that would continue the legacies of Afro-futurism of OutKast, of Rick James's freak, of the queer Afro–South Asian thematics of both James and OutKast, but would also and simultaneously speak to the elided sexual politics of and for Black women. The Black woman rapper was Melissa "Missy" Elliott, and the song was "Get Ur Freak On."

When the Freak Meets the ATLien, She Get Her Freak On

When Elliott and her production partner Timothy "Timbaland" Mosley went to the studio in early 2001 to record Elliott's upcoming third album, they had one plan in mind: "Pretend nobody else in the world existed."[67] The result was an album, *Miss E . . . So Addictive*, that did not sound like anything else in the world, and that did not sound like anything else *of* this world. For this record, Timbaland and Elliott continued their well-known history of creating futuristic-sounding music—unusual drum patterns, robotic sound effects, and synths—and added instruments and voices from Asia and Africa. And when it came time to select the first single, and therefore the representative for *Miss E . . . So Addictive*, Elliott chose "Get Ur Freak On," and with it, released a song that musically and visually reimagined the queer possibilities and potentiality of and for Afro–South Asian collaborative sounds, of and for the other side of things.

To do so, Elliott revisits the figure of the freak. Like Lisa Lowe's use of the "coolie" figure in rendering legible the "intimacies of four continents"— the imbricated processes of settler colonialism, slavery and the transatlantic slave trade, and imported indentured labor that were central to the formation of European liberalism and that tied the geographically disparate Africa, Asia, Europe, and the Americas—the figure of the freak similarly (but in pointedly different ways) binds people of color, queer people, and people with disabilities whose marginalization as nonnormative subjects—as freaks— prop(ped) up the systems and violences of white supremacy, heteronormativity, and able-bodiedness. As critical race, feminist, queer, and disability studies scholars compellingly articulate, an array of scientific, medical, and colonial institutions used black bodies and other bodies of color (e.g., Sarah Baartman / Hottentot Venus), bodies with disabilities (e.g., Chang and Eng, the conjoined twins), nonnormative gendered and sexed bodies (e.g., Peter Sewally / Mary Jones), and bodies that sit at the intersections of all three marginalizations, as primitive and monstrous and proof that such communities were "foreign and biologically degenerate curiosities, if not outliers, in the mythic nation."[68] "Get Ur Freak On" signals and makes intimate these histories. By intimate, I again draw on Lowe to express an intimacy in the formal (what she calls "dominant") sense of sex(uality) and reproduction as well as what Lowe calls "emergent" and "residual" definitions of intimacy that treat them as "close connexion" or "the implied but less visible forms of alliance, affinity, and society among variously colonized peoples beyond the metropolitan national center."[69]

Visually, we see such intimacies take shape in the "Get Ur Freak On" music video, which is set in a dark, underground, futuristic lair removed from white people. This underground space solely comprises Black people, Asian people, people of color with disabilities (via norms of mobility), butch women of color, gender nonconforming people of color, and figures (aliens?) whose relationship to the human is (purposely) unclear—figures for whom L. H. Stallings deems as the hallmarks of the freak: "the otherly human, inhuman, or nonhuman" (Figures 10a and 10b).[70] Within this underground, the freaks live and collectively and sexually dance with one another. This point of collective erotic dance is important because not only was "the freak" a 1970s funk dance, but also, following Stallings, Black culture has long linked Black dance and the Black orgy.[71] It is thus against this historical backdrop that "Get Ur Freak On" directs viewers to bear witness to the erotic attachments of the freak and the ways in which such an underground space is a site by and for freaks, that houses and affirms freaks, that marries the otherworldly with the otherly human, and that is a space for freak fucking and other forms of collective freak action.

Musically, "Get Ur Freak On" sounds such collective action, especially as it concerns Afro–South Asian relationalities. The track opens with a Japanese lyrical phrase—"korekara min-na-de mecha-kucha odotte sawago sawago"— and then proceeds to an interplay between an Indian stringed *tumbi*, tabla drum patterns, and Afro-diasporic syncopated rhythms. Such an Afro–South Asian sonic interplay anchors "Get Ur Freak On," and becomes the foundation from and through which Elliott raps. It is with this Afro–South Asian collaboration of sounds that Elliott deploys a stuttering rhyme of "getcha getcha getcha getcha getcha freak on" that signals solidarity with disabilities. And it is with this Afro–South Asian musical interplay that Elliott launches her chorus to "go get your freak on." Similar to the slippage between "funk" and "fuck" that I discussed above, "freak" is also a euphemism for "fuck," and as such to "get your freak on" is to also "get your fuck on," an erotic call to which the characters in the video adhere and allude. And in this way, to "get your freak on" can also be understood to mean to produce more freaks through fucking. It is a call, an anthem of sorts, to reproduce, expand, and build a community of queer of color and disabled freaks. I, of course, use anthem here deliberately to draw parallels between Rick James's "Freak Flag" and Elliott's "Get Ur Freak On." Indeed, we might read Elliott's call to "get your freak on" as a twenty-first-century extension and iteration of James's call to rally around the freak (flag). It is through and with the freak that a coalition can be built, and as such "Get Ur Freak On" insists on a development of more underground—more southern—spaces through which to support and reproduce a queer Afro–South Asian politics of the freak.

Unlike *The Flag*, however, "Get Ur Freak On" became a commercial and critical success. Missy Elliott scored her first Grammy award with the song, and it was also a top-ten Billboard hit. The popularity and praise of "Get Ur Freak On" began to influence the music market, and rap and R&B labels started to release music that featured South Asian instrumentation and artists. These records were, however, released amid the growing war on terror

a

b

Figure 10. (a) "Get Ur Freak On" music video, by Missy Elliott, Atlantic Records, 2001. Directed by Dave Meyers. (b) "Get Ur Freak On" music video, by Missy Elliott, Atlantic Records, 2001. Directed by Dave Meyers.

(something that Elliott's "Get Ur Freak On" missed by a few months) and the surveillance, detention, and disappearance of Muslim and Middle Eastern peoples (and those assumed to be Muslim / Middle Eastern, including tur-baned people). And with that, the stakes of drawing on South Asian culture became an even more complicated field. In the following two chapters, I address this complexity, and how Black artists developed new approaches to the other side of things that created alternative expressions of Afro–South Asian collaborative sounds.

4

Recovering Addict(ive)

The Afro–South Asian Sexual Politics of Truth Hurts's "Addictive"

My back is achin' from our love makin'.

—Truth Hurts, "Addictive"

On September 13, 2002, African American entertainment attorney Dedra S. Davis issued a press release on behalf of the Indian film and music company Saregama India Ltd. The document announced that Saregama was filing a $500 million copyright infringement lawsuit against hip-hop producer Dr. Dre, his label Aftermath Records, and Aftermath's parent labels Interscope and Universal Music Group. The lawsuit centered on a spring 2002 hit titled "Addictive" by R&B singer Truth Hurts and featuring rapper Rakim—Rakim and Hurts were at the time of the song's release Aftermath/Interscope/Universal artists. Davis makes three allegations in her press release: (1) that "Addictive," which was produced by rapper and producer DJ Quik, samples music and lyrics from the Bollywood film song "Thoda Resham Lagta Hai" from the film *Jyoti*; (2) that Saregama is the proper copyright holder of "Thoda"; and (3) that Quik / Dr. Dre / Aftermath / Interscope / Universal sampled and released "Addictive" without securing Saregama's permission. Oddly enough, the main focus of Davis's allegations was not actually about a violation of her client's intellectual property, but rather a violation of cultural propriety. Davis claims that "Addictive" contains "obscene and offensive" lyrics that "cause extreme offense . . . to the company's owners and to the sensibilities of the many Hindu and Muslim people," a remark that she would later amend to suggest that Hindus were the sole victims in the purported offense.[1] A week later, in an interview with *MTV News,* Davis discussed her press release and revealed that the specific obscenities in "Addictive" were Rakim's use of "fuck" in his featured rap and Truth Hurts's sung lines "'I like it rough' and 'He makes me scream.'"[2] Such sexual lyrics, for Davis, stood in stark contrast to the sampled Hindi lyrics in "Thoda," which focused on flowers, love, and romance. As such, Davis argued that the song's sexually explicit lyrics along with the unauthorized sampling of "Thoda" evidence "the misuse of the company's copyright [and] threatens its reputation and standing."[3]

Much has been written about "Addictive" since its 2002 release. It reached the top ten of the Billboard Hot 100 and, using the momentum of Missy Elliott's "Get Ur Freak On," played a crucial role in increasing U.S. popular music interest in sampling Bollywood and other forms of South Asian music.[4] Perhaps due to its popularity as well as Davis's press release announcing the impending lawsuit, the music director of "Thoda," Bappi Lahiri, later joined Saregama's lawsuit claim and, together, they won an injunction against the sale of "Addictive" and Truth Hurts's debut album, *Truthfully Speaking*. And so, because of all of this, "Addictive" made an apt case study for scholarly theorizations of copyright, capital, and (cultural) appropriation. Joanna Demers, for instance, argues that "Addictive" is indicative of a 2000s trend in U.S. popular music where producers sample non-Western music without permission because of non-Western music's purported exoticism and because copyright licensing is problematically framed as less strict and/or the non-Western identities of proper copyright holders are seemingly less defined.[5] Wayne Marshall and Jayson Beaster-Jones also take up the issue of copyright, but do so by examining how the large number of remixes and interpolations of "Addictive" within and outside of South Asia ultimately "unsettle easy charges of appropriation, whether cross-cultural or illegal, as well as notions of ownership, whether national or personal."[6]

Scholars have also considered how the issues of copyright and capital surrounding "Addictive" intersect with race. Specifically, many scholars have used Orientalism as a productive framework through which to analyze the representations of South Asia on "Addictive." Orientalism helps contextualize the release and popularity of "Addictive" during the period after 9/11 and at the start of the U.S. invasion in Iraq, and it works as a lens through which to make sense of the complexities of such purported imperialist representations taking place within the Afro-diasporic forms of R&B and rap. For example, Nitasha Sharma points out that while Blackness complicates facile and imperialist charges against Truth Hurts and DJ Quik's appropriations of Bollywood, she reads the music video for "Addictive," which problematically conflates South Asia and the Middle East into an exotic harem-like other, as representing "a type of Western cultural imperialism over the East, shaping and reflecting national perspectives not limited to Blacks, music, or the present moment."[7] T. Carlis Roberts, in almost a reverse position of Sharma, argues that while we cannot elide the Orientalist fantasies presented in "Addictive," we must also remain attuned to and hold in tension moments like Truth Hurts's performance of "Addictive" at the 2002 Zee Gold Bollywood Awards, which "allowed for the continued evolution of the meanings of the song and the cultural exchange it fostered."[8]

This chapter builds on such scholarship by paying special attention to, as Dedra Davis's press release that opened this chapter gestures toward, the place and politics of gender and sexuality in "Addictive." In particular, I am interested in exploring and centering the intersections of Black and South Asian women's sexualities in the song. In so doing, I draw on and complicate T. Carlis Roberts's framework of "Afro Asian critique," which Roberts proposes as a specific musical approach that allows for "signs of interracial promise such as shared experiences or understanding, joint counterhegemonic gestures, and non-essentialist representations."[9] For Roberts, such critique lays bare the kinds of Afro-Asian alliances that are "missed in clichéd, and now hegemonic, dominant–subdominant analyses and [is] poised to pinpoint progressive political potential amidst racial faux pas."[10] To pursue a Roberts-style "Afro Asian critique," then, is to resist starting from a perspective that interprets the relationship between African Americans and South Asians as adversarial and conditioned by nationalist and imperialist oppositionality. It is to challenge and complicate the conditions that produce such an assumption, to consider the power dynamics shaping the relationality of African and Asian diasporic communities, and to consider the possibilities for Afro-Asian minoritarian alliances. And so I'm interested in expanding Roberts's critique to take into account how such a framework of race and ethnicity intersects with gender and sexuality, and interrogating how an intersectional approach to such a critique might consider and reveal the overlapping politics of sexuality between "Thoda" and "Addictive."

It's instructive to go back to Dedra Davis's copyright infringement announcement to think through this question. Her assertion that Hurts's lyrical references to and pleasures in rough sex on "Addictive" are vulgar, and

that they remake "Thoda" in such a way that offends Hindu people, intimates two things. First, it taps into the gender and sexual politics of antico-
lonial Hindu nationalist thought and cinematic representations that figure
the imperial lasciviousness of Western modernity as an affront to the traditions of South Asian female purity.[11] Second, as a Black woman discussing
the performance of another Black woman, Davis's categorical rather than
relational reference to Hurts's lyrics as "obscene"—that the lyrics are intrin-
sically rather than relatively offensive because they compete with Hindu
nationalist discourse—evidences a politics of respectability and silence that,
because of the long history of stereotypes of Black women that prop(ped)
up sexual violence, discourages explicit representations of Black women's
erotic lives.[12]

It is at this nexus of Black and South Asian female sexual dissidence that
this chapter grapples with Truth Hurts's "Addictive." Rather than solely reading "Addictive" as sexualizing "Thoda," I want to pursue the other side of
things and argue that the expressions of female sexuality on "Addictive" productively, and at times queerly, entangle African American and South Asian
female erotics. Indeed, despite Davis's intimation that the sexually explicit
lyrics of "Addictive" egregiously altered the meaning of "Thoda," the vocalist
on "Thoda," famed Bollywood playback singer Lata Mangeshkar, claimed
that she neither objected to DJ Quik's sampling of her voice nor felt that he
"tampered with" the song.[13] To engage and practice the other side of things
is to take seriously Mangeshkar's remarks and consider the ways "Thoda"
complements rather than contrasts the female erotic pleasures and practices in "Addictive." It is to see, as I explicate below, how "Addictive" brings
together the historical and moralistic silencing of Black and South Asian
women's sexuality in U.S. and South Asian popular culture, and how it creates a space from which Black and South Asian female sexual pleasure can
be imagined, expressed, and experienced.

Sexually Addictive

The production history of "Addictive" helps elucidate the workings of Afro–
South Asian female sexualities. In an often-told story, DJ Quik first encountered "Thoda" at home when *Jyoti*, the film in which the song is featured,
was playing on the Bollywood television channel Zee-TV:

I woke up one morning . . . I turned on the TV and landed on this Hindi channel and I just turned it up real loud. . . . There was a commercial on, and I just
got up and went into the bathroom and started brushing my teeth. I'm brushing, and before I knew it I was grooving . . . [the beat] was just in my body. I
went back in there and looked at the TV—there was a girl on there bellydanc-
ing [sic], just like real fly. So I pushed record on the VCR.[14]

DJ Quik's viewing and recording/sampling "Thoda" from his television is
important because it not only potentially informs the eroticism of "Addictive" (more on that later), but also because, contrary to the lyrics of "Thoda"
as well as Dedra Davis's contention that "Thoda" was not sexually explicit,
the visualized song and dance performance of "Thoda" centers female sex
work. The character from *Jyoti* who DJ Quik (mis)read as a belly dancer was
Mallika (played by actress Aruna Irani). Mallika is a courtesan or *tawayaf*,
who is performing a dance known as a *mujra* in an urban salon called a
kotha. As Beaster-Jones and Marshall explain, *kothas* are "highly erotic spaces
within the conventions of Hindi film, the *kotha* sometimes represented as
little more than a brothel, the *tawayaf* as little more than a prostitute."[15]
Wayne Marshall and Jayson Beaster-Jones go on to note that the Orientalist
otherness that DJ Quik perceived as belly dancing—the conflation of South
Asia (via Bollywood) and the Middle East (via belly dancing) into a homogenous East—is "not so far from eroticized *tawayaf* representations in Hindi
films."[16] Indeed, the song and dance number for "Thoda" opens in a *kotha*
where a landowner's son, Niranjan (played by Vijayendra Ghatge), intimately
whips Mallika (Figure 11a). After playfully struggling with the whip and dodg-
ing Niranjan's attempts to kiss her on the lips, Mallika pushes Niranjan onto
a couch and begins to perform the *mujra* dance for him. The scene consists
of Mallika thrusting her breasts forward while crawling on the floor, wink-
ing at Niranjan, seductively biting her bottom lip, and playfully dangling
grapes between Niranjan's and her lips (Figure 11b).

Such a scene is indicative of what ethnomusicologist Regula Qureshi
describes as the place of *kothas* as stigmatized spaces of erotic performance,
sex work, and nonnormative sexual activities and desires, as "licentious and
immoral social space[s] where a woman offers her art and, by implication,
herself."[17] Following independence in 1947, Indian elite and middle-class social
reformers vilified *kothas* and *tawayafs* as threats to women's respectability

a

b

Figure 11. (a and b) "Thoda Resham Lagta Hai" song and dance sequence, *Jyoti*, 1981. Directed by Pramod Chakravarty.

and Indian nationalism, and sought to curtail representations of *tawayaf* culture in Indian popular music and film. Despite these efforts, Bollywood films continue to depict *tawayaf* culture, but do so in ways that shore up rather than circumvent middle-class notions of femininity and respectability. For example, as Beaster-Jones and Marshall explain, these films often portray *kothas* "within the context of an exoticized historical past," and therefore as sites of premodern, backwards, and uncivilized cultural practices.[18]

Remarkably, DJ Quik's sampling of "Thoda" as well as Truth Hurts's lyrics on "Addictive" refuse the relegation of the sexual impropriety of "Thoda" to a historical past; they instead create and imagine an erotic Afro–South Asian present and future elsewhere, an erotic expression of the other side of things. When I interviewed Truth Hurts, she informed me that the recording process for "Addictive" stalled for six months because, "until Static came into the studio," DJ Quik, Dr. Dre, and Hurts were unable to find and work with a songwriter capable of capturing their vision for the song.[19] Static was the professional name of the late singer-songwriter Stephen Garrett. Known in R&B circles for being a member of "Da Bassment crew" musical collective that included Missy Elliott and Timbaland, Static became famous for writing sexually forward songs like Ginuwine's 1996 hit "Pony" as well as hit R&B songs that sample non-Western, and especially Middle Eastern, music like Aaliyah's 2002 "More Than a Woman." In enlisting Static to take the lead in writing "Addictive," Hurts, DJ Quik, and Dr. Dre found someone who had the background to fully address and (re)imagine the eroticism (via "Pony"), South Asian (via his association with Elliott and Timbaland who, as described in the previous chapter, ushered in a new iteration of Afro–South Asian music), and Middle Eastern (via "More Than a Woman") backing of "Thoda." With Static, as Truth Hurts explained to me, they found someone who could, and did, establish the necessary "pace and sexuality" of "Addictive" that resulted in the "marriage between the beat, the melody, and the lyrics."[20]

Such a marriage on "Addictive" articulates with the sexual and kink aesthetics of the original's song and dance performance. "Addictive" opens with a sample from "Thoda" in which Lata Mangeshkar sings "kaliyon ka chaman tab banta hai" (translated as "a flower garden is then made"). DJ Quik plays a bass line to underlie the opening sample, and then uses renowned percussionist Bryan Brock to provide added rhythmic textures to the song. Trained in Afro-diasporic and South Asian instruments, Brock informed me that DJ

Quik hired him to play drum patterns on "Addictive" that could bridge and accentuate the musical similarities between other sampled instrumental elements from "Thoda" with the sampled backbeat from "Do It ('Til You're Satisfied)" by funk band B. T. Express.[21] It is with Brock that we glean the ways in which DJ Quik does not attempt to draw out the exoticism of "Thoda" and South Asia, to highlight its supposed sonic difference from the rest of recording. DJ Quik's approach is to sonically create Afro–South Asian linkages that illuminate the braided percussive elements and cultural histories of Afro-diasporic and South Asian culture as well as, via the sexually suggestive title and lyrics in "Do It ('Til You're Satisfied)," set and sustain the sexual spirit of the "Thoda" song and dance sequence and "Addictive."

Split into three verses with Hurts singing the first two and Rakim delivering a sixteen-bar rap, "Addictive" tells the story of a woman who believes that she's found the male companion of her dreams, or perhaps better yet, her desires. "Addictive" is not a romantic narrative that sidesteps or euphemistically approaches sex and pleasure. It is a song in which Hurts describes a woman's general love of sex, particularly sex involving her drug-dealing male partner (Rakim) with whom she finds such activities utterly irresistible, contagious, and otherwise "addictive." Rakim's rap articulates a man who cosigns his female lover's addictive sexual relationship, revealing that although he sells drugs, it is their sex that produces and maintains their addiction to and for each other. Rough sex, as I noted above, sits at the heart of Hurts's character's insatiable sexual pleasure. And while listeners are not privy to the specific forms of rough or kinky sex, both Rakim and Hurts allude to erotic asphyxiation—Rakim raps, "[You're] breathing hard while I'm squeezing your lungs"—and flogging—Hurts sings, "My back is achin' from our love makin'"—a possible allusion to Niranjan whipping Mallika during the "Thoda" song and dance performance that DJ Quik recorded. The "Addictive" music video opens with a shot of Truth Hurts's back, which sports a *mehndi* (henna) spelling of her name down her back in red dye as a gesture toward blood, and she is later seen in the bed with her hands positioned as if she were tied up (Figure 12).

In explicitly singing about a Black woman's sexual practices and desires, and especially those that are rough and kinky and that involve whipping and bondage, Truth Hurts taps into misogynoir representations that pathologize Black women as subservient and excessively sexual and that articulate with Black women's institutional and interpersonal experiences of sexual violence

Figure 12. "Addictive" music video, by Truth Hurts, Aftermath Records, 2002. Directed by Phillip Atwell.

during and after U.S. slavery.[22] It is perhaps these kinds of dehumanizing stereotypes, or "controlling images" as Patricia Hill Collins famously describes them, that informed Dedra Davis's assessment of "Addictive," irrespective of its relation to South Asian religious traditions, as "obscene."[23] Richard Zumkhawala-Cook makes similar critiques of "Addictive" when he posits that Hurts's masochistic narrative portrays a "sex-crazed" woman who "reproduces the most retrograde male fantasies," and that such acquiescence to patriarchy implicates "Thoda" and Lata Mangeshkar by "globally pluralizing the glorified female submission . . . as if it should be understood that Mangeshkar's aural presence articulates the same position."[24] And while T. Carlis Roberts resists such a sex-negative approach to "Addictive," noting the relation of "Thoda" to *kothas* and *tawayafs*, they still locate a particular patriarchal impulse in "Addictive." In particular, Roberts argues that DJ Quik's use of Mangeshkar's vocals for "Addictive" strips her of any agency and determines "what she would say, when, and the tempo and pitch, the source material altered to support the new song's content."[25]

I want to briefly complicate these readings that bind "Addictive," "Thoda," and Mangeshkar to heterosexism because I believe that such arguments belie the ways the lyrics and production of "Addictive" refuse to solely express male pleasures and center the male gaze. While Truth Hurts uses "he" throughout much of "Addictive," such use is always in relation to her own pleasure, sexual or otherwise. "Addictive" is focused on the steps a man makes to materially, romantically, and sexually fulfill the desires and pleasures of his female partner. Remember, it's Truth Hurts who sings, "I like it rough." She is the one who directs the narrative of the relationship, and her "addiction" to her male partner is due to her continued (sexual) satisfaction with him: "He makes me scream . . . he hits the spot." In other words, he works to please her; she does not work to please him. Moreover, Rakim's verse is one that one might expect an expression of phallocentrism and male sexual prowess. Instead, Rakim spends most of the verse discussing his drug-dealing practices, and makes only one reference to his relationship with his female companion— "Just me and you high off sex and twisted"—a nod to shared sexual desire and pleasure. The only implication of female submission in "Addictive," then, is the expression of sadomasochism.

But the logic that links S/M sex to heterosexism is one born out of second-wave feminism (radical and liberal, Black and non-Black) that only imagines S/M within the boundaries of sexual violence. And here we must go back to Dedra Davis's press release. Her use of the word "obscene" to describe "Addictive" was not simply a personal feeling stemming from a politics of morality, but also a legal argument that recalls the ways anti-pornography feminists of the 1970s and 1980s attempted to use the U.S. obscenity laws to define such materials as obscene and ban them from existence. As anti-anti-pornography activists like Lisa Duggan, Nan Hunter, Carole Vance, Pat Califia, Amber Hollibaugh, and Cherrie Moraga have argued, anti-pornography feminism uses images of S/M pornographic material to promote the banning of porn, and (further) demonizing S/M culture as dangerous, violent, and patriarchal.[26] Which is to say, and to quote Amber Jamilla Musser, anti-pornography feminists saw S/M as a "pernicious extension of patriarchy because it coerced women into participating in this masculine sphere of unequal power distribution through a cooptation of eroticism."[27]

Truth Hurts resists such a narrative on "Addictive" by locating S/M sex as a site of Black female pleasure and power, and not pathology. And in so doing, she makes intimate what Ariane Cruz calls the "politics of perversion" and what Joan Morgan calls the "politics of pleasure." Hurts's lyrics locate a Black woman's pleasure in the erotic forms of whipping and asphyxiation, and as a result, finds S/M as a "subversive, transformative power of perversion" that resists the politics of respectability and silence governing Black women's sexuality and that makes room for "honest bodies that like to also fuck."[28]

And it is in relation to this kind of female pleasure in S/M sex on "Addictive," this kind of melding of the politics of perversion and the politics of pleasure, that I argue that Mangeshkar's lyrics and vocals are not altered to support patriarchy, but rather perform a subversion of such norms that seek to curtail women's sexual dissidence. Indeed, Bollywood playback singers (singing prerecorded vocals for use in movies) like Mangeshkar have been central to Bollywood's attempt to reconcile visual erotic representations with middle-class notions of sexual morality. Mangeshkar rose to fame alongside, and consequently informed, post-Indian independence notions of proper womanhood that rendered women's sexual subjectivity and desires (queer and non-queer) as at least domestic and at most nonexistent. Regarded as "virginally pure" and displaying an "adolescent-girl falsetto," Mangeshkar's voice performed nationalist middle-class ideals of femininity, providing female characters in popular Indian cinema with the forms of innocence and chastity, irrespective of a female character's story line, that the gender politics of Indian nationalist discourses demanded.[29] As Pavitra Sundar argues, Mangeshkar's "desexualized vocal style helped contain the dangerous visual" presence of nonnormative female subjectivities and pleasures represented in Bollywood film scenes; her "pure" vocal performance "thinned" and "cleansed" nonnormative representations.[30] In other words, to the ears of many Bollywood elite and middle-class audiences, the "purified" voice of Lata Mangeshkar rescripted nonnormative scenes and/or characters to conform to the normative logics of the Indian popular film industry, the Indian state, and the dominant milieu.

DJ Quik's coupling of Truth Hurts and Mangeshkar for "Addictive," then, works to undo the ways in which Mangeshkar's vocals and lyrics render illegible the kinky female sexual desires advanced in the song and dance number of "Thoda." Recall that while the film performance in "Thoda" features whipping and sexual flirtations, Mangeshkar's lyrics use desexualized language of flowers and romantic attachment. On "Thoda," the sonic betrays the visual. One could listen to "Thoda" without knowing the impropriety of the song and dance performance, and one could watch and listen to the film performance, as DJ Quik did, in ways that fail to hear Mangeshkar's voice and lyrics as containing and buffering the visual representations of erotic nonnormativity. For "Addictive," however, there isn't a visual to which Mangeshkar's lyrics and voice respond. Instead, "Addictive" finds Hurts and Mangeshkar residing in entangled tension of female sexual dissidence. DJ Quik's sampling of certain phrases in "Thoda" limits and contains the respectability of Mangeshkar's lyrics. Because he does not sample the entire song or long verses from "Thoda," Mangeshkar's voice and lyrics are unable to fully excise the nonnormativity of the song and dance sequence that DJ Quik initially saw and recorded. And because of this, Truth Hurts is able to express Black female sexual desires and pleasures denied under the demands of the politics of respectability while simultaneously revealing and aligning with the erotic past of the song's filmic representation that Lata Mangeshkar's voice initially and supposedly masked. "Addictive" thus sutures and subverts Black and Indian nationalist middle-class norms of morality that disavow the erotic, and in so doing offers a cross-cultural recording that centers and articulates shared Afro–South Asian (Hurts and Mangeshkar) nonnormative female sexual pleasure, desire, and practices. In other words, "Addictive" creates space for an Afro–South Asian sociality of sexual dissidence.

(S)he Makes Me Scream

We can also read the Afro–South Asian sociality of "Addictive" as a queer performance, especially if we further analyze its relation to the "Thoda" song and dance number. In addition to its depictions of sex workers, brothels, and S/M-related flagellation, the scene is also about deception. Much of the performance centers on Niranjan eagerly attempting to respond to Mallika's flirtations with a kiss, but to no avail—she always eludes his grasp, but still continues to flirt. Near the end of the scene, Niranjan chases Mallika around the *kotha* and suddenly collapses and passes out on the floor. Much to the surprise of the audience, Mallika begins to steal Niranjan's rings and other personal items. But it soon becomes apparent that Mallika's flirtatious activities were not genuine, and that Mallika conspired with Amirchand, a character closely tied to Mallika and Niranjan and who lurks behind the scenes out of Niranjan's view, to rob Niranjan. Realizing Niranjan's general wealth and infatuation with Mallika, Mallika and Amirchand decided to exploit such lust by portraying Mallika as equally, if not more, obsessed with Niranjan.

She seduces Niranjan while Amirchand slips an incapacitating agent into his drink, and then robs him of consciousness and wealth. Thus, rather than an uneven and unidirectional romantic desire with Niranjan at the center and Mallika hopelessly attached to him, this act of deception reverses such perceptions. The film's acknowledgment of the deception repositions Mallika as the relationship's main focal point and seductive and financial consumer, with Niranjan serving as the lone sexually addicted partner.

I go back to the song and dance performance because, as I outlined above regarding DJ Quik's sampling of the picturized performance of it as well as the two songs' shared thematics of kink play, the visual memories of "Thoda" bear on "Addictive." In particular, I want to think through the ways in which audiences' (and not to mention Niranjan's) deception in the song and dance sequence might provide a way to read "Addictive" in such a way that Truth Hurts similarly dupes her male partner, Rakim, and its listeners in "Addictive." If the concluding scene in "Thoda" reveals to viewers that Mallika's interest in Niranjan is simply an act to trick him into providing her with wealth, then perhaps we could also read Truth Hurts as similarly tricking listeners and Rakim into believing that she is the one addicted to Rakim, that his pleasure is her main concern. Hurts's lyrics briefly allude to such a possibility when she sings, "He takes care of home / but he's not alone." Placing Hurts's implication that Rakim is not her only sexual partner in relation to Mallika's conning of Niranjan gestures toward two things. First, as the playback singer for the "Thoda" song and dance number, Lata Mangeshkar's sampled voice on "Addictive" serves as a haunting reminder that Hurts is potentially feigning fixation, a pretense of docility in order to fulfill her own sexual and economic desires—an act that re-centers Hurts as the subject of her own sexual narrative and foregrounds instead of subsumes her pleasure. Second, and more to the point on the subject of queerness, because "Thoda" and "Addictive" share narratives of women deceiving male interests/sexual partners (not to mention women-centered pleasures with kink play fantasies), I want to push for a reading of Lata Mangeshkar's role on "Addictive" as one that partly plays as Hurts's lyrically absent and unnamed partner. If "Addictive" at most restages and at least parallels the "Thoda" song and dance sequence, then "Addictive" must also have three characters who overlap with the three characters in the picturized performance in "Thoda." As such, Hurts, Rakim, and Mangeshkar's characters in "Addictive" resonate with Mallika, Niranjan, and Amirchand: Hurts/Mallika play up attraction to

Rakim/Niranjan, only to hold ulterior motives that involve Mangeshkar/ Amirchand. Importantly, like Amirchand, Mangeshkar is literally and figuratively in the background of the sonic scene of "Addictive." But whereas Amirchand is strictly written in the scene as a character with whom Mallika conspires, Hurts's lyrics on "Addictive" suggest that Mangeshkar is her coconspirator and her significant other who, in addition to Rakim, "takes care of home," a double entendre that dually signals an ability to adequately address the needs of the house as well as an ability to satisfy the sexual needs within another domestic space: the bedroom.[31] Rakim alone does not, and perhaps cannot, solely or fully satisfy Hurts. She also has to rely on Mangeshkar to provide such addictive pleasures as well.

Nabeel Zuberi persuasively argues that Mangeshkar's moaning on "Addictive" serves as the song's affective register.[32] Zuberi reads Mangeshkar's vocables during Truth Hurts's sung lyrics as "exhalations of sexual ecstasy," and he interprets similar sounds during Rakim's rhymes—particularly those concerning Rakim's potential incarceration for dealing drugs—as "discomfort and loss." I agree with Zuberi that Mangeshkar's moans mediate and "materialize" the relations between Rakim and Hurts, but I want to further expand this line of thinking to read such vocalizations as also signifying opposition to Rakim's boasts of his sexual prowess and/or general presence on the record itself. That is, I want to read Mangeshkar's nonverbal sonic expressions as also critiques of patriarchy and/or heteronormativity, and by extension a longing for an alternative and queer sexual relation. Lata Mangeshkar's vocables, her non-lexical guttural sounds, serve as a sonic extension of Hurts's sexual satisfaction and as possible markers of Mangeshkar's own enjoyment in Truth Hurts's practice of rough sex. If sampling characterizes an extraction of music from the past and inserting it into a present recording, then "Addictive" brings the lyrics and sounds of Mangeshkar on "Thoda" back to life, allowing Mangeshkar's "oohs" on "Addictive" to operate as visceral reactions to Hurts's sexually charged lyrics.[33] Hurts also returns the favor by providing background vocals of heavy panting and rising orgasmic sounds during Mangeshkar's sampled Hindi lyrics. Hurts's expirated erotic performance over and under Mangeshkar's lyrics of desexualized romance dually makes audible the sexual activity and allusions in the filmic performance of "Thoda" that Mangeshkar's original lyrics worked to erase, and it also marks Mangeshkar's voice as a site through which Hurts directs desire and finds pleasure. Which is to say, even as Hurts discusses the ways that she is sexually addicted

to her male sexual partner—Rakim—her aural expressions of sexual pleasure that are sung in relation to Mangeshkar casts such articulations of heteronormative monogamy in doubt. It is a doubt that consequently allows
"Addictive" to voice a narrative of queer sexualities between Mangeshkar
and Hurts and/or Mangeshkar, Hurts, and Rakim.

Mangeshkar and Hurts's lyrical and vocal encounters on "Addictive,"
then, where, as Roberts notes, "one voice sings words, while the other shifts
to vocables that accent the lead voice," engender a "geographically and tem-
porally displaced duet" that relies on and materializes through the syncing
up of same-sex bodies and pleasures across time and space.[34] Truth Hurts's
verses and voice demystify Mangeshkar's orgasmic expressions, and Lata
Mangeshkar provides a sonic illustration of Hurts's description of her sexual
practices and pleasures. Both artists perform and sound a queer binding that
collectively shapes and informs each recording's and artist's female-derived
enjoyment of rough sex, and form a sonic exploration and articulation of
Afro–South Asian female same-sex pleasure that is emblematic of what Juana
María Rodríguez calls queer perverse sociality.[35]

In so doing, "Addictive" challenges contentions that the lyrics and sound
of "Addictive" construct an Orientalist narrative where Truth Hurts ostensibly acquiesces to patriarchal sexual pleasure, and, through Lata Mangeshkar's
voice on the song, produces India as a feminine spectacle subordinate to the
masculine United States. I posit, instead, that "Addictive" elides such heteronormative logic and illustrates a shared female-centered account of pleasure,
a gendered, temporal, and racialized lateral connection made along the
margins of erotic practices and pleasures. "Addictive" and "Thoda Resham
Lagta Hai" serve as mutually constitutive songs that uphold each track's
female-centered shared pleasure and refusals of patriarchy. The visuality of
the "Thoda" song and dance performance accompanies "Addictive," and dis-
rupts readings of "Addictive" that use Truth Hurts's references to rough sex
and sexual fixation as tied to fulfilling heterosexual male fantasies. Further,
Hurts's lyrics highlight and literally keep alive the queer memories and reading practices that Dedra Davis aimed to obfuscate through her press release
and lawsuit. Simply put, rather than sampling a non-Western record and
using its exoticness to explore and shore up African American sexual politics,
the music and lyrics of "Addictive" bring these seemingly disparate songs
and communities together in ways that produce new meanings to both songs.
This allows listeners to experience and interpret queer female pleasures and

practices that are too often silenced and rendered impossible within mainstream rap, Indian popular film/music circles, Black respectability politics,
and Indian nationalist moralities.

Recovering Addict(ive)

In her 2005 essay "Bollywood Spectacles: Queer Diasporic Critique in the
Aftermath of 9/11," cultural and queer theorist Gayatri Gopinath explores the
ostensible paradox of the commercialization of Bollywood cinema among
non–South Asian audiences in the United States simultaneously occurring
alongside the policing and disappearing of South Asian bodies and communities in the wake of 9/11. Grappling with these seemingly "curious and contradictory" processes, Gopinath invokes a "queer diasporic critique" in order
to expose the highly gendered and sexualized underpinnings of Bollywood's
popularity among Western audiences, revealing the ways in which its intel-
ligibility in the United States is predicated on the effacement of queer female
bodies, subjectivities, and desires.[36] Yet, while Gopinath's use of queer diasporic critique astutely highlights the false paradox of the visibility of South
Asians on the silver screen with the heightened *invisibility* of such bodies
within the state, this chapter has illustrated the ways in which a turn to the
other side of things, to the sonic and specifically Black popular musicians'
engagements with South Asian cultural production, can open up spaces where
such female queerness is expressed and experienced horizontally between
racially marginalized communities.

Examining "Addictive" through the other side of things illustrates how,
rather than engaging in dominant reading practices of "Addictive" that auto-
matically contextualize the song as an extension of the imperialist and Orientalist Indo-chic period and the post-9/11 war on terror, we need to explore
the relationship between South Asian cultural production and U.S.-based
hip-hop as their own relationship, independent of white consumption of
South Asian cultural commodities. In so doing, we find new understandings of this Afro–South Asian cultural moment. My use of the other side of
things here is not an attempt to deny that "Addictive" or similar songs engage
in Orientalist tropes. But what I am pointing out is that often these same
songs are involved in other progressive politics, and that is what makes the
other side of things a necessary reading practice and analytic. Specifically,
a turn to the workings of gender and sexuality in "Addictive" lays bare the

numerous ways that the song complicates approaches that solely analyze it through lenses of race, imperialism, and Orientalism. The politics of gender and sexuality in "Addictive" offer another way, an imagining elsewhere that I call the other side of things. If Orientalism is an imperialist binary logic of difference that shores up norms of race (whiteness), gender (patriarchy), and sexuality (heteronormativity), then it might mean that a turn toward the anti-Orientalist manifestations of "Addictive" challenges such dominant formations and opens up Afro–South Asian, feminist, and queer possibilities.

In the midst of the lawsuit, Truth Hurts was invited to perform this intercultural, cross-spatial, and cross-temporal queer sociality to a majority–South Asian audience in the summer of 2002. Given the commercial success of "Addictive" in the United States, Kamal Dandona, the chairman of the Zee Gold Bollywood Awards, asked Hurts to perform the song as part of their annual awards show at the Nassau Coliseum on Long Island, New York. According to Hurts, she was the first "American artist" ever, and by extension first African American artist, to perform at the event.[37] The history-making set is also notable because it did not include Rakim. Instead, the set featured Hurts, surrounded by women of color dancers, singing "Addictive" alongside the sampled voice of Lata Mangeshkar. This all–women of color performance both figuratively and literally stages a queer collectivity that visually and sonically links the bodies and voices of such women of color through the practice of and pleasure in rough sex. As music journalist Corey Takahashi wrote about the proceedings, after the conclusion of Hurts's set, "teenage girls shrieked with glee; sari-wearing grandmothers gasped."[38] Takahashi's description speaks to a generational shift in the audience response to Hurts's performance, and one that is specific to and ostensibly centered on sexual (im)propriety. Hurts's set was a transgression of gender and sexual norms of respectability within Indian nationalist and Black cultural formations that animated the Afro–South Asian female queerness of "Addictive" and Saregama's copyright infringement lawsuit.

But, in the end, this lawsuit stalled Hurts's career, the financial potential of "Addictive," and the song's Afro–South Asian queer sociality. Saregama won an injunction against Dr. Dre / Aftermath Records / Interscope / Universal in 2002 (despite later losing the lawsuit), and it halted the sales of "Addictive" and the Truth Hurts album that included it. To this day, "Addictive" isn't available for purchase or streaming via normative channels Spotify, iTunes, and Tidal. The injunction, the multimillion-dollar lawsuit itself, and the attendant media attention placed too much of a burden on Hurts, and she and Dr. Dre agreed to part ways in late 2002 / early 2003.[39] The legal fallout affected how Black hip-hop artists and producers approached the inclusion of and engagement with South Asian music. Some producers, like the Black Eyed Peas' will.i.am, obtained permission before releasing any recorded material that sampled Bollywood music; while other producers, like DJ Quik, abandoned the whole project.[40] But as we will see in the next chapter, some Black rap producers, notably Timothy "Timbaland" Mosley, saw the controversy surrounding "Addictive" as an opportunity to imagine and pursue a new way of working with South Asian music in his songs—and importantly, this was an other side of things that kept in play the queer and feminist impulses that "Addictive" compellingly engendered and explored.

5

Do(ing) Something Different

Cross-Cultural Collaboration in the Work of Timbaland and Rajé Shwari

Tim was pretty much doing a lot of Indian stuff at the time. But he wanted to do something different.

—Bill Pettaway, interview

Several years ago, I interviewed guitarist and music executive Bill Pettaway, who is most known for cowriting Milli Vanilli's "Girl You Know It's True" and for discovering Toni Braxton. But at the time of my interview with him, he was the A&R (artists and repertoire) head for rap producer Timothy "Timbaland" Mosely, for whom he was developing a pool of South Asian American talent. Timbaland, as discussed in chapter 3, produced Missy Elliott's hit "Get Ur Freak On," and soon produced other chart-topping songs that sampled South Asian music—Tweet's "Oops (Oh My)" and "Call Me" and Bubba Sparxxx's "Ugly" being the exemplary recordings—that, along with Truth Hurts's "Addictive," helped usher in the mainstream popularity of and visibility to South Asian music in U.S. (Black) popular music.[1] But then things started to slightly change for Timbaland. He stopped sampling South Asian music and started to create songs with a South Asian American singer named Rajé Shwari. Shwari, born Rajeshwari Parmar, had enjoyed minor success in Europe in 2000 and 2001 while working with house producer Todd Terry, and had begun working on a demo in the summer of 2002 in the hopes of securing a record deal with a major label. Shwari's work soon landed in the hands of Pettaway, who was impressed with it, and then took it to

123

Timbaland. Timbaland, like Pettaway, loved Shwari's demo, quickly signed her to his production company, which Pettaway ran, and started to work with her on his upcoming projects with Jay-Z, Kanye West, Beenie Man, and his own solo efforts. When I asked Pettaway about what drew Timbaland to Shwari, he told me, "Tim [Timbaland] was pretty much doing a lot of Indian stuff at the time. But he wanted to do something different. He was tired of everyone sampling. So he wanted to change music again—he's the king of that, you know—and Rajé [Shwari] fit where he was going."[2]

This chapter explores Timbaland's desire to "do something different," and in particular his collaborations with Rajé Shwari that such a desire engendered. I read the music that they created together, their collective effort to "do something different," as a form of what I've called throughout this book as the other side of things—an alternative imaginative space of Afro–South Asian music making that holds cross-cultural coalitional and queer political implications and possibilities. Timbaland and Shwari extended the queer Afro–South Asian impulse of Truth Hurts's "Addictive" that I discussed in the previous chapter, but they did so with a twist. Rather than a sample serving as the South Asian representational construct in U.S.-based rap and R&B, as it had with "Addictive," Shwari's presence on songs and her coproduction and cowriting with Timbaland shifted focus to the agential. That is, the music that Timbaland and Shwari collectively developed brings to the fore the collaborative and the face-to-face contact of what performance theorist Patrice Pavis calls the "intercorporeal," and how such intercultural music making practices shape the racial, gender, and sexual meanings of Afro–South Asian music during this moment of increased sampling of South Asian sound. I'm interested, in other words, in the queer and cross-racial musical solidarities that potentially arise within, are cultivated out of, and expressed through the Afro–South Asian interpersonal collaborative workings of the other side of things.

Shwari and Timbaland's tapping into and elaboration of the other side of things most chiefly recalls the collective work between Miles Davis and Badal Roy that I addressed in chapter 2. In both examples, we find a famous and influential African American artist working with a lesser-known South Asian (American) musician. But there are two significant differences between these two collective groups and moments that explicate how Timbaland and Shwari continue the legacies of these Afro–South Asian collaborative efforts. First, while *On the Corner* was a response to Black Power politics, formal politics did not drive Shwari and Timbaland's creative processes. As noted above, the popularity of South Asian samples in U.S.-based Black popular music led them to work together. Timbaland noticed the ubiquity of music producers sampling South Asian music, and consequently sought other ways to include South Asian cultural production in his music that didn't contribute to the trend's oversaturation.[3] As for Shwari, as she informed the *New York Times,* while she was working on her demo in the summer of 2002, she was "hearing Indian samples in hip-hop, so I sang some background vocals and made them sound like samples, because of Timbaland."[4] In order to make her vocals "sound like samples," Shwari recorded herself in Hindi, and used software that filtered her voice to emphasize high and mid-range frequencies in such a way that they produced a vocal tone like that coming from a telephone receiver. This altered vocal sound is key for Shwari's demo and career because it resembles and mimics the timbral, temporal, and spatial characteristics commensurate with digital sampling. But more than the mechanics of sounding like a sample, Shwari's statement to the *New York Times* points to how Timbaland's popularity and association with sampling South Asian music was the impetus to her sample-sounding demo—it was her way to appeal to Timbaland's aesthetic as well as get his attention. And so, when Timbaland heard Shwari's demo, it coincided with his desire to "do something different" with South Asian music. It was Shwari's emulation of samples that was that difference. It illustrated what a South Asian (American) social actor, and not simply a sampled object, could sound like in hip-hop.

The second way that Timbaland and Shwari's collaborations differ from Davis and Roy concerns gender. Shwari's gender as a woman informs her sample-sounding demo and work with Timbaland. While *On the Corner* is an all-male affair, Shwari and Timbaland's cowriting and coproduction work took place between a woman and man. I draw attention to the gender difference between Shwari and Timbaland because, at this time, hip-hop producers disproportionally sampled South Asian women's voices (usually Bollywood) for their songs, which, in return, exacerbated critiques that such producers and sampling practices were Orientalist—the masculine as West and the feminine as East. Shwari's sample-sounding demo and performance, then, contends with this narrative. But, like Timbaland, Shwari is interested in doing, and then later very much does, something different: she gives the sample agency. Rather than the status of a static sampled South Asian woman—a commodity that a rap producer manipulates or to whom a featured artist (i.e., singer/rapper) references in their song—Shwari's performance as this gendered sample allows the recording to address its surroundings—the featured artist(s), the theme of a song, the pitch and rhythmic patterns of a song—and further contributes to the meaning making of the song. Shwari, and I'm alluding to Fred Moten (who was drawing on Marx) here, creates a space from which the commodity, the gendered sample, can speak (back).[5] As we'll soon see, Shwari kept and made central the sample-sounding demo performances and effects for her future collaborations with Timbaland. And in so doing, Shwari and Timbaland's intercultural collaborative work complicates and challenges the Orientalist framings of Afro–South Asian rap that predominated this kind of music at the time. In moving from object to subject, Shwari and Timbaland produce new racialized, gendered, and sexual narratives of and for Afro–South Asian music.

In order to explicate these new narratives, I want to consider Shwari and Timbaland's two most prominent songs: "The Bounce," which Timbaland produced for Jay-Z, which is Kanye West's first featured performance in a major rap track, and which is Timbaland and Shwari's first collaborative release; and "Indian Flute," which Timbaland produced for his and his longtime rap partner Magoo's album, which features a rap from Timbaland's brother Sebastian, and which was the last single that Timbaland and Shwari released together.[6] These songs are thus bookends of Shwari and Timbaland's Afro–South Asian collaborative projects, and I argue that they illuminate the breadth and complexity of Shwari and Timbaland's dual desire to "do something different." This difference, as we will see and which has been highlighted throughout this book, is a difference that sits at the intersections of race and sexuality, a difference produced through Black and South Asian (diasporic) relationalities, and a difference that facilitates queer Afro–South Asian bonds.

What's Beneath the Bounce?

Soon after signing Shwari, Timbaland enlisted her assistance in writing and producing a song titled "The Bounce" for Jay-Z, a song that features the then-emerging rapper/producer Kanye West, and which was slated for Jay-Z's highly anticipated album *The Blueprint 2: The Gift & the Curse*.[7] By the time Shwari entered the studio, Timbaland had finished the beat, Jay-Z had already recorded his verses and his chorus, and West had completed his verse. The song's beat is sparse and heavy. It comprises a steady yet syncopated non-pitched tabla that underlies an interplay between a hard-hitting kick drum and a slapping clap. "The Bounce" also features an array of synthesizer-based sounds that give the song a strong base but fail to render a melodic impulse. Jay-Z's verses center on him boasting to male rappers about the success of his previous album, *The Blueprint*—"Rumor has it / *The Blueprint* [*sic*] classic"—and how its and his success are causing other rappers to mimic his style, his proverbial blueprint—"It's like you tryin' to make *The Blueprint 2* before Hov."[8] Kanye West, who produced a significant portion of *The Blueprint* and became famous for his contributions to its sound, complements Jay-Z's verses with similar gendered boasts—"Magazines call me a rock star, girls call me cock star / Billboard pop star, neighborhood block star." And Jay-Z uses part of the chorus to instruct male listeners that he can teach them how to become a star like him—"Point out the bounce! / Ima show you how to get this dough in large amounts 'til it's hard to count." With most of the song recorded, Timbaland asked Shwari to add to Jay-Z's chorus. Given that her demo featured her singing songs like a sample, she decided to record a short rendition of the chorus of the 1993 Bollywood film song "Choli Ke Peeche" and use that to add to and overlap with Jay-Z's voice and lyrics in chorus of "The Bounce." Additionally, Shwari placed the same sample effect on her voice while she recorded her cover of "Choli Ke Peeche" for "The Bounce," and the contrast between Jay-Z's present and strong voice against the distant and faint voice of Shwari gave the song's chorus added texture, depth, and melody. Jay-Z and his record label apparently liked the final version of "The Bounce" enough that they kept Shwari's vocals, included it on *The Blueprint 2,* and even made "The Bounce" the B-side single to his soon-to-be crossover and Grammy-nominated hit "Excuse Me Miss."

It is somewhat poetic that "The Bounce" is the B-side to "Excuse Me Miss." While "Excuse Me Miss" is a song about heterosexual romance, "The Bounce," as the B-side, as the flip side, as the other side (of things), is quite queer. And it is queer precisely because of Shwari's lyrical and vocal performance in the song's chorus. Her rendition of "Choli Ke Peeche" indexes the representations and history of queer female expressions tied to the song. Monika Mehta notes that "Choli Ke Peeche" engendered enormous national debate in India for its purportedly explicit discussion of Indian female sexuality, a topic rendered unimaginable and impermissible within patriarchal Indian popular film industry and print media. Specifically, many saw the chorus of "Choli Ke Peeche," which is "choli ke peeche kya hai" and translates from

Hindi to English as "what's beneath the blouse?" as a "veiled sexual reference" intended to transmit "improper sexual mores." At the height of this
controversy, the chairman of the Central Board of Film Certification of
Bombay received more than two hundred letters and petitions calling for
(among other things) the deletion of the song from the film it was set to
appear in, titled *Khalnayak*. Eventually, out of concern for the film itself and
the song and dance number that accompanies "Choli Ke Peeche," the Bombay Film Examining Committee reached a compromise with the director
of the film, Subhash Ghai, to edit scenes from the song and dance sequence
in order for *Khalnayak* to receive a "parental guidance [rating] for children
under twelve years old."[9]

However, despite the changes, certain gestures involving sexual desire
remained in the scene, and for many, these gestures were queer. The scene in
Khalnayak in which "Choli Ke Peeche" is performed centers on the interplay
between two women who use the song to seduce, and eventually capture, the
male antagonist of the film. For Gayatri Gopinath, while the scene takes place
between two women and one man, *Khalnayak* sets up a "structure of female
homosociality," where female homoerotic desire between two of the film's
heroines is articulated via the "triangulated relation to the male character."
Both female characters appear on a stage presumably as spectacles for the
male antagonist's gaze, but once the scene begins, the male figure increasingly
"becomes peripheral to the scene of desire as it takes shape between the two
women, who are clearly more engaged with each other than with him."[10]

I want to mine this queer visual scene in *Khalnayak* in order to think
through the queer musical moments in "The Bounce." That is, I want to shift
Gopinath's analysis from a reading practice of visual culture to that of an
interpretive frame of aurality. And to do so I want to further analyze Shwari's
performance as a sample on "The Bounce." I'm particularly interested in
thinking through how Shwari sounds and what she does when she sings
her rendition of "Choli Ke Peeche." On the original version, Bollywood playback singer Alka Yagnik sings "choli ke peeche kya hai / choli ke peeche"
twice at the beginning and end of the song, in a loud, confident, and crisp
voice. Conversely, Shwari's voice is soft, seductive, and distant, and she sings
the chorus as follows: "choli ke peeche kya hai / choli ke peeche kya hai /
ke peeche / peeche kya hai/kya hai / [pause] / choli ke peeche kya hai / choli ke
peeche kya hai / choli choli / ke peeche/peeche kya / kya hai." Shwari's rendition constitutes what Jason King refers to as "reconstruction," a performance

that "restructures the original in ways that reorient both the melodic and lyric foundations of the original, as well as its performative cultural and political effects."[11] Shwari's seductive vocals and lyrical repetition of "choli"—"blouse"—and "ke peeche"—"beneath," emphasize and announce a queer female erotics that the original song did not and could not. Indeed, while the original song teases female sexual desire, Yagnik resolves the question of "choli ke peeche kya hai"—"what's beneath your blouse?"—by singing in the next line "choli me dil hai mera"—"in my blouse there is my heart." Here, by moving from a gesture toward breasts to a focus on the heart, Yagnik mutes the erotic potentiality of "Choli Ke Peeche"; she shifts the possibility of prurience to a reality of normative romance. Shwari's interpolation, on the other hand, refuses this kind of de-eroticized resolution. Her repeated use of "choli ke peeche" ensures that listeners' attention will be on women's breasts in general and the queer female controversy around them in particular. We might imagine the relationship between Yagnik and Shwari on "Choli Ke Peeche" and "The Bounce" as resembling that of Lata Mangeshkar and Truth Hurts on "Thoda" and "Addictive." Hurts's lyrics and Shwari's performance as a sample (re)center the (queer) female sexual dissidence that Yagnik's lyrics and Mangeshkar's voice seek to curtail. And in so doing, Shwari's sample-like reconstruction of "Choli Ke Peeche" is a resurrection—it raises/razes the queer memories and queer pasts of "Choli Ke Peeche."

My use of resurrections and razings is deliberate here because I want to take seriously Shwari's status as a sample, and read it as a performance that sits at the nexus of the temporal turn in queer studies and what Jason Stanyek and Benjamin Piekut call "deadness" and "intermundane collaborations." In their article "Deadness: Technologies of the Intermundane," Stanyek and Piekut use posthumous duets, like Nat King and Natalie Cole's 1991 "Unforgettable," to think through the late capitalist colaboring between "the worlds of the living and dead" marking much of post–World War II recorded music.[12] Intermundane collaborations challenge predominant, but in no way exclusive, scholarly and popular assumptions around the split between presence and absence in performance, and help us to see how various spatiotemporal patterns and repatternings that animate and (re)frame the interlocking and colaboring practices of intermundane collaborations, provide alternative imaginings of sound recordings and recording studios.[13] Stanyek and Piekut thus seek to illustrate how collaborations are not bound to face-to-face interpersonal encounters, but instead spatiotemporal colaborings that engage with and engender the entanglements of life and death, presence and absence, past and present in formations of capital, sound, agency, and kinship.

Although absent from Stanyek and Piekut's article, the potential for deadness and the intermundane to produce and highlight unexpected meetings of and exchanges between bodies and subjectivities through and across space and time dovetails with queer studies' recent focus on temporality. Queer temporalities refuse the Western schism between and chronology of past, present, and future precisely because such organizations of time and history are violent to queers. They negate, for example, the ways in which the past has often been a site of queer subject formation in the present, and how the rhetoric of "growing up" and the demands of futurity are often tied to and privilege reproduction and normative ways of life. As such, queer temporalities focus on disruptions to the normative logics of time, the "straightness" of time (e.g., the linear, progressivist divides of past, present, future; and birth, marriage, child, death), and how such disruptions can produce queer subjectivities and forms of desire and pleasure. Queer temporalities open up, as Elizabeth Freeman notes, "a set of possibilities produced out of temporal . . . difference" that afford new and exciting approaches to and inhabitations of queerness. They allow us to imagine queerness differently.[14]

Thus, as I explained in the previous chapter, if sampling is a schizophonic, mimetic practice that splits sound material from old recordings (the past) and then inserts and reorganizes this material into "new patterns" (the present), then Shwari, as someone performing as well as transforming into a sample, must in some degree inhabit the past; she must constantly attempt to reach across time and tap into the past.[15] Shwari's repetition of lyrics and the differences between her and Yagnik's tone highlight how her relation to "Choli Ke Peeche" mark a channeling of and connection to the past. The past exists in and is expressed through Shwari's voice, speaking to and through her like the mediums that scholars such as Molly McGarry read as queer. For McGarry, mediums channel "the voices of the dead as a means of connecting with the past . . . imagining both worldly and otherworldly figures."[16] As a sonic medium on "The Bounce," Shwari's vocal and lyrical gestures dually summon the queer memories and ghosts of the visual and material history of "Choli Ke Peeche" and enacts a haunting of such ghosts on "The Bounce." Shwari, through her vocal and lyrical transformation of "Choli Ke Peeche" into a sample intimates a calling for the pastness of the latent female homoeroticism within the song's eponymous song and dance performance as well as demands for such a past to take root in the present particularities of "The Bounce" and the presence of Jay-Z and Kanye West. This move of temporal dissonance and re/misalignment reorients the heteronormative and masculinist frame of "The Bounce" (sans Shwari, "The Bounce" is a fully male-dominated production, Jay-Z and West's imagined listeners are men, and West boasts that "girls call me cock star") to one that centers on queer female possibilities. It is with "The Bounce" that Shwari performs temporal drag, to borrow from Elizabeth Freeman. Shwari indexes and inhabits this queer and erotic past in ways that resist how the Indian film company in 1993 and Jay-Z and Kanye West's lyrics in 2002 render such queer, female, and queer female articulations invisible and inaudible.

Shwari's invocation of "choli ke peeche kya hai" not only engenders a queer sonic space on "The Bounce" in general, but also potentially queers Jay-Z in particular. By creating a South Asian diasporic queer soundscape on "The Bounce," Shwari interpellates Jay-Z within this South Asian queer narrative, history, and imagining. Rather than upholding the male rapper as active speaker to the passive woman sample that dictates most practices of sampling South Asian music in the United States at this time, Shwari's position as a sample allows her to, at minimum, reverse the (aural) gaze and, at most, render such heterosexist logics useless. To explicate this point, I want to briefly explore the chorus of "The Bounce," which, as a reminder, centers on the interplay between Jay-Z, who raps, "Point out the bounce! / Ima show you how to get this dough in large amounts 'til it's hard to count," and Shwari's reconstruction of "choli ke peeche." If we read the chorus as a dialogue between Shwari and Jay-Z, a queer situation emerges. While Jay-Z informs Shwari that he will show her how to increase her wealth, Shwari's response of "choli ke peeche kya hai"—with, again, emphasis on "choli" (blouse) and "ke peeche" (beneath)—is directed toward Jay-Z. And in so doing, her answer to Jay-Z dually queries and points to Jay-Z's supposed blouse and what lies beneath it. The juxtaposition of Shwari's lyrics with the presence of Jay-Z on the track produces a reading of "The Bounce" that renders Jay-Z queer or genderqueer in the sense of cross-dressing, and potentially as a sex worker as well—he uses what's "beneath the blouse" to earn money. It is, then, in the interplay between Shwari and Jay-Z that he emerges, is queered, as someone whose gender expression and wage-earning practices are trans(gressive) and nonnormative within the dominant logics and articulations of labor and Black male masculinity.[17]

While these queer valences of "The Bounce" highlight Black male queerness and provide useful ways to imagine queerness within hip-hop, I propose that specifically analyzing Shwari's lyrics in relation to the song and dance sequence of "Choli Ke Peeche" allows us to glean the ways in which Shwari's queer positionality articulates queer female South Asian diasporic desire. Moving back to McGarry's contention of mediums' desire to connect to the past, I want to suggest that the consistent and *incessant* repetition of the words "choli ke peeche kya hai" act as a chant, a calling for another female voice to enter the song and successfully reenact the song and dance performance of "Choli Ke Peeche." To put it another way, and to allude to "Addictive," because the visual scene of "Choli Ke Peeche" features two women and a man, and because only Jay-Z and Shwari occupy the space of the chorus in "The Bounce," "The Bounce" subsequently fails to restage this scene—another female voice is required. Shwari's repetition of the phrase "choli ke peeche kya hai" serves as an invitation for and interpellation of a second female presence. This ghostly call aims to replicate the scene in general and the latent female queer desire imbued in the scene as well.

As Shwari's status as a sample attempts to allow for a reopening of the queer memories of "Choli Ke Peeche," her positionality recalls what lesbian musicologist Elizabeth Wood theorizes as "sapphonics." Analyzing nineteenth-century operas as illustrative case studies, Wood defines sapphonics as "a mode of articulation, a way of describing a space of lesbian possibility, for a range of erotic and emotional relationships among women who sing and women who listen."[18] My use of sapphonics is in no way an attempt to impose a Euro-American lesbian identity on the queer female sonic space of "The Bounce" or queerness within Shwari's vocal performance. As this book has articulated, the queerness of the other side of things, of these Afro–South Asian genealogies of sound, refuses an easy lining up with such an identity. But I find sapphonics a useful and compelling framework because of its allusions to transgression; of destabilizing normative boundaries, binaries, and logics; and its ability to vocalize, as Wood notes, "inadmissible sexualities."[19] These are similar sexualities and pleasures that the Indian film industry and nationalist politics aimed to censor "Choli Ke Peeche" (the song as well as song and dance sequence). Using sapphonics, Rajé Shwari, as a living sound of the past, functions as the queer female singer calling on past queer female desires and subjects. Yet, because sapphonics is predicated on the female singer *and* female listener tied by the erotic bonds of desire, we must then ask who constitutes the female listener?

While in Wood the listener is the queer female audience member attending an opera, in "The Bounce" it seems as if the listener is the sonically *absent* woman whose presence completes the sonic restaging and translation of the "Choli Ke Peeche" song and dance performance. Because of this, I want to consider the multiple desires that might emerge from Shwari's use of "Choli Ke Peeche." Her repetition of "choli ke peeche kya hai" attempts to sonically re-create, via the absent listener, those queer desires and pleasures found in the visual rendition of "Choli Ke Peeche." It articulates a desire for the listener to hear and share Shwari's queer calling. Applying this to "The Bounce," we can glean the ways in which Shwari invokes these queer intimacies between her and her listeners. She articulates an affective longing for such a queer listener, a politics centered on queer desire that is rendered impossible in the Bollywood film from which it is associated. It is a desire for such a queer desire to exist, a desire that Wood powerfully notes is "the desire for desire itself."[20]

It is perhaps Shwari's indexing of "Choli Ke Peeche" on "The Bounce," and its attendant queer female desires and memories, that forced the Bollywood film's director, Subhash Ghai, to threaten a lawsuit. In a similar move to, and on the heels of, "Addictive," Ghai informed news outlets that he was considering taking legal action against everyone involved in the recording and release of "The Bounce." He noted, "[It's] more than just a line, it is an entire concept they've taken."[21] As the director of the film, Ghai's statement, particularly his contention that the song's concept had been appropriated, points to a recognition of "The Bounce," via Shwari's status as a living sample, as a song indexing and potentially reopening the queer memories, voices, desires, pleasures, and possibilities inherent in "Choli Ke Peeche." But because of how Shwari performed "Choli Ke Peeche," how she reconstructed it as a sample, "The Bounce" did not qualify as copyright infringement. Ghai was unable to sue, and so "The Bounce" avoided the fate of being another "Addictive."

Blowing the Indian Flute

After "The Bounce," Timbaland and Shwari began working on more songs. They created a track for a multimillion-dollar KMart and Joe Boxer underwear ad campaign, Timbaland introduced Shwari to his friend and colleague Pharrell Williams who enlisted her to sing on a song for the *Charlie's Angels* movie sequel, and Timbaland and Williams agreed to coproduce Shwari's debut album and help her obtain a record deal with a major label. In order to further advertise Shwari's work, Timbaland collaborated with her as a singer and writer on his and his rap partner Magoo's third studio album, *Under Construction Part II*. Together, Shwari and Timbaland developed a song on the album titled "Indian Flute" that, once released, they believed would be "the most amazing Indian urban record yet," and a song that would further evidence their Afro–South Asian pursuit of "doing something different." Notably, "Indian Flute" was going to be Shwari's first A-side single and her first track to have an accompanying music video.

Divided into three verses (and an eight-measure bridge), "Indian Flute" centers on flirtatious dialogue between Shwari and Timbaland, Magoo and Shwari, and Sebastian and Shwari, respectively. In the first verse, Timbaland remarks that he has been "eyeing you [Shwari] from afar"; the second verse features Magoo informing Shwari that sleeping on the same bed and watching late-night movies would inevitably lead to a sexual encounter; and in the last verse, Sebastian advises Shwari on how to keep their imminent sexual relationship a secret. Shwari engages the sexual advances of Timbaland, Magoo, and Sebastian, but does so speaking in what Nabeel Zuberi defines as "Punjabi-inflected Hindi."[22] For example, she queries Timbaland "zara sa choom loo to kya?" (why don't you give me a little kiss?). The trading of pickup lines within each verse concludes with a linguistic crossing and exchange—Shwari sings a line in English, and her male interlocutors respond in Hindi.

It is within these linguistic exchanges that we begin to understand why Shwari heralded "Indian Flute" as a groundbreaking Afro–South Asian hip-hop recording. As the previous chapter illustrated, mainstream Afro–South Asian rap in the United States predominantly concerned the interfaces between African American artists and producers and sampled South Asian musical phrasings. "Indian Flute" completely shifts this dominant way of engaging South Asian music. Instead of sampling a song from an Indian film recording, Timbaland, Magoo, and Sebastian directly worked with a South Asian American artist in Rajé Shwari. Moreover, in having the African American male artists rap in Hindi and Shwari sing in English during the closing couplets of each verse, "Indian Flute" explodes the linguistic limits placed on previous mainstream Afro–South Asian hip-hop, where African American rappers rap in English and use the Hindi sample as the sonic representation of South Asia. In "Indian Flute," Shwari's use of English and the male performers' utilization of Hindi breaks from this normative script, and as such broadens the potential listeners and prospective fans of the song to communities that understand English and/or Hindi. The track's use of English and Hindi provides a space for Hindi- and English-speaking South Asian and South Asian diasporic as well as African American communities to mutually engage one another on this record. Indeed, although (and because of being) mediated by capitalist interests, the song also sought to forge bonds between the two communities (Black and South Asian) rather than produce a distance and mark them as disparate.

When I interviewed hip-hop producer Hannon Lane, who was Timbaland's protégé and Shwari's close friend at the time of the recording of "Indian Flute," and who was present at the recording of the song, I asked him to tell me about the recording session for "Indian Flute." Lane eagerly responded:

> Tim one day came to Magoo and said, "I got this beat, Magoo, I got this beat I want you check out." You know that's how Tim talks. So he played the joint. He was like "I wanna go like [in the song's melody] 'I got my Indian flute, boo da doo da doo da doo, sing it to me.' And then I think Rajé should sing in Hindi." It was like he premeditated that song. Like how you heard the song was exactly how he sung it to Magoo . . . and then he went into the booth, and did some mumbo jumbo [a common practice in rap where a rapper uses non-lexical phrases to establish a vocal cadence, rhythm, or flow for a particular verse, and later replaces them with words that conform to this rhythmic vocal structure]. And then Magoo turned Tim's shit into words. And then Rajé came in and did her verses in Hindi. And then she started teaching them how to say certain things in Hindi. . . . So Magoo was like "How do you say this in your language?" And so she taught them how to sing whatever the line was, *she taught them how to say it*, so they learned how to say it and then incorporated it into they [*sic*] rap . . . so it was kind of cool to see the process. That's how Tim, Magoo, and Rajé made the song. It was kind of cool to see that whole process, and them working together like that. It was kind of cool.[23]

The sequence of events that Lane outlines highlights the collaborative beginnings of "Indian Flute." Initially, each performer—Timbaland, Magoo, and Shwari—added on to the previous performer's work—Magoo reinterpreted Timbaland's nonsensical phrasings into intelligible words; Shwari complemented Magoo's rapping with sung lyrics; and then at some point during the recording of "Indian Flute" the session became a collective, dialogic, and intercultural endeavor. Ostensibly searching to enhance his rap verses (both for himself as well as for Timbaland), Magoo asked Shwari to teach him not only how to translate certain English verses into Hindi, but also how to pronounce the verses in Hindi. Lane's emphasis on "she taught them how to say it" suggests a pedagogical aspect of the song, a critical and mutual site of teaching and learning that bridges and intertwines cultures and languages. Furthermore, Lane's repeated phrasing of "she taught them how to say it," works to highlight the centrality of Shwari in the music making process. Rather than simply being told what to do and/or how to sing certain things, Shwari had agency and shaped the entire form of the song. She helped move it from an African American rap song featuring a South Asian American singer, to an experience in Afro–South Asian collectivity. Indeed, I interviewed Timbaland's longtime recording engineer Jimmy Douglass who, like Lane, attended and participated in the recording of "Indian Flute," and I asked him about Shwari and Timbaland's recording process for the song. Douglass was initially frustrated with my question because, as he explained to me, far too frequently people ask such questions to pit Timbaland and Shwari against each other in discerning who should receive "credit" for the creation of "Indian Flute." Douglass then curtly informed me, "It was a collaborative thing, OK? And people that are creative realize that."[24] We should not ignore the significance of the place of communal activities, of being a "collaborative thing" for Douglass or "working together" in the words of Lane's reflective awe. Instead, we should read Douglass's exasperation and Lane's excitement as constitutive of the song's mutual authoritative structure. Interpreting their experience in this way illumines the potential for "Indian Flute" to envelop listeners into similar forms of the communal and the collective.

It was perhaps this aim to produce Afro–South Asian alliances that led Shwari to inform the *New York Times* that she saw "Indian Flute" as a response to "these MC's [*sic*] who sample Indian music without understanding it."[25] Shwari's statement was a thinly veiled critique of African American rapper Erick Sermon and his 2002 hit song "React." "React" features a sample from the Bollywood film song "Chandi Ka Badan," and specifically a vocal line from the song's playback singer Asha Bhosle: "Kisi ko khudkushi ka shok ho tow uh huh kya kare." The sampled lyric translates into English as "If someone wants to commit suicide, what am I to do?" Sermon was unaware that the sampled line was about suicide, and rapped alongside the sampled verse with his own line, "Whatever she said then I'm that." The song features the Bhosle sampled lyric throughout the song, and Sermon refers to Bhosle as an "Arabic chick" to whom he makes sexual advances and mocks her accent. Erick Sermon's misogyny—his use of "chick," his dismissiveness, and his unprompted sexual advances—xenophobia—his mocking of non-English speech—and Orientalism—his conflation of Hindi and Arabic as homogenous—on "React" illustrate, as Nitasha Sharma rightly posits, "a general American ignorance of both geography and non-European languages . . . [and] relays the message, though, that artists who have become commercially viable do not need to do their homework."[26]

For Rajé Shwari, then, "Indian Flute" is a corrective to songs like "React." It dares to "do something different." And Shwari's position as a sample on "Indian Flute," much like on Jay-Z's "The Bounce," operates as a mode of critique. "Indian Flute" addresses a similar thematic and story-line structure to that of "React": African American heterosexual male rapper makes sexual advances toward a South Asian (diasporic) woman (one whose sexuality is unknown and rendered irrelevant to the male character); South Asian (American) woman responds in a South Asian language (Hindi, in both cases); male rapper confesses that he does not, cannot, and will not try to translate or locate a shared and equal form of communication, and thus maintain his misogynist pursuits. Shwari, Timbaland, Magoo, and Sebastian signal these narratives on "Indian Flute," but, in a shift in standard hip-hop practice, allow the sample (i.e., Shwari) to respond to these propositions. Upon first listen to "Indian Flute," Shwari seemingly constructs a reverse discourse in which she performs the role of the active subject who initially pursues Timbaland, Magoo, and Sebastian. She sings with verses in Hindi that translate to "why don't you give me a kiss?" which position her as an erotic and desiring (active) subject who also desires and enjoys pleasure from someone else. While it is apparent to listeners of the record that Shwari is shaping the contours of the flirtatious conversation, the masculinist rappers on the song imagine themselves to be the ones holding that position.

But despite the attempt at heterosexual consummation, audiences are left without any confirmation of successful and mutual heterosexual erotic pleasure. The chorus of "Indian Flute" highlights the degree to which Timbaland, Sebastian, and Magoo love Shwari's "Indian flute" (what some have posited connotes her clitoris), but the chorus ends with them lamenting that they "can't understand a word you're sayin'."[27] Interestingly, they use Hindi as an attempt to "understand" Shwari, but it is at the moment that they speak in Hindi that Shwari begins to sing in English, producing another layer of misunderstanding, missed connection, and failed heterosexual erotic fulfillment.

"Indian Flute" is, in other words, a song about arrested heterosexuality. By performing as a sample on "Indian Flute," and using that status to create a parody of songs like "React," Shwari enacts a queer of color feminist critique that lyrically—through the literal misunderstandings that occur between Shwari and her African American male counterparts—and sonically—the temporal and spatial distance produced by Shwari's status as a sample—arrests heterosexual pleasure, and renders it unimaginable and impossible.

And in this way, "Indian Flute" offers a response to and critique of the theme of romance that looms large in Afro-Asian studies. From the real-life marriage of James and Grace Lee Boggs to the fictionalized story of Matthew Townes and Princess Kautilya in W. E. B. Du Bois's *Dark Princess,* Afro-Asian studies scholarship has long privileged romance narratives. Vanity Reddy and Anantha Sudhakar argue that Afro-Asian studies scholars are drawn to these stories because they ostensibly bear "potential as a political strategy to denaturalize the production of racial divisions under global capitalism and produce new forms of community."[28] And yet these narratives are disproportionately heterosexual and racially gendered in such a way that the African (diasporic) subject is a man and the Asian (diasporic) subject is a woman. "Indian Flute" takes this narrative and refuses to make it celebratory. The inability of Timbaland, Magoo, and Sebastian to develop a romantic relationship with Shwari forces us to consider new ways we might imagine Afro-Asian relationalities. It was the rubric of failure rather than success, misconnections instead of connections, queerness instead of heteronormativity, and difference rather than sameness—what Stuart Hall sees as the power of articulation—that served as the foundation for their Afro-Asian exchange.[29]

With "Indian Flute" recorded, with the decision that it would be an A-side single, and with Timbaland's record label greenlighting a music video for the song, it seemed like Timbaland and Shwari would have a platform for their collaborative project of doing something different, of articulating an intercultural production of the other side of things. However, a few weeks before the shoot for the "Indian Flute" video, Timbaland and Shwari parted ways. The reason for the split remains vague (Pettaway informed me that "Tim and I had a plan, but she wanted to do things her way").[30] Regardless of the reason, Timbaland decided to move forward with shooting "Indian Flute" without Shwari.

The "Indian Flute" music video failed to visually restage and translate the song's sonic and lyrical critique of heteronormativity and Orientalism in songs like "React." It opens with a computer-generated view of the front entrance to the Taj Mahal. The camera then takes the viewer into the assumed interior of the space, where an older South Asian male snake charmer plays his flute (it resembles a recorder, not a *pungi* or *been*). Instead of a snake, however, a brown-skinned woman slowly emerges from the basket. The camera moves from the snake charmer to an open, harem-like area where multiple women of color surround and caress Timbaland, Magoo, and Sebastian. Their raps are predominantly shot within this space, with belly dancers performing in the background, and with other women of color lip-syncing Shwari's verses. The camera then pans to the snake charmer, who throws away his flute and begins to grab his penis and simulate various sexual positions. The spot ends with him "charming" his female partner back into the basket, and the camera zooming out of the interior room and back to the full shot of the front of the Taj Mahal.

If the musical recording of "Indian Flute" marked another sonic site of Afro–South Asian connectivity and South Asian female diasporic queerness, the song's video betrays such equitable and progressive politics. Orientalist fantasies are on display throughout the clip. The older male snake charmer in general, and his seated position during most of the video in particular, represents a South Asian antiquity in relation to the modern U.S. nation, embodied in Timbaland's, Magoo's, and Sebastian's upright and youthful performance. Further, the video's mixing of South Asian and Middle Eastern cultural commodities and performances (i.e., belly dancing) expresses an imaginary of a homogenous and mysterious Orient.[31] Moreover, gender and sexuality shaped these racialized representations. The women of color function as objects of the male characters' heterosexual desires and pleasures, through their caressing and flirtations with Timbaland, Magoo, Sebastian; and the snake charmer's literal control over his female partner's moves. In essence, rather than parody songs and videos like "React," the "Indian Flute" video parroted them instead, and raises the question whether Timbaland was truly interested in the kind of pursuit of the other side of things that Bill Pettaway called "doing something different."

From Bollywood to Bollyhood

But such a question was perhaps premature. Following their split, Timbaland and Rajé Shwari continued to create music that centered on collaborations between African American and South Asian (diasporic) artists. Timbaland has worked with British Asian singer Amar, British Asian singer and rapper M.I.A., South Asian American emerging artist Shakti, and most recently South Asian American breakout singer and rapper Raja Kumari. With some of these artists—Amar and Shakti—they've performed on his productions as samples, while others—M.I.A. and Kumari—have used their natural/human voices. Regardless, Timbaland's previous and current South Asian (diasporic) collaborators illustrate that he remains committed to "do something different" collectively, to develop an Afro–South Asian sound that further pushes the boundaries of music.

Similarly, Rajé Shwari has also remained steadfast in her pursuit of doing something different. After she and Timbaland parted ways, she started to work exclusively with Hannon Lane. Lane and Shwari's shared experiences with Timbaland seemed to have led them to work together. Lane recalls his work with Shwari as a collective endeavor: "We kind of fell in love with each other's work. Kind of just married ourselves, our music together. You know what I'm saying? We just was vibing. So I'd go to Philly [Shwari's hometown] all the time. *Allllllllll the time, man . . .* working with Rajé was definitely an amazing experience."[32] Lane's use of "marriage" to describe his collaborations with Shwari not only suggests an Afro-Asian sonic, interracial, and cross-cultural union, but also a oneness implicated within the realm of the intimate. In other words, Lane's interpretation of his work with Shwari illuminates a central argument of this chapter as well as this book: that the musical, the racial, the cultural, and the sexual conspire within the articulations of Afro–South Asian sonic music making practices in Black popular music—that the other side of things is a space where race, gender, and sexuality meet in an expression of Afro–South Asian collective music.

Recently, Timbaland and Shwari have reconnected, creating music for her upcoming album *The Queen of Bollyhood*. The title of this work seeks to bridge the South Asian film industry, and cultural space of South Asian and South Asian diasporic identity formations (Bollywood), with the "hood," a space, much like the street corner in Miles Davis's *On the Corner,* that confers African American identity and political consciousness within hip-hop culture.[33] At the time of writing this book, these songs have not been released, and so it is unclear if they will speak directly to formal political situations or if Shwari will perform like a sample. What is clear, however, is that Timbaland and Rajé Shwari are still dedicated to working together, to doing something different, and to pursuing the other side of things.

Epilogue

Let's end how we began: with a story. It was a Sunday night—February 7, 2016, to be exact. I was on my couch eating ice cream and cake when I received a text from a friend: "Did you watch it? What did you think of it?" The "it" in question was the Super Bowl 50 halftime show, where Coldplay, Beyoncé Knowles, and Bruno Mars performed. I informed my friend that I had, indeed, watched the set, and that I found Coldplay's performance a bit confusing. My friend responded, "I know, right?!? It should have just been Beyoncé! Or maybe Beyoncé featuring Bruno. But definitely Beyoncé! I know she headlined a few years ago, but still. She's grown so much since then. She's basically a different artist now. Her performance now would look nothing like her performance then." I agree that Knowles had developed into a different artist during the intervening three years. By 2016, Knowles was increasingly interested in recording and releasing concept albums like her self-titled audiovisual work *Beyoncé,* in which she explicitly proclaimed that she was a feminist. Moreover, one day prior to her 2016 Super Bowl performance, Knowles released the "Formation" song and video, the latter of which addressed issues of environmental racism—via the U.S. government's response to Hurricane Katrina—police brutality, and other forms of anti-Black violence, especially as they manifest in the South. "Formation," of course, set the stage for her album *Lemonade,* which centered the social lives of Black women in the South. With all of that said, however, I still disagreed with my friend that Knowles's 2013 and 2016 Super Bowl halftime sets did/could/would not share anything. In particular, I believe that both performances overlap in their engagements with South Asian music and culture.

Knowles headlined the 2013 Super Bowl halftime show in New Orleans. Her set comprised an array of her recent solo hits—"Run the World (Girls)" and "Love on Top"—her classic hits—"Crazy in Love"—and even a reunion with the members of her former girl group Destiny's Child—"Bootylicious" and "Independent Women Part 1." While I was impressed with the complexity and sharpness of Knowles's halftime show, I was most struck by her performance of her 2003 Billboard #1 hit song "Baby Boy," and how it resonates with the framework of the other side of things. An electric sitar–driven song, and one that is part of the litany of South Asian–inspired rap and R&B songs that Truth Hurts's "Addictive" inspired and that Rajé Shwari's sample-like demo responded to, Knowles's Super Bowl rendition of "Baby Boy" upped the South Asian cultural aesthetic by fusing "herself into an image of Mahadevi . . . the female deity that serves as the foundation of [the Hindu goddesses] Durga and Kali" (Figure 13).[1] Rebecca Kumar rightly points out that Beyoncé's performative allusion to Durga, and its workings alongside her all-female band and dancers, operates as a women of color feminist "interruption" of the heteropatriarchal impulse of the National Football League.[2] While her engagements with Indian spirituality and its disruption of heteronormativity recalls John Coltrane's similar approaches to Indian spiritual traditions and how they helped to mark his illegible masculinity and place him outside the normative jazzman archetypes, Knowles's invocation of Durga also occurs alongside a powerful display of Black women's eroticism. Her Super Bowl performance of "Baby Boy" involve her slowly caressing her inner thighs and crotch. Such sexually explicit acts performed in relation to punctuated sitar plucks powerfully signify on Truth Hurts's erotic play in "Addictive." But given that "Baby Boy" is also a dancehall-inspired recording that features Sean Paul (whose voice plays during this Super Bowl rendition), her crotch and autoerotic play situate this set within Black Caribbean women's "punany powah" erotics that Carolyn Cooper famously describes in her analyses of Black women's sexual politics in Caribbean music culture.[3] In so doing, Knowles taps into much broader African and South Asian diasporic connections. Her halftime performance of "Baby Boy" makes use of South Asian and Black Caribbean culture in ways that bridge feminist, sexual, and spiritual politics, and that are exercised in New Orleans, a port city known for its (both violent and nonviolent) racial and cultural migrations, meetings, and mixings. As Daphne Brooks has argued, Knowles often embraces her creole heritage and ties to New Orleans.[4] But her use of Durga also speaks to another kind of New Orleans history, one that, as Vivek Bald notes, involves Indian immigrant men who settled in New Orleans and married and had children with Black women and other women of color during the early and mid-twentieth century.[5] Knowles's Super Bowl version of "Baby Boy," then, is a layered performance of Afro–South Asian sound that is feminist, erotic, and transnational in politics and scope. It continues to express the import of the other side of things in Black popular music.

And it's against this backdrop that we can analyze Knowles's return to the Super Bowl in 2016 in Santa Clara, California. As mentioned above, Knowles was not the sole performer for this show; Coldplay and Bruno Mars joined her. The set went as follows: Coldplay opens with a medley of their hits, Bruno Mars then takes the stage to do "Uptown Funk," Knowles follows Mars and performs "Formation," Mars and Knowles do a collaborative mash-up of "Uptown Funk" and "Crazy in Love," and the set closes with all three acts performing another Coldplay medley.

What interests me here is the connection, or disconnection as it were, between Coldplay and Knowles during their respective solo sets. A couple of months prior to the event, critics attacked Knowles and Coldplay for engaging in cultural appropriation for the music video to their collaboration "Hymn for the Weekend." The video features Knowles as a Bollywood figure and Coldplay, a white British rock band, participating in the *holi* festival. Many charged Coldplay and Knowles with "perpetuating a colonial trope

Figure 13. "Baby Boy" sequence by Beyoncé, Super Bowl halftime performance, 2013.

that misrepresents India as an exotic playground or Orientalist fantasy . . . [and] consolidates singular narratives about India that romanticize color and song at the expense of Indians' everyday lives."[6] Perhaps because of the backlash, Knowles and Coldplay do not perform "Hymn for the Weekend" during their halftime show. But Coldplay does open their set on a stage inspired by the 1960s white hippie counterculture movement in San Francisco, replete with Hindi writing and South Asian–inspired "marigold flowers and colourful garlands."[7] Knowles (and Bruno Mars for that matter) continues the Bay Area 1960s theme, but does so in such a way that places her set strictly within Black Power politics.[8] She performs her brand-new single "Formation" while occasionally pumping a Black Power fist and while an all-Black-female dancing crew dressed in Black Panther–inspired garb (the Panthers originated in Oakland) support her. The song and Super Bowl performance of "Formation" also include Knowles using Black queer vernacular (e.g., "slay").[9] Importantly, there is not a stage change for Mars and Knowles's sets, and so they perform on the same Indophilic stage on which Coldplay opened.

This fact of Knowles and Coldplay using the same South Asian–inspired stage for their respective sets is important because it encapsulates what I've framed throughout this book as the other side of things. While the shared stage becomes the site from which Coldplay and Knowles perform in general and engage with South Asian culture in particular, their performances as well as the space of the stage hold and produce different meanings. With songs like "Yellow" and "Adventure of a Lifetime," Coldplay's set taps into the 1960s hippie culture, and involves South Asian culture (again via the stage) as a site from which to articulate universality and love. Conversely, Knowles uses that same stage, that same foundation of South Asian culture, for "Formation" and lyrically expresses pride in Black hairstyles—Afros—and gay slang derived fantasies of Black women's sexual pleasure—"If he hit it right, I might take him on a flight on my chopper ('cause I slay)"—and sartorially signal Black Power—Knowles's backup dancers' Black Panther–inspired outfits (Figure 14). For Knowles, South Asian culture both figuratively and literally sets the stage for her Black feminist and queer political performance. And so this is all to say, and to illustrate, that the other side of things demands that we must refuse to use white artists' engagements with South Asian culture as an origin point or a nexus of comparison through which to analyze Black musicians' South Asian musical encounters and/or collaborations. The other side of things illuminates how Afro–South Asian music making endeavors

Figure 14. "Formation" sequence, by Beyoncé, Super Bowl halftime performance, 2016.

produce their own knowledges and envision their own possibilities that are often distinct from those performed by white artists. The other side of things demands that we understand Afro–South Asian collaborative sounds as musical performances that imagine coalitions and relationalities differently.

Of course, the Super Bowl performance ends with Knowles, Mars, and Coldplay collectively performing on that same stage and singing Coldplay's "Up & Up," a song that posits universal love as the solution to systemic inequities like poverty. Some might arguably read Knowles's participation in such neoliberal logics and liberal politics of equality as depoliticized practices that undermine her performance of "Formation." But I choose to see the performances of "Formation" and "Up & Up" differently and separately. As we saw with the short-lived performance of Truth Hurts or the largely forgotten Rick James album The Flag, the other side of things often resides in spaces of limited temporality. It manifests and creates meaning in the brief and the overlooked. And so both of Knowles's performances of "Baby Boy" and "Formation" carry the Afro–South Asian political impulse of the other side of things. They are a part of the Afro–South Asian genealogy of sound that I've discussed throughout this book. Whether it was John Coltrane, Miles Davis, Rick James, André 3000, Missy Elliott, Truth Hurts, or Timbaland and Rajé Shwari, each artist's music during the civil rights, Black Power, 1980s AIDS, 1990s model minority, and post-9/11 eras joined aesthetics and politics in ways that transgressed assumed boundaries of and between race, culture, nation, gender, and sexuality. This music moves beyond vertical interactions that (re)centered whiteness, and instead gestures toward horizontal alliances, to the political struggles and possibilities of creating music among and between the margins. The music that these artists created highlights the braided histories, overlapping presents, and connected futures of the African and South Asian diasporas. And it is this music that articulates an imaginative space that queerly fosters and foregrounds Afro–South Asian bonds. It is an alternative guiding political vision of the world that I call and will forever hold on to as the other side of things.

Acknowledgments

So this is going to be long. And it's going to be long because there are a number of people to whom I express and owe my most immense and immediate gratitude. It's a gratitude that is not simply tied to the research and writing of this book. It's more than that. The people named in this book also greatly shaped and informed my life. I deeply value the relationships I have with those named here because, whether they know it or not (and because I am a deeply reserved person, most probably do not), they came into my life (and are still present in my life) when I need(ed) them the most, professionally and personally. The people named here are thus folks who helped me think differently, write differently, and live differently.

When I was a student at the University of Chicago, I had an idea that there was something to be said about the sampling of South Asian music in U.S.-based hip-hop. I didn't know at the time what exactly needed to be said, but I was lucky enough to be around and learn from people (faculty, graduate students, and staff) who facilitated my critical thinking about this idea, which would later (after a number of twists and turns) become this book. Maria Mendonça, you were the first person I remember talking to about this idea. You listened to me and encouraged me to write about it, and that encouragement has sustained me all these years. Philip Bohlman, I learned so much from you about how to analyze and consider South Asian music, and those approaches are very much central to this work. George Chauncey, you were the first person to see something queer about this music, and encouraged me to consider how sexuality operates in these sono-racial formations. Mae Ngai, you introduced me to Asian American and immigration studies, which led me to think more historically about the implications of this music. Wayne Marshall, your analyses of sampling and other forms of technomusicology are beyond reproach, and I'm fortunate that our paths crossed. Judy Wu, I learned about Afro-Asian studies, the chief field that this book engages, from you; without your class and your mentorship, I don't know if I could write a book like this. To Sareeta Amrute and Elizabeth Todd-Breland, you both helped me to locate and embrace interdisciplinary research. Darryl Heller, our multiple conversations about the sociocultural implications of rap's sampling of South Asian music helped me get to a point to consider the intersections of aesthetics and politics. Elise LaRose, you made sure that I had all the necessary resources to think about this idea and make it something that I could develop; thank you for doing that. To Jonathan Rosa, you're a model for work–life balance and for what critical scholarship looks like. You saw value in this idea I had, and continue to see value in everything I do. No matter the day, time, or place, you were there to help me with anything and everything I needed. I hope one day I can be as good of a friend to you as you have been to me. Lastly, Travis Jackson . . . I could honestly write another book about what your mentorship and friendship has meant to me. Almost everything I do is modeled after you. You saw and continue to see things about my work that productively push it in the right direction. You're an incredible scholar and teacher, and even a better person. I can't thank you enough for being a constant presence and influence in my life and work.

Like most first academic books, much of the work here began as a doctoral dissertation, which I wrote as a graduate student in American studies at New York University. I was lucky to be around and learn from the faculty, graduate students, and staff while I was there. To Jack Tchen, I could not have asked for a better chair. You helped inform how I approach cultural objects and the questions that I ask. Gayatri Gopinath, you do the kind of queer work that I (and many others) can only attempt to do. You are central to how I think through issues of queerness and cultural production. And you kept me in grad school when I wanted to drop out; I'll forever be grateful for that. Maureen Mahon, my dissertation and book would not be what they are without you. There are very few who have the kind of musical knowledge that you have, and I still pinch myself that I was able to learn from you. Nikhil Pal Singh, thank you for pushing me to think more about the historical and political implications of my work. To Travis, again, thank you. Other faculty as well as staff at NYU also deserve recognition for devoting time, no matter how brief, to talk with me about and by extension helped enrich my work: the late and great José Esteban Muñoz, Arlene Dávila, Cristina Beltrán, Lisa Duggan, Phillip Brian Harper, Jennifer Morgan, Crystal Parikh, Andrew Ross, María Josefina Saldaña-Portillo, Julie Elman, Thuy Linh Tu, Michael Ralph, Andrew Sartori, Andrew Needham, Martin Daughtry, Jason King, Marty Correia, Noeva Wong, Candyce Golis, Raechel Bosch, Ramona Knepp, Alyssa Burke, and Madala Hilaire.

I was also fortunate to be in grad school at NYU at the same time as a number of brilliant students. To that end, I want to acknowledge the following people for their friendship and assistance in helping me navigate the institution: Eva Hageman, Elizabeth Mesok, Zenia Kish, Emma Kreyche, Emily Williamson, Leigh Dodson, andré carrington, Leticia Alvarado, Lezlie Frye, Lena Sze, Marlon Burgess, Liza Williams, Jan Padios, Dacia Mitchell, Rana Jaleel, Ronak Kapadia, Dawn Peterson, Khary Polk, Rich Blint, Frank Leon Roberts, Allison Janae Hamilton, Amaka Okechukwu, Stuart Schrader, Grace Helton, Lydia Brawner, Shannon Wearing, Josh Ye, Mosarrap Hossain Khan, Vanessa Casado-Pérez, Sarah Klevan, Mick Hattaway, Ruth Tucker, Philippa Robinson, Ruth Dear, Becca Howes-Mischel, Andy Cornell, Samuel Ng, Devin Murphy, Barrak Alzaid, Amalia Mallard, Vanessa Agard-Jones, Zach Schwartz-Weinstein, Johana Londoño, Claudia Sofía Garriga López, Ariana Ochoa Camacho, Manijeh Nasrabadi, Miabi Chatterji, Jennifer Kelly, Jessica Nydia Pabón-Colón, James Rodriguez, A. J. Bauer, Roy Pérez, and Joan Morgan. There are a few other people who were graduate students with me whom I especially want to thank. Vivek Bald, you gave and continue to give me confidence in my work. You do comparative scholarship in the way that it needs to be done, and I'm immensely honored that you're someone I know. Shanté Paradigm Smalls, I can't say enough how much it meant to know there was someone else doing queer hip-hop and queer Afro-Asian music. I value the times we get to spend with each other to share work and break bread. Marisol LeBrón, our constant conversations about all things music and pop culture have made it into this book in some way or another. Also, you're just so dope—you really are. To Emily Hue, I look forward to every text and every message you send me. Your brilliance and love know no bounds; thank you for being a friend. MJ Grier, you're one of the smartest and magnanimous people I know. At some point, I think we should publish some version of our hours-long conversations about race, sexuality, and

Black popular music and culture. You're one of the reasons why I came to NYU and one of the reasons why I remain in the academy. Lastly, Carmen L. Phillips, I don't think there's anyone I talk to more on a daily basis than you, and I wouldn't have it any other way. You think about pop culture in a way that most do not, and you write with the kind of care that I wish most would. You're truly in a league of your own. And, whether you knew so before reading this book or not, you're the reason that Beyoncé is discussed herein.

During my time as a graduate student, I also had the chance (through conferences, writing workshops, and other professional settings) to meet and learn from others outside of NYU who were also graduate students at the time. The conversations that we had then and those we have now continue to sustain me intellectually and personally. I'm grateful to the following: Anjali Nath, Meenasarani Linde Murugan, Sunny Yang, Fritz Schenker, Mark Padoongpatt, Lata Murti, Chris Eng, Douglas Ishii, Deborah Al-Najjar, Aymar Jean Christian, Mark Villegas, Laurence Ralph, Monica Muñoz Martinez, Reginald Wilburn, Chera Reid, Freda Fair, Darius Bost, Josen Masangkay Diaz, Meghan Drury, Hentyle Yapp, Sriya Shrestha, and Kwami Coleman. I want to especially acknowledge madison moore, R. Benedito Ferrão, and Jih-Fei Cheng, who were at the time and who continue to be integral to my intellectual and personal growth. madison, I'm a better writer and thinker of popular culture because of you. You're pushing the boundaries of cultural studies, and I couldn't be prouder of you for it. Bene, your critical eye on South Asian diasporic studies has immensely helped my thinking around key issues concerning my book, and your humor and wit have kept me in high spirits during dark times. Jih-Fei, I'm so deeply appreciative of your generosity and willingness to help me articulate my ideas when they're just a string of thoughts.

After NYU, I spent two years at the University of Rochester as a Fellow in the Department of Music, the Frederick Douglass Institute for African and African-American Studies, and the Susan B. Anthony Institute for Gender, Sexuality, and Women's Studies. My time there was critical in helping me reimagine my work, and I thank John Covach, Elaine Stroh, Beth Olivares, Cilas Kemedjio, Ghislaine Radegonde-Eison, Jeffrey Tucker, Eleana Kim, Jeffrey Runner, Sarah Seidman, Jennifer Kyker, and Douglas Flowe for such assistance. I also owe an enormous debt of gratitude to Ed Brockenbrough, Lauron Kehrer, and Tiffany E. Barber. Ed, I can't thank you enough for your amazing feedback on my work and for helping me navigate Rochester as a queer Black man. Lauron, your critical work on queerness and hip-hop have greatly informed my own thinking, and I'm happy that we were able to work together through these issues of race, sexuality, and popular music. Tiffany, I'm so grateful that we were at Rochester at the same time. I always looked forward to (and continue to look forward to) our late-night bar talk. I'm so grateful for our friendship.

This book was written while I was assistant professor of American studies at the University of Minnesota. I'm so lucky to be in such a welcoming department and to be able to research, write, and conspire with so many amazing colleagues and friends. Jennifer Pierce and Bianet Castellanos have been the best mentors I could have ever imagined. You carefully read and gave invaluable feedback on my book and ensured that it was in the best possible shape. David Karjanen, thank you for being so generous with your work and helping to demystify the publishing process. Kale Fajardo and Brenda Child, I am grateful for your mentorship and for providing necessary resources to write this book. Elaine Tyler May, I still can't believe I'm in the same department with someone of your stature and someone whose work I've admired since I was in college. You've been such a great colleague and model of rigorous scholarly work. Riv-Ellen Prell, your suggestion that I play with my narrative voice has informed the structure of this work, and I thank you for it. Martin Manalansan, although you're a recent addition to the department, we've known each other for a while and your mentorship and feedback on my work is invaluable. Lorena Muñoz and Terrion Williamson, you both entered the department at the same time and, for me at least, at the right time. I can't say enough about what a joy it's been to be able to work with you all. I can't imagine my time at Minnesota without y'all. Angela Boutch, Deja Just, Hongna Bystrom, Melanie Kelly, Colleen Hennen, Zach Rakke, Lauren Sietsema, Rodrigo Sanchez-Chavarria, Christina Martinez, and Christine Powell have been staff in the Department of American Studies who greatly assisted in my writing and research of this book, and I am thankful for their work. While technically not in the American studies department, Kevin Murphy served as chair on two separate occasions while I was writing this book. Kevin, during and in between those stints, you have been pivotal to my development as a scholar. You have an incredibly big heart, and your willingness to take time to listen to my ramblings about my scholarship, provide detailed feedback on my work, and help make contacts with people who could and have facilitated the writing of this book have all truly meant a lot to me. I'm lucky to have you as a colleague, and even luckier to have you as a friend.

Outside the American studies department at the University of Minnesota, I've been fortunate to be surrounded by and work with amazing scholars who offered assistance with this book, namely Matt Rahaim, Michael Gallope, Sumanth Gopinath, Beth Hartman, Rachmi Diyah Larasati, Edén Torres, Jimmy Patiño, Gabriela Spears-Rico, Miranda Joseph, Erin Durban, Jenn Marshall, Karen Ho, Kat Hayes, Jeani O'Brien, Jennifer Gunn, Doug Hartmann, Charles Doss, Keith Mayes, Yuichiro Onishi, Maggie Hennefeld, Tracey Deutsch, David Chang, Sugi Ganeshananthan, J. B. Mayo-Moschkau, Ananya Chatterjea, David Pellow, Teresa Gowan, Susan Craddock, Richa Nagar, Kate Derickson, David Valentine, Vince Diaz, Sonali Pahwa, Zenzele Isoke, Diane Willow, Josephine Lee, and Catherine Squires. A special recognition goes to Jigna Desai for being such a fierce colleague and friend and for modeling how to do transformative work and mentoring. I also want to acknowledge the faculty and staff of the U's Asian American Studies Program—Lisa Park, Teresa Swartz, Jigna Desai, Kale Fajardo, Karen Ho, Erika Lee, Vichet Chhuon, Josephine Lee, Mai Na Lee, Richard Lee, Bic Ngo, Yuichiro Onishi, Juliana Hu Pegues, Moin Syed, Martin Manalansan, and Saymoukda D. Vongsay—for being a significant source of support, community, and organizing.

Much of this book was written, rewritten, and (differently) imagined over the course of two writing groups and late-night dinner conversations with some amazing thinkers at the U. At the start of my time at Minnesota, I was a part of a writing group that comprised, at various points, Aren Aizura, Annie Hill, Siri Suh, Lena Palacios, Kari Smalkoski, and Lorena Muñoz. I learned so much from your feedback as well as reading your works-in-progress, and I am inspired by all the great writing that you all are putting out in the world. I was also fortunate to be a part of and share my work with the Bodies and Borders (aka B2) writing/working group that Sandy Soto and Cindy García organized during my fourth year at Minnesota. I am indebted to my fellow B2 members Cindy García, Sandy Soto, Aren Aizura, Kari Smalkoski, Juliana Hu Pegues, Sima Shakhsari, Jennifer Row, Sayan Bhattacharya, Naimah Petigny, Kevin Murphy, and Jose Meño Santillana. Lastly, there's no doubt in my mind that this book couldn't have been written without the dinner events that Siri Suh, Terrion Williamson, and I had over the past several years. Through the laughs, food, and OFs and Sprites, I was able to think through complex ideas about my work.

This book could also not have been written without the amazing graduate students at the U. Thanks go out to Robert Smith III, Amber Annis, Rudy Aguilar, Sarah Atwood-Hoffman, Christine Bachman-Sanders, Matthew Boynton, Michelle "Chip" Chang, Karla Padrón, Kidiocus Carroll, Agléška Cohen-Rencountre, Vanessa Guzmán, Michelle Lee, Amanda Lugo, K. Mohrman, Mia Fischer, Jessica Lopez Lyman, Hana Maruyama, Brendan McHugh, Soham Patel, Thomas Seweid-DeAngelis, René Esparza, Sasha Suarez, Angela Carter, Rose Miron, Nick-Brie Guarriello, Karisa Butler-Wall, Simi Kang, AK Wright, Alex Mendoza Covarrubias, Waleed Mahdi, Aaron Mallory, Tia Simone-Gardner, Shannon Flaherty, Matthew Tchepikova-Treon, Joe Whitson, Lei Zhang, Mario Obando Jr., and Mingwei Huang. I especially want to thank the graduate students in my "Queer Temporalities" and "Black Cultural Studies" seminars for helping me think through ideas and scholarship that were and are integral to this book: Christine Bachman-Sanders, Shannon Flaherty, Mario Obando Jr., AK Wright, Colin Wingate, Kidiocus Carroll, Noah Barth, Gabriel Schwartzman, Jonelle Walker, Julio Vega Cedeño, and Roy G. Guzmán. I acknowledge and thank the late Jesús Estrada-Pérez, who was the first graduate student I met when I arrived at Minnesota, whose office was across from mine, and whose dedication to justice still inspires.

I workshopped most of this book over a series of conference presentations, invited talks, and writing retreats hosted by the American Studies Association, the Association for Asian American Studies, the Society for Ethnomusicology, the International Association for the Study of Popular Music, the Ford Foundation (which supported my research for this book during my tenure as a Ford Postdoctoral Fellow), the Woodrow Wilson Foundation Career Enhancement Writing Retreat (which also supported my work during my time as a Woodrow Wilson Career Enhancement Fellow), and the Andrew W. Mellon Foundation and the Social Science Research Council (which provided resources and other forms of support for me as Mellon Mays Fellow). Through these events and programs I was able to get feedback on my work and build relationships with people who continue to inform my thinking and way of life. To that end, I thank Alex Weheliye, Cally Waite, Caryl McFarlane, Michelle Scott, Anita Mannur, Jordan Stein, Aaron Lecklider, Brian Halley, Kwame Holmes, Quincy Mills, Keith Miyake, Vijay

Shah, Kareem Khubchandani, Duchess Harris, Shana Redmond, Deborah Wong, Nicole Fleetwood, Derrais Carter, Chandan Reddy, Marlon Bailey, Nicolas Pillai, Jayna Brown, Mejdulene Shomali, Sa'ed Atshan, Leila Ben-Nasr, Jina Kim, Pahole Sookkasikon, Cathy Schlund-Vials, Ashon Crawley, Eric Hung, Kim Park Nelson, Tom Sarmiento, Christina Hanhardt, Cathy Cohen, Robin D. G. Kelley, Roderick Ferguson, Jeffrey McCune, Cassius Adair, Timothy Stewart-Winter, Mpalive Msiska, Ekua Andrea Agha, Hoang Tan Nguyen, Eli Meyerhoff, Jecca Namakkal, Sheela Namakkal, Birgitta Johnson, Adam Radwan, Kadji Amin, Jarvis McInnis, Julius Fleming Jr., Gabriel Solis, Chad Shomura, Roshy Kheshti, Trung PQ Nguyen, Aimee Bahng, C. Riley Snorton, Imani Owens, Natasha P. Bissonauth, Dennis Tyler, Judith Casselberry, Nic John Ramos, Rashida Braggs, Koritha Mitchell, Amber Musser, Thea Quiray Tagle, Andreana Clay, Emily Lordi, Janaka Lewis, Imani Johnson, Jeffrey K. Coleman, Nigel Hatton, Nick Jones, Ryan Ku, A. Naomi Paik, Marcia Ochoa, Jennifer Devere Brody, Fareeda Griffith, Anthony Kwame Harrison, Ali Colleen Neff, Jennifer Stoever, Justin Burton, Griff Rollefson, Sarah Jane Cervenak, Jack Hamilton, Wendy Sung, Jang Wook Huh, Molly McGarry, Jules Gill-Peterson, Summer Kim Lee, John Paul Catungal, Lauren Michele Jackson, J. Lorenzo Perillo, Jenny James, Elizabeth Ault, Alexandra Vazquez, Ashvin Kini, Ernesto Martínez, Jodi Byrd, Kyla Wazana Tompkins, Chinua Thelwell, Jason Ruiz, Regina Kunzel, Treva Lindsey, Matthew Morrison, Karma Chávez, Hilarie Ashton, Teresa Gonzales, Dhiren Panikker, Eva Pensis, Huan He, Karen Jaime, Uri McMillan, Gayle Wald, Fredara Hadley, George Lewis, LaMonda Horton-Stallings, T. Carlis Roberts, and the inimitable Julio Capó Jr. I particularly want to acknowledge Octavio González, Alisha Lola Jones, Regina Bradley, Steven Thrasher, Fred Moten, and Sony Coráñez-Bolton for helping me make it to the finish line. Tavi, thank you for always being there when I need guidance on something or need to figure out an idea. Alisha, we're two peas in a pod whenever we get together, and you seem to always know when to call and text—I appreciate you. Regina, you're an inspiration, a model scholar and person, and I could not have done some things in this book without you. Steven, to quote Charmaine's note to Blanche in the "Sisters and Other Strangers" episode of *The Golden Girls,* you have inspired me more than you'll ever know. Fred, you gave me advice during my first year in grad school that I have held on to and used throughout my career. I thank you for sharing those words with me so many years ago, and I always look forward to reconnecting with you because I always leave a better scholar and person after we talk. Lastly, Sony, your brilliance is only matched by your generosity as a friend. I always marvel at, and am thankful for, both.

The University of Minnesota Press has been amazing to work with in publishing this book. Danielle M. Kasprzak, you understood and saw potential in this work even before I saw it. Thank you for your dedication to seeing this through. Jason Weidemann, you've been an incredibly supportive editor during this whole process. Zenyse Miller, thank you for your assistance and patience with me in putting all the pieces together. I also thank the anonymous two readers for their insightful, necessary, and generative feedback.

Outside the academy, a number of people have been key to keeping me afloat during the time I was working on this book. They are a reliable support network and, being an only child, I consider them family. I love them all, and I hope I can be the kind of rock for them that they have been for me. Jesse Dunbar and TJ Moore, thank you for making sure I have a life outside of writing and teaching, making sure I have fun beyond the page. Elliot James, even though you're fully within the academy like me, what has meant the most to me in terms of our friendship is how little we talk about work. We're invested in each other's wellness in a way that is tied to but also separate from our professional lives; I thank you for making such a friendship possible. While working on the final stages of this book, I met Chris Stedman, and Chris, our frequent music musings have not only greatly informed my book, but they are parts of my day that I often look forward to the most. Roy G. Guzmán, we've been friends since college, and I am thankful for our enduring friendship; your frequent check-ins and words of support mean so much to me. John Orduña, you've always had your door open for me, and you've been there for me through everything: thank you. Aron William Christopher Cobbs, you're a fantastic artist and even better friend, and I wouldn't trade that for anything in the world. Ivan Anderson, I always look forward to our music debates not simply because you're usually wrong (had to get that in there), but because you push me to think about what and how I hear. José Salas, thank you for your wit and humor. Angel Ochoa, you're still my partner in crime, and can always bring a smile to my face. Scott Baillie-Hinojosa, I can always be at my most raw and vulnerable with you, and you've always listened and given me the necessary advice to make it through the day. Ashley Davis, you're a true ride or die, and I'm always humbled by your support. Also, I can't wait for our next trip to party! And lastly, to Tamilia D. Reed, my fellow Floridan, you have such a rare and beautiful gift, and I am honored that you share it with me. You bring joy with you wherever you go, and when I get an email, text, or phone call from you, I am always smiling because I know, whatever the message, it's going to warm my heart. As you and I say, reciprocity is the key to every human relation in life, and so even though I don't have your gift, I'll continue to try my hardest to return the favor.

None of this would have been possible without the love and support from my parents, Patricia and Errol. Thank you for allowing me to be me. More important, thank you for reminding me to be me. I love you fiercely and I love you always.

Notes

Introduction

1. Raga rock is the term used to describe the subgenre of music that (predominantly) white rock bands of the 1960s and 1970s created that contained some sort of Indian influence (via instrumentation and/or structure). These were predominantly, but not exclusively, English artists and bands, and while the Beatles may be the face of raga rock, acts like the Rolling Stones, the Yardbirds, and the Kinks are often associated with the subgenre. As for Madonna, the *Ray of Light* album features Madonna singing a Hindu prayer on "Shanti/Ashtangi." Moreover, Madonna frequently wore temporary henna tattoos and/or bhindis for most of her promotion for the album, including the "Frozen" music video. Like the Beatles with raga rock, Madonna was not the only artist involved in this kind of mainstream commodification of South Asian culture; other stars like Liv Tyler and Gwen Stefani also donned similar style commodities during this period.

2. See particularly Jonathan Bellman, "Indian Resonances in the British Invasion, 1965–68," in *The Exotic in Western Music,* ed. Jonathan Bellman (Boston: Northeastern University Press, 1998), 292–306; Carl Clements, "John Coltrane and the Integration of Indian Concepts in Jazz Improvisation," *Jazz Research Journal* 2, no. 2 (2008): 155–75; Carl Clements, "Musical Interchange between Indian Music and Hip Hop," in *Critical Minded: New Approaches to Hip Hop Studies,* ed. Ellie M. Hisama and Evan Rapport (Brooklyn, N.Y.: Institute for Studies in American Music, 2005), 125–41; Gerry Farrell, "Reflecting Surfaces: The Use of Elements from Indian Music in Popular Music and Jazz," *Popular Music* 17, no. 2 (May 1988): 189–205; Brian Ireland and Sharif Gemie, "Raga Rock: Popular Music and the Turn to the East in the 1960s," *Journal of American Studies* 10, no. 10 (2017): 1–38; Kevin Miller, "Bolly'hood Remix," *Institute for Studies in American Music Newsletter* 34, no. 2 (Summer 2004): 6–8; Sarah Hankins, "So Contagious: Hybridity and Subcultural Exchanges in Hip-Hop's Use of Indian Samples," *Black Music Research Journal* 31, no. 2 (2011): 193–208;

David B. Reck, "The Neon Electric Saraswati: Being Reflections on the Influence of Indian Music on the Contemporary Music Scene in America," *Contributions to Asian Studies* 12 (1978): 3–20; and David B. Reck, "Beatles Orientalis: Influences from Asia in a Popular Song Form," *Asian Music* 16, no. 1 (1985): 83–150. I borrow the term "Indochic" from Sunaina Maira, "Indo-Chic: Late Capitalist Orientalism and Imperial Culture," in *Alien Encounters: Popular Culture in Asian America*, ed. Mimi Thi Nguyen and Thuy Linh Nguyen Tu (Durham, N.C.: Duke University Press, 2007), 221–43.

3. Here, I am in conversation with T. Carlis Roberts's conception of "sono-racial collaboration." But I differ from Roberts, as we will see throughout this book, by not necessarily treating these collective acts as "intentional engagements in which artists employ racialized sound to form and perform interracial rapport." I'm interested in intentional acts as well as collaborative practices that exceed intentionality. For more on sono-racial collaboration, see T. Carlis Roberts, *Resounding Afro Asia: Interracial Music and the Politics of Collaboration* (London: Oxford University Press, 2016).

4. Roberts, *Resounding Afro Asia*, 3.

5. Michel Foucault, *"Society Must Be Defended": Lectures at the Collège de France, 1975–1976*, ed. Mauro Bertani and Alessandro Fontana, trans. David Macey (New York: Picador, 2003), 10.

6. Stuart Hall, "What Is This 'Black' in Black Popular Culture?" *Social Justice* 20, nos. 51–52 (Spring–Summer 1993): 109; Stuart Hall, "Race, Articulation, and Societies Structured in Dominance," in *Sociological Theories: Race and Colonialism* (Paris: UNESCO, 1980), 305–45.

7. Robin D. G. Kelley, *Freedom Dreams: The Black Radical Imagination* (Boston: Beacon Press, 2002).

8. Kelley, *Freedom Dreams*, 2.

9. There was, of course, Afro-Asian work that predated the early 2000s. For exemplary writings, see David Hellwig, "The Afro-American and the Immigrant, 1889–1930: A Study of Black Social Thought" (PhD diss., Syracuse University, 1978); Arnold Shankman "Black on Yellow: Afro-Americans View Chinese Americans, 1850–1935," *Phylon* 39, no. 1 (1978): 1–17; and Gary Y. Okihiro, "Is Yellow Black or White?" in *Margins and Mainstreams: Asians in American History and Culture*, ed. Gary Y. Okihiro (Seattle: University of Washington Press, 1994), 31–63.

10. See, for example, Gerald Horne, *The End of Empires: African Americans in India* (Philadelphia: Temple University Press, 2009); Nico Slate, *Colored Cosmopolitanism: The Shared Struggle for Freedom in the United States and India* (Cambridge, Mass.: Harvard University Press, 2012); Vijay Prashad, *Darker Nations: A People's History of the Third World* (New York: New Press, 2007); Sudarshan Kapur, *Raising Up a Prophet: The African-American Encounter with Gandhi* (Boston: Beacon Press, 1992); Judy Tzu-Chun Wu, *Radicals on the Road: Internationalism, Orientalism, and Feminism during the Vietnam Era* (Ithaca, N.Y.: Cornell University Press, 2013); Nitasha Tamar Sharma, *Hip Hop Desis: South Asian Americans, Blackness, and a Global Race Consciousness* (Durham, N.C.: Duke University Press, 2010); Yuichiro Onishi, *Transpacific Antiracism: Afro-Asian Solidarity in 20th Century Black America,*

Japan, and Okinawa (New York: New York University Press, 2013); Sohail Daulatzai, *Black Star, Crescent Moon: The Muslim International and Black Freedom beyond America* (Minneapolis: University of Minnesota Press, 2012); Laura Pulido, *Black, Brown, Yellow, and Left: Radical Activism in Los Angeles* (Berkeley: University of California Press, 2006); Scott Kurashige, *The Shifting Grounds of Race: Black and Japanese Americans in the Making of Multiethnic Los Angeles* (Princeton, N.J.: Princeton University Press, 2008); Andrew F. Jones and Nikhil Pal Singh, eds., "The Afro Asian Century," special issue of *Positions: East Asia Cultures Critique* 11, no. 1 (March 2003); and Diane Fujino, *Heartbeat of Struggle: The Revolutionary Life of Yuri Kochiyama* (Minneapolis: University of Minnesota Press, 2005).

11. Robin D. G. Kelley, "People in Me," *Colorlines* 1, no. 3 (Spring 1999): 5–7; Bill V. Mullen, *Afro-Orientalism* (Minneapolis: University of Minnesota Press, 2004), xviii; Vijay Prashad, *Everybody Was Kung-Fu Fighting: Afro-Asian Connections and the Myth of Cultural Purity* (Boston: Beacon Press, 2001). For other works that resonate with Afro-Asian polyculturalism, see Heike Raphael-Hernandez and Shannon Steen, *AfroAsian Encounters: Culture, History, Politics* (New York: New York University Press, 2006); Shannon Steen, *Racial Geometries of the Black Atlantic, Asian Pacific, and American Theatre* (New York: Palgrave Macmillan, 2010); Fred Ho and Bill V. Mullen, *Afro Asia: Revolutionary Political and Cultural Connections between African Americans and Asian Americans* (Durham, N.C.: Duke University Press, 2008); Roberts, *Resounding Afro Asia*; Vivek Bald, *Bengali Harlem and the Lost Histories of South Asian America* (Cambridge, Mass.: Harvard University Press, 2013); Sunaina Marr Maira, *Desis in the House: Indian American Youth Culture in New York City* (Philadelphia: Temple University Press, 2002); and Crystal S. Anderson, *Beyond the Chinese Connection: Contemporary Afro-Asian Cultural Production* (Jackson: University Press of Mississippi, 2013).

12. See, for example, Vanita Reddy and Anantha Sudhakar, eds., "Feminist and Queer Afro-Asian Formations," special issue of *Scholar & Feminist Online* 14, no. 3 (2018), http://sfonline.barnard.edu/feminist-and-queer-afro-asian-formations/; Vanita Reddy, "Afro-Asian Intimacies and the Politics and Aesthetics of Cross-Racial Struggle in Mira Nair's *Mississippi Masala*," *Journal of Asian American Studies* 18, no. 3 (2015): 233–63; and Lisa Lowe, *The Intimacies of Four Continents* (Durham, N.C.: Duke University Press, 2015).

13. Vanita Reddy and Anantha Sudhakar, "Introduction: Feminist and Queer Afro-Asian Formations," in "Feminist and Queer Afro-Asian Formations," special issue of *Scholar & Feminist Online* 14, no. 3 (2018), http://sfonline.barnard.edu/feminist-and-queer-afro-asian-formations/introduction-feminist-and-queer-afro-asian-formations/.

14. Kimberlé W. Crenshaw, "Demarginalizing the Intersection of Race and Sex: A Black Feminist Critique of Antidiscrimination Doctrine, Feminist Theory and Antiracist Politics," *University of Chicago Legal Forum* 140 (1989): 139–67; Mari J. Matsuda, "Beside My Sister, Facing the Enemy: Legal Theory out of Coalition," *Stanford Law Review* 3, no. 6 (July 1991): 1183–92.

15. Matsuda, "Beside My Sister, Facing the Enemy," 1189.

16. Grace Kyungwon Hong and Roderick A. Ferguson, "Introduction," in *Strange Affinities: The Gender and Sexual Politics of Comparative Racialization*, ed. Grace Kyungwon Hong and Roderick A. Ferguson (Durham, N.C.: Duke University Press, 2011), 2; Roderick A. Ferguson, *Aberrations in Black: Toward a Queer of Color Critique* (Minneapolis: University of Minnesota Press, 2004), 137. See also *Aberrations in Black* for a more detailed discussion of queer of color critique.

17. Cathy J. Cohen, "Punks, Bulldaggers, and Welfare Queens: The Radical Potential of Queer Politics?" *GLQ* 3, no. 4 (1997): 438, 441.

18. Cohen, "Punks, Bulldaggers, and Welfare Queens," 442.

19. Hortense Spillers, "Mama's Baby, Papa's Maybe: An American Grammar Book," *Diacritics* 17, no 2 (Summer 1987): 64–81; Eric Hayot, *The Hypothetical Mandarin: Sympathy, Modernity, and Chinese Pain* (New York: Oxford University Press, 2009), 139; Nayan Shah, *Stranger Intimacy: Contesting Race, Sexuality, and the Law in the North American West* (Berkeley: University of California Press, 2012); Cathy J. Cohen, "The Radical Potential of Queer? Twenty Years Later," *GLQ* 25, no. 1 (2019): 142; Jasbir K. Puar and Amit Rai, "Monster, Terrorist, Fag: The War on Terrorism and the Production of Docile Patriots," *Social Text* 20, no. 3 (Fall 2003): 117–48; Jasbir K. Puar, *Terrorist Assemblages: Homonationalism in Queer Times* (Durham, N.C.: Duke University Press, 2007); Hong and Ferguson, "Introduction," 18.

20. @tomorrowmanx, "Listen . . . when all the Black producers started infusing Bollywood samples in everything . . . you wanna talk about a fuggin ERA in hip hop/R&B??" Twitter, October 12, 2019, https://twitter.com/tomorrowmanx/status/11 82912204699508736.

21. There's a similar slippage that happens with ERA for "era" as well as ERA for the Equal Rights Amendment, which further adds to how I want to think through these kind of Afro–South Asian collaborative sounds as highly gendered and sexualized formations. I want to thank Jennifer Pierce for helping me with this point.

22. @tomorrowmanx, "Listen . . ."

23. See for example George Lipsitz, *The Possessive Investment in Whiteness: How White People Profit from Identity Politics* (Philadelphia: Temple University Press, 1998); and Greg Tate, ed., *Everything but the Burden: What White People Are Taking from Black Culture* (New York: Broadway, 2003). For a more complicated assessment of cultural appropriation in this way, see Lauren Michele Jackson, *White Negroes: When Cornrows Were in Vogue . . . and Other Thoughts on Cultural Appropriation* (Boston: Beacon Press, 2019).

24. Sunaina Marr Maira, *Desis in the House: Indian American Youth Culture in New York City* (Philadelphia: Temple University Press, 2002).

25. Nitasha Tamar Sharma, *Hip Hop Desis: South Asian Americans, Blackness, and a Global Race Consciousness* (Durham, N.C.: Duke University Press, 2010), 237, 245.

26. Salome Asega, Homi K. Bhabha, Gregg Bordowitz, Joan Kee, Michelle Kuo, Ajay Kurian, and Jacolby Satterwhite, "Cultural Appropriation: A Roundtable," *Artforum*, Summer 2017, 270.

27. Claire Jean Kim, *Bitter Fruit: The Politics of Black–Korean Conflict in New York City* (New Haven, Conn.: Yale University Press, 2000); Helen Heran Jun, *Race for Citizenship: Black Orientalism and Asian Uplift from Pre-Emancipation to Neoliberal America* (New York: New York University Press, 2011).

28. Asega et al., "Cultural Appropriation," 269.

29. Deborah Wong, *Speak It Louder: Asian Americans Making Music* (New York: Routledge, 2004), 190. For more recent works that share and inform my challenge of the "good versus bad" narrative of cultural appropriation, see Lauren Michelle Jackson, *White Negroes: When Cornrows. Were in Vogue . . . and Other Thoughts on Cultural Appropriation* (Boston: Beacon Press, 2019); and Minh-Ha T. Pham, "Why We Should Stop Talking about 'Cultural Appropriation,'" *The Atlantic*, May 15, 2014, https://www.theatlantic.com/entertainment/archive/2014/05/cultural-appropriation-in-fashion-stop-talking-about-it/370826/.

30. Stuart Hall, "Notes on Deconstructing 'The Popular,'" in *People's History and Sociality Theory*, ed. Raphael Samuel (London: Keagan Paul-Routledge, 1981), 227–40.

31. Jack Halberstam, *Female Masculinity* (Durham, N.C.: Duke University Press, 1998), 13; Gayatri Gopinath, *Impossible Desires: Queer Diasporas and South Asian Public Cultures* (Durham, N.C.: Duke University Press, 2005), 22.

1. A Desi Love Supreme

1. Louise Davis Stone, "The Jazz Bit: John Coltrane," *Baltimore Afro-American*, September 1, 1962, 12.

2. Louise Davis Stone, "The Jazz Bit: Record Ratings Charlie Mingus," *Baltimore Afro-American*, February 3, 1962, 15.

3. Ben Ratliff, *Coltrane: The Story of a Sound* (New York: Picador, 2007), 57.

4. John Coltrane, "Interview with Michiel de Ruyter, Part 1," November 19, 1961, https://www.johncoltrane.com/interviews.

5. Stone, "Jazz Bit: John Coltrane," 12.

6. Within the context of this book, "Sonny's Blues" is also noteworthy for its allusions to India.

7. See for example Lindsay Barrett, "The Black Artist in Exile," *Revolution—Africa, Latin America, Asia* 11, no. 1 (March 1964): 131–38; LeRoi Jones and Larry Neal, eds., *Black Fire: An Anthology of Afro-American Writing* (New York: William Morrow, 1968); Ingrid Monson, *Freedom Sounds: Civil Rights Call Out to Jazz and Africa* (New York: Oxford University Press, 2007); Eric Nisenson, *Ascension: John Coltrane and His Quest* (New York: Da Capo Press, 1993); Sonia Sanchez, *We a BaddDDD People* (Detroit: Broadside Press, 1970); Scott Saul, *Freedom Is, Freedom Ain't: Jazz and the Making of the Sixties* (Cambridge, Mass.: Harvard University Press, 2003).

8. See Monson, *Freedom Sounds*.

9. Erica Edwards, *Charisma and the Fictions of Black Leadership* (Minneapolis: University of Minnesota Press, 2012), xviii–xix.

10. James Baldwin, "The Dangerous Road before Martin Luther King," *Harper's Magazine*, February 1961, 42.

11. James Baldwin, Leverne McCummins, and Malcolm X, "Black Muslims vs. the Sit-ins," April 25, 1961, New York, WBAI radio broadcast.

12. Here, I'm thinking especially of *Another Country.*

13. Erica Edwards, "Baldwin and Black Leadership," in *The Cambridge Companion to James Baldwin*, ed. Michele Elam (New York: Cambridge University Press), 150.

14. Lawrie Balfour, "Finding the Words: Baldwin, Race Consciousness, and Democratic Theory," in *James Baldwin Now,* ed. Dwight A. McBride (New York: New York University Press, 1999), 83.

15. Monson, *Freedom Sounds*; Lewis Porter, *John Coltrane: His Life and Music* (Ann Arbor: University of Michigan Press, 2000).

16. James Scott, *Domination and the Arts of Resistance: Hidden Transcripts* (New Haven, Conn.: Yale University Press, 1990), 183.

17. See Gerald Horne, *The End of Empires: African Americans in India* (Philadelphia: Temple University Press, 2009); Nico Slate, *Colored Cosmopolitanism: The Shared Struggle for Freedom in the United States and India* (Cambridge, Mass.: Harvard University Press, 2012); Prashad, *Darker Nations*; Sudarshan Kapur, *Raising Up a Prophet: The African-American Encounter with Gandhi* (Boston: Beacon Press, 1992).

18. Gerald Early, "Ode to John Coltrane: Jazz Musician's Influence on African American Culture," *Antioch Review* 57 (Summer 1999): 372.

19. Mark Anthony Neal, *Looking for Leroy: Illegible Black Masculinities* (New York: New York University Press, 2013), 4.

20. John Coltrane, "Interview with August Blume," June 15, 1958, https://www.johncoltrane.com/interviews.

21. Peter Lavezzoli, *The Dawn of Indian Music in the West* (New York: Continuum, 2006), 277.

22. Francesca T. Royster, *Sounding Like a No-No: Queer Sounds and Eccentric Acts in the Post-Soul Era* (Ann Arbor: University of Michigan Press, 2013), 8.

23. Coltrane, "Interview with August Blume."

24. See, for example, Hafez Modirzadeh, "Aural Archetypes and Cyclic Perspectives in the Work of John Coltrane and Ancient Chinese Music Theory," *Black Music Research Journal* 21, no. 1 (Spring 2001): 75–106.

25. Carl Clements, "John Coltrane and the Integration of Indian Concepts in Jazz Improvisation," *Jazz Research Journal* 2, no. 2 (2008): 161.

26. Monson, *Freedom Sounds*, 298.

27. Jean Clouzet and Michel Delorme, "Entretien avec John Coltrane," *Les Cahiers du Jazz* 8 (1963): 13.

28. Melani McAlister, *Epic Encounters: Culture, Media, and U.S. Interests in the Middle East since 1945* (Berkeley: University of California Press, 2001), 7.

29. John Coltrane, *A Love Supreme,* recorded December 9, 1964, Impulse! Records, B0000A118M, 2003 (1965), compact disc, liner notes.

30. Don DeMichael, "John Coltrane and Eric Dolphy Answer the Jazz Critics," *Down Beat,* April 12, 1962, 22.

31. Clouzet and Delorme, "Entretien avec John Coltrane," 14.

32. Porter, *John Coltrane*, 237.

33. Saul, *Freedom Is, Freedom Ain't*, 257.

34. Saul, *Freedom Is, Freedom Ain't*, 238. Coltrane sought, and this comes through later in my analysis, to connect all sections of *A Love Supreme*, and as a result, each song begins where the last track ends.

35. Ashley Kahn, *A Love Supreme: The Story of John Coltrane's Signature Album* (New York: Da Capo Press, 2002), 104.

36. Olly Wilson, "'It Don't Mean a Thing If It Ain't Got That Swing': The Relationship between African and African American Music," in *African Roots / American Cultures: Africa in the Creation of the Americas*, ed. Sheila S. Walker (Lanham, Md.: Rowman & Littlefield, 2001), 161.

37. Olly Wilson, "The Significance of the Relationship between Afro-American Music and West African Music," *Black Perspective in Music* 2, no. 1 (Spring 1974): 3–22.

38. Kahn, *Love Supreme*, 101.

39. John Coltrane, "Interview with Michiel de Ruyter, Part 4," July 27, 1965, https://www.johncoltrane.com/interviews.

40. Clements, "John Coltrane."

41. Moustafa Bayoumi, "'East of the Sun (West of the Moon)': Islam, the Ahmadis, and African America," *Journal of Asian American Studies* 4 (2001): 261.

42. Porter, *John Coltrane*, 242; Saul, *Freedom Is, Freedom Ain't*, 258.

43. It's worth noting that, given *A Love Supreme*'s ties to sobriety, there's a potential overlap between Coltrane's transposition of the motif in all twelve keys and the Alcoholics Anonymous twelve-step program (the chromatic scale comprises twelve half *steps*). Thus, with the broad conception of God within AA, we can also read the final part of Coltrane's solo not only as an allusion to this more expansive perspective, but also as a statement on and embrace of the various ways in which people believe in a Higher Power.

44. Bayoumi, "East of the Sun," 257.

45. For more on Islam in the United States, see Sohail Daulatzai, *Black Star, Crescent Moon: The Muslim International and Black Freedom beyond America* (Minneapolis: University of Minnesota Press, 2012).

46. Bayoumi, "East of the Sun," 253.

47. Tony Whyton, *Beyond A Love Supreme: John Coltrane and the Legacy of an Album* (Oxford, UK: Oxford University Press, 2013), 19–20.

48. Coltrane, *Love Supreme*, liner notes.

49. Porter, *John Coltrane*, 244.

50. Quoted in Kahn, *Love Supreme*, 124.

51. Porter, *John Coltrane*; Saul, *Freedom Is, Freedom Ain't*.

52. Kahn, *Love Supreme*; Porter, *John Coltrane*, 247

53. I use "known" here to signal the possibilities of other performances that have yet to be analyzed and published as aligning with this style of performance and composition.

54. The family of the fourth girl, Carole Robertson, decided to hold a separate, private funeral.

55. Quoted in Kahn, *Love Supreme*, 79.

56. Ben Ratliff, "Pieces of Jazz History Head to Auction Block," *New York Times*, January 20, 2005, E2; Ratliff also references the auction in his book *Coltrane: The Story of a Sound* (New York: Picador, 2007).

57. Whyton, *Beyond A Love Supreme*, 20.

58. Nikky Finney, "Playing by Ear, Praying for Rain: The Poetry of James Baldwin," *Poetry* 203, no. 6 (March 2014): 582.

59. Fred Moten, *In the Break: The Aesthetics of the Black Radical Tradition* (Minneapolis: University of Minnesota Press, 2003), 186.

60. José Esteban Muñoz, *Disidentification: Queers of Color and the Performance of Politics* (Minneapolis: University of Minnesota Press, 1999); Ashon T. Crawley, *Blackpentecostal Breath: The Aesthetics of Possibility* (New York: Fordham University Press, 2016), 2.

61. Clements, "John Coltrane," 161.

62. Kahn, *Love Supreme*, 123.

63. George Ruckert, *Music in North India: Experiencing Music, Expressing Culture* (New York: Oxford University Press, 2003), 22.

64. Cuthbert Ormond Simpkins, *Coltrane: A Biography* (New York: Herndon House, 1975), 58. The analysis of this section draws partly on Marc Howard Medwin, "Listening in Double Time: Temporal Disunity and Structural Unity in the Music of John Coltrane, 1965–67" (PhD diss., 2008).

65. Ingrid Monson, "Oh Freedom: George Russell, John Coltrane, and Modal Jazz," in *In the Course of Performance: Studies in the World of Musical Improvisation*, ed. Bruno Nettle and Melinda Russell (Chicago: University of Chicago Press, 1998), 162.

66. James Baldwin, *The Fire Next Time* (New York: Vintage Books, 2013), 90.

67. José Esteban Muñoz, *Cruising Utopia: The Then and There of Queer Futurity* (New York: New York University Press, 2009).

68. See Franya Berkman, *Monument Eternal: The Music of Alice Coltrane* (Middletown, Conn.: Wesleyan University Press, 2010).

2. Corner Politics

1. John S. Wilson, "Jazz Returning to Village Gate: But Hereafter Bands Will Have to Risk Low Payment," *New York Times*, December 12, 1969, 74.

2. Hollie I. West, "Changing Trends: Nightclubs Fight Inflationary Cycles," *Los Angeles Times*, June 14, 1969, A6.

3. The sitarist was most likely Khalil Balakrishna, who joined Davis's band in 1972 and befriended Davis only a month prior to the Gate's reopening.

4. Richard Pryor, *Pryor Convictions and Other Life Sentences* (New York: Pantheon Books, 1995), 98.

5. Pryor, *Pryor Convictions*, 100. Pryor recounts the performance as occurring in 1968, but the historical advertisements do not support this, instead indicating 1969 as

the year. This information then suggests that Pryor's infamous trip to Berkeley and involvement with the Black Panthers took place in 1970, not 1969. Pryor's story about Davis kissing Gillespie contributed to the long-standing rumors that Davis was queer. Indeed, Wynton Marsalis once described Davis as having "bisexuality in his sound" and compared Davis to Lester Young, another jazz musician rumored to be queer. For more on queerness and Miles Davis, see Elliott H. Powell, "Queering Miles: Black Masculinity and the Disidentification Praxis of Miles Davis," in *Rethinking Miles Davis*, ed. Nicolas Pillai (Oxford, UK: Oxford University Press, 2021).

6. Jeremy Smith, "'Sell It Black': Race and Marketing in Miles Davis's Early Fusion Jazz," *Jazz Perspectives* 4 (2010): 10.

7. Stephen Davis, "My Ego Only Needs a Good Rhythm Section," in *Miles on Miles: Interviews and Encounters with Miles Davis*, ed. Paul Maher Jr. and Michal K. Dor (Chicago: Lawrence Hill Books, 2009), 145.

8. Davis, "My Ego Only Needs a Good Rhythm Section," 136; Miles Davis, *Miles: The Autobiography* (New York: Smith and Schuster, 1990), 328.

9. Cathy J. Cohen, "Deviance as Resistance: A New Research Agenda for the Study of Black Politics," *Du Bois Review* 1, no. 2 (2004): 29.

10. See Phillip Brian Harper, *"Are We Not Men?" Masculine Anxiety and the Problem of African-American Identity* (London: Oxford Press, 1996); Tracye Matthews, "'No One Ever Asks What a Man's Role in the Revolution Is': Gender and the Politics of the Black Panther Party, 1966–1971," in *The Black Panther Party Reconsidered*, ed. Charles E. Jones (Baltimore: Black Classic Press, 1998), 167–304.

11. For discussions of the Afro-Asian coalitional politics of the Panthers, see Robin D. G. Kelley and Betsy Esch, "Black Like Mao: Red China and Black Revolution," *Souls* 4, no. 1 (1999): 6–41; Diane C. Fujino, *Samurai among Panthers: Richard Aoki on Race, Resistance, and a Paradoxical Life* (Minneapolis: University of Minnesota Press, 2012). For texts on South Asian (Americans) and the Asian American power movement and pan-ethnic identity, see Lavina Dhingra Shankar and Rajini Srikanth, *A Part, Yet Apart: South Asian in Asian America* (Philadelphia: Temple University Press, 1998); Yen Le Espiritu, *Asian American Panethnicity: Bridging Institutions and Identities* (Philadelphia: Temple University Press, 1992); and Nazli Kibria, "Not Asian, Black, or White? Reflections on South Asian American Racial Identity," *Amerasia Journal* 22 (1996): 77–86.

12. bell hooks, *Feminist Theory: From Margin to Center* (Boston: South End Press, 1984).

13. Nikhil Pal Singh, *Black Is a Country: Race and the Unfinished Struggle for Democracy* (Cambridge, Mass.: Harvard University Press, 2004), 193.

14. Marlon B. Bailey and Rashad Shabazz, "Gender and Sexual Geographies of Blackness: Anti-Black Heterotopias (Part 1)," *Gender, Place, & Culture: A Journal of Feminist Geography* 21, no. 3 (2014): 316–21.

15. Michel Foucault and Jay Miskowiec, "Of Other Spaces," *Diacritics* 16, no. 1 (Spring 1986): 22–27; Katherine McKittrick and Clyde Woods, *Black Geographies* (Boston: South End Press, 2007); Bailey and Shabazz, "Gender and Sexual Geographies," 318.

16. See, for example, Davis, *Miles*; Pearl Cleage, *Mad at Miles: A Black Woman's Guide to Truth* (Southfield, Mich.: Cleage Group, 1990); Hazel Carby, *Race Men* (Cambridge, Mass.: Harvard University Press, 2000); Farah Jasmine Griffin and Salim Washington, *Clawing at the Limits of Cool: Miles Davis, John Coltrane, and the Greatest Jazz Collaboration Ever* (New York: St. Martin's Press, 2008); and Farah Jasmine Griffin, "Ladies Sing Miles," in *Miles Davis and American Culture*, ed. Gerald Early (St. Louis: University of Missouri Press, 2001), 180–87.

17. Cohen, "Punks, Bulldaggers, and Welfare Queens," 480. Cohen's concept of "principled coalition work" is in conversation with how Bernice Johnson Reagon frames coalitions. For more information, see Bernice Johnson Reagon, "Coalition Politics: Turning the Century," in *Home Girls: A Black Feminist Anthology*, ed. Barbara Smith (New York: Kitchen Table Press, 1983), 356–68.

18. Examples include Sly and the Family Stone's *There's a Riot Goin' On*, the Impressions' "This Is My Country," Curtis Mayfield's "The Other Side of Town," Aretha Franklin's "Think," Vicki Anderson's "Message from the Soul Sisters," and James Brown's "Say It Loud—I'm Black and I'm Proud."

19. Davis, *Miles*, 298.

20. Kevin Fellezs, *Birds of Fire: Jazz, Rock, Funk, and the Creation of Fusion* (Durham, N.C.: Duke University Press, 2011), 7–9.

21. Fellezs, *Birds of Fire*, 55.

22. Tanisha C. Ford, *Liberated Threads: Black Women, Style, and the Global Politics of Soul* (Chapel Hill: University of North Carolina Press, 2015).

23. To help provide some contextualization to the making of the album, I initially contacted a few musicians who were listed in the liner notes of the most recent reissue of *On the Corner*. Each artist eventually declined my requests for an interview because, contrary to what was written in the record's liner notes, it turned out that they were not involved in the recording sessions.

24. By "various accounts," I'm referring to my use of Davis's autobiography, secondary works on Davis, published interviews with Davis and musicians in Davis's band at the time, and my own interviews with those involved in the recording of *On the Corner*. And I pinpointed shared information among these sources that were related to *On the Corner*'s personnel.

25. Jesse L. MacBurnie Stewart, "Call and Recall: Hybridity, Mobility, and Dialogue between Jazz and Hip Hop Culture" (PhD diss., University of Guelph, 2008).

26. For examples of the various critiques of *On the Corner*, see Paul Tingen, *Miles Beyond: Electric Explorations of Miles Davis, 1967–1991* (New York: Billboard Books, 2001).

27. Tingen, *Miles Beyond*.

28. Davis, *Miles*, 322.

29. Davis, *Miles*, 329.

30. We might interpret Davis's decision to remove the names of the musicians who worked on the album as an insistence on this kind of collectivity.

31. Wilson, "Significance of the Relationship."

32. Badal Roy and Geeta Roy Chowdhury, interview by the author, July 26, 2016. Chowdhury played with Roy on albums featuring Dave Liebman and Lonnie Liston Smith.

33. Other examples include Stevie Wonder's "I Was Made to Love Her," the Spinners' "It's a Shame," the Stylistics' "You Are Everything" and "You Make Me Feel Brand New," and Freda Payne's "Band of Gold."

34. Tingen, *Miles Beyond,* 130.

35. Roy and Chowdhury interview.

36. Matt Rahaim, "Badal Roy," in *The New Grove Dictionary of American Music,* ed. Charles H. Garett (New York: Oxford University Press, 2013), 250.

37. Roy and Chowdhury interview.

38. Vijay Prashad, *The Karma of Brown Folk* (Minneapolis: University of Minnesota Press, 2000), 179.

39. Susan Koshy, "Morphing Race into Ethnicity: Asian Americans and Critical Transformations of Whiteness," *Boundary 2* 28, no. 1 (Spring 2001): 153–94.

40. Mae M. Ngai, *Impossible Subjects: Illegal Aliens and the Making of Modern America* (Princeton, N.J.: Princeton University Press, 2004); Ian Haney-López, *White by Law: The Legal Construction of Race* (New York: New York University Press, 1997).

41. For an incisive critique of state-sanctioned pathologizing of Black households as nonnormative, see Roderick Ferguson, *Aberrations in Black: Toward a Queer of Color Critique* (Minneapolis: University of Minnesota Press, 2004).

42. The pimp / sex worker analysis is informed by Stewart, "Call and Recall."

43. See for example Arnold Hirsch, *Making the Second Ghetto: Race and Housing in Chicago, 1940–1960* (Cambridge, UK: Cambridge University Press, 1983); Thomas Sugrue, *The Origins of the Urban Crisis, Race, and Inequality in Postwar Detroit* (Princeton, N.J.: Princeton University Press, 1996); Robert O. Self, *American Babylon: Race and the Struggle for Postwar Oakland* (Princeton, N.J.: Princeton University Press, 2003); and Howard Gillette Jr., *Camden after the Fall: Decline and Renewal in a Post-Industrial City* (Philadelphia: University of Pennsylvania Press, 2005).

44. Singh, *Black Is a Country*; Robert O. Self, "The Black Panther Party and the Long Civil Rights Era," in *In Search of the Black Panther Party: New Perspectives on a Revolutionary Movement* (Durham, N.C.: Duke University Press, 2006), 15–58; Frantz Fanon, *Les Damnés de la Terre* (Paris: François Maspero, 1961), first published in English as *The Wretched of the Earth* (New York: Grove Press, 1963), 135. Citations are to the Grove Press edition.

45. Ford, *Liberated Threads.*

46. Davis, *Miles,* 322.

47. L. H. Stallings, *Funk the Erotic: Transaesthetics and Black Sexual Cultures* (Urbana: University of Illinois Press, 2015), 69.

48. Sandra McCoy, interview with the author, February 24, 2017.

49. Muñoz, *Cruising Utopia,* 65

50. Corky McCoy, interview with the author, September 26, 2016.

51. During my interviews with both Sandra and Corky McCoy, they alleged that Miles Davis frequently assisted James Baldwin with his mortgage payments for his Saint-Paul-de-Vence home in France. With respect to Vernon Davis, Hazel Carby argues that Davis's embrace of violence against women as a signifier for masculinity was, in part, a way for him to distance himself from Vernon and queerness in general. The *On the Corner* cover's nod to Vernon (and Baldwin) bring some nuance to this argument.

52. Corky McCoy interview.

53. Here I am inspired by Roderick Ferguson's contention about Black queer subjects: "It is not enough to merely recognize their existence. In this moment of transgressions and regulations, we must approach these subjects as sites of knowledge." See Roderick A. Ferguson, *Aberrations in Black: Toward a Queer of Color Critique* (Minneapolis: University of Minnesota Press, 2004), 148

54. Cohen, "Punks, Bulldaggers, and Welfare Queens," 438.

55. Albertson, "The Unmasking of Miles Davis," *Saturday Review*, November 27, 1971, 68.

56. Blair Sobol, "Rock Threads," *Show Magazine*, March 1970, 31–34.

57. I want to thank George Chauncey for his assistance with this.

58. Davis, *Miles*, 310.

59. Davis, *Miles*, 310.

60. Roy and Chowdhury interview.

3. Punks, Freaks, OutKasts, and ATLiens

1. Rick James, *Glow: The Autobiography of Rick James* (New York: Atria Books, 2015), 276.

2. Rick James, *The Flag*, recorded 1985–86, Gordy Records /Motown Records, GCD06185GD, 1986, compact disc, liner notes.

3. OutKast's venture into Afro-futurism and the evil entity Nosamulli is reminiscent of the Afro-futurist funk band Parliament and the frequent villain in their songs, Sir Nose D'Voidoffunk.

4. OutKast, *ATLiens*, OutKast, recorded 1995–96, LaFace Records, 73008-26029 -2, 1996, compact disc, liner notes by Ruben "Big Rube" Bailey.

5. Following the release of *ATLiens*, André 3000 became heavily interested in the work of John Coltrane. For the OutKast double album *Speakerboxxx / The Love Below*, André sampled and covered Coltrane's rendition of "My Favorite Things" (whose version was purportedly based on an Indian cover of the Rodgers and Hammerstein standard), he has spoken in interviews about his frequent listening of *A Love Supreme*, and he even sports a Coltrane poster in one of his musical workspaces.

6. I borrow "outsider racialization" from Angelo Ancheta, *Race, Rights, and the Asian American Experience* (New Brunswick, N.J.: Rutgers University Press, 1998).

7. Sources differ on whether he was Shankar's cousin or another relative. For more information see James, *Glow*; Rick James, *The Confessions of Rick James: Memoirs of*

a Super Freak (Phoenix: Colossus Books, 2007); and Peter Benjaminson, *Super Freak: The Life of Rick James* (Chicago: Chicago Review Press, 2017).

8. James, *Glow*, 151.

9. LeRoi Johnson, interview with the author, October 20, 2017.

10. Johnny Lee, interview with the author, December 1, 2017.

11. Johnson interview.

12. Alexandra T. Vazquez, "Salon Philosophers: Ivy Queen and Surprise Guests Take Reggaetón Aside," in *Reggaetón*, ed. Raquel Z. Rivera, Wayne Marshall, and Deborah Pacini Hernandez (Durham, N.C.: Duke University Press, 2009), 301.

13. Vazquez, "Salon Philosophers," 301; Barbara Johnson, *A World of Difference* (Baltimore: Johns Hopkins University Press, 1989).

14. Young, Palmer, St. Nicholas, and McJohn would have significant careers in their own right. Young, most prominently, as a solo artist as well as for his work in Buffalo Springfield and Crosby, Stills, Nash, and Young; Palmer became a member of Buffalo Springfield as well; and St. Nicholas and McJohn were members of Steppenwolf.

15. For a classic work that unsettles the association of Canada and whiteness, and focuses on Blackness instead, see Rinaldo Walcott, *Black Like Who? Writing Black Canada* (Toronto: Insomniac Press, 1997).

16. See for example Sanjay Sharma, John Hutnyk, and Ashwani Sharma, *Dis-Orienting Rhythms: The Politics of the New Asian Dance Music* (Atlantic Highlands, N.J.: Zed Books, 1997); Jacqueline Warwick, "'Make Way for the Indian': Bhangra Music and South Asian Presence in Toronto," *Popular Music & Society* 24, no. 2 (2000): 25–44; Jerome Teelucksingh, "A Global Diaspora: The Indo-Trinidadian Diaspora in Canada, the United States, and England, 1967–2007," *Diaspora Studies* 4, no. 2 (2011): 139–54; Nabeel Zuberi, *Sounds English: Transnational Popular Music* (Urbana: University of Illinois Press, 2001); and Nabeel Zuberi and Jon Stratton, eds., *Black Popular Music in Britain since 1945* (Farnham, UK: Ashgate, 2014).

17. James, *Glow*, 195. James uses the term "rebellious" in *Confessions of a Superfreak*.

18. Jayna Brown, Patrick Deer, and Tavia Nyong'o, "Punk and Its Afterlives," *Social Text* 31, no. 3 (2013): 5.

19. See for example Tavia Nyong'o, "Punk'd Theory," *Social Text* 23, nos. 3–4 (2005): 19–34; Tavia Nyong'o, "Brown Punk: Kalup Linzy's Musical Anticipations," *TDR: The Drama Review* 54, no. 3 (2010): 71–86; and Brown, Deer, and Nyong'o, "Punk and Its Afterlives."

20. Jennifer C. Nash, *The Black Body in Ecstasy: Reading, Race, and Pornography* (Durham, N.C.: Duke University Press, 2014), 439.

21. Cohen, "'Deviance as Resistance,'" 29.

22. Cohen, "'Deviance as Resistance,'" 29–30.

23. L. H. Stallings, *Funk the Erotic :Transaesthetics and Black Sexual Cultures* (Champaign: University of Illinois Press, 2015), 90. It is also worth noting that, as Peter Benjaminson suggests in his biography of Rick James, James's solo career began in gay bathhouses in the U.S. South. His first single, "You and I," from his 1978 debut album *Come Get It!,* stalled on radio, and so James soon suggested to a gay friend DJ

to play it in an Atlanta bathhouse. The single quickly gained momentum first in bathhouses and then reached dance floors and radio stations.

24. Janet M. Davis, "Spectacles of South Asia at the American Circus, 1890–1940," *Visual Anthropology* 6, no. 2 (1993): 121–38; Shah, *Stranger Intimacy*; Puar, *Terrorist Assemblages*; Susan Koshy, *Sexual Naturalization: Asian Americans and Miscegenation* (Palo Alto, Calif.: Stanford University Press, 2005).

25. James's sitar performance can be heard on "You Are My Heaven" and "Lonely."

26. Examples of the Mary Jane Girls' erotic songs include "All Night Long," "In My House," "Wild and Crazy Love," and "Leather Queen." For more information on the history of the PMRC, see Claude Chastagner, "The Parents' Music Resource Center: From Information to Censorship," *Popular Music* 18, no. 2 (May 1999): 179–92.

27. Robert Hilburn, "Flamboyant Rick James Earns a Split Decision: Rick James," *Los Angeles Times*, August 22, 1983, G1.

28. An alternate version of this back cover exists with James wearing a long jewelry-studded black coat, his hand still on his popped-out hip, he's still carrying the freak flag, and he is wearing thigh-high red leather heels that are similar to those seen on the back cover of *Street Songs*. This cover further evidences what I'm reading as the Black queer aesthetics of James on *Street Songs* and *The Flag*.

29. James, *The Flag*, liner notes.

30. I interviewed Chris Callis, who photographed *The Flag*, and asked him about the photo shoot. While the interview discussed everything from who Rick James was as a celebrity to his rivalry with Prince, Callis repeatedly informed me that he could not "remember much" about the photo shoot other than that "it was different" from previous album photo shoots that Callis had with James. Despite not recalling details of the session, Callis's memory of difference underscores my argument that James saw *The Flag* as a site for new creative expression. Chris Callis, interview with the author, November 20, 2017.

31. Lee interview.

32. Lee interview.

33. Albums on vinyl and CD refer to the track as "Om Raga," but streaming platforms like Spotify and Tidal call it "Rick's Raga."

34. Anne Danielsen, *Presence and Pleasure: The Grooves of James Brown and Parliament* (Middletown, Conn.: Wesleyan University Press, 2006), 73.

35. This use of "shame and pity" is reminiscent of James's 1981 song "Mr. Policeman" from *Street Songs*. It's on "Mr. Policeman" that James refers to racist and anti-sex work police surveillance and violence as a "shame and disgrace." In connecting the two, we might read "Funk in America / Silly Little Man" as a transnational iteration of "Mr. Policeman," putting the military–industrial complex and prison–industrial complex in conversation.

36. Stallings, *Funk the Erotic*, xii.

37. Lee interview.

38. Shana L. Redmond, *Anthem: Social Movements and the Sounds of Solidarity in the African Diaspora* (New York: New York University Press, 2014), 2.

39. Here, I'm especially considering the resonances between James's *The Flag* and Marlon Riggs's 1991 film *Anthem*.

40. Prince is actually an interesting bridge between Rick James and André 3000. Prince was James's contemporary, but also someone who opened for James and, according to James, stole much of James's act. Most interesting, however, is that there is, or perhaps was, a South Asianness to Prince that connects all three artists. Following James's release of *The Flag*, Prince released his own political album, *Sign o' the Times*. The record initially featured the Revolution member Wendy Melvoin playing the electric sitar. But after Prince fired the band, he removed and/or lowered the levels of Melvoin's sitar. Faint remnants of her playing can be heard on the tracks "Strange Relationship," "The Cross," and "Adore."

41. Imani Perry, *Prophets of the Hood: Politics and Poetics in Hip Hop* (Durham, N.C.: Duke University Press, 2004), 103.

42. Perry, *Prophets of the Hood*, 107.

43. Perry, *Prophets of the Hood*, 103.

44. Samuel A. Floyd, *The Power of Black Music: Interpreting Its History from Africa to the United States* (New York: Oxford University Press, 1996).

45. Regina N. Bradley, "*ATLiens* Turns 20: OutKast's Past–Future Visions of the Hip-Hop South," *Black Perspectives*, September 7, 2016.

46. Vince Robinson, interview with the author, December 8, 2017.

47. Robinson interview, December 8, 2017.

48. C. Riley Snorton, *Nobody Is Supposed to Know: Black Sexuality on the Down Low* (Minneapolis: University of Minnesota Press, 2014), 122.

49. *Driven*, season 3, episode 23, "OutKast," aired April 25, 2004, on VH1.

50. For more on this kind of historical racialized violence, see Joan M. Jensen, *Passage from India: Asian Indian Immigrants in North American* (New Haven, Conn.: Yale University Press, 1988).

51. Vince Robinson, interview with the author, December 5, 2017.

52. Vivek Bald, *Bengali Harlem and the Lost Histories of South Asian America* (Cambridge, Mass.: Harvard University Press, 2013), 50.

53. Bald, *Bengali Harlem*, 50.

54. Quoted in Meenasarani Murugan, "Exotic Television: Technology, Empire, and Entertaining Globalism" (PhD diss., 2015), 81; quoted in Bald, *Bengali Harlem*, 50. Original citations are as follows: "How to Solve the Race Problem," *Ebony* 13, no. 3 (January 1958): 80; and "How Dark Negroes 'Pass' Down South," *Jet Magazine*, September 8, 1955, 10–12.

55. Bald, *Bengali Harlem*, 50.

56. Paul A. Kramer, "The Importance of Being Turbaned," *Antioch Review* 69, no. 2 (Spring 2011): 208–11.

57. Further examples of turbaned African American male musicians include Chuck Willis, the Turbans, Screamin' Jay Hawkins, Lonnie Smith, and Rudy Ray Moore.

58. Puar, *Terrorist Assemblages*, 169.

59. Bradley, "*ATLiens* Turns 20."

60. OutKast, *ATLiens,* liner notes.

61. Kelley, *Freedom Dreams,* 2.

62. Sohail Daulatzai, *Black Star, Crescent Moon: The Muslim International and Black Freedom beyond America* (Minneapolis: University of Minnesota Press, 2012), 109.

63. Royster, *Sounding Like a No-No,* 170. Royster also discusses Sun Ra's other queer gestures like his rumored dissident sexual practices and nonnormative musical and visual aesthetics.

64. Alondra Nelson, "Afrofuturism: Past–Future Visions," *Color Lines,* Spring 2000, 34–37; Ramzi Fawaz, *The New Mutants: Superheroes and the Radical Imagination of American Comics* (New York: New York University Press, 2016), 147.

65. Khyati Y. Joshi and Jigna Desai, "Discrepancies in Dixie: Asian Americans and the South," in *Asian Americans in Dixie: Race and Migration in the South,* ed. Khyati Y. Joshi and Jigna Desai (Urbana: University of Illinois Press, 2013), 1.

66. Fawaz, *New Mutants,* 28.

67. Quoted in Sarah Hankins, "So Contagious: Hybridity and Subcultural Exchange in Hip-Hop's Use of Indian Samples," *Black Music Research Journal* 31, no. 2 (Fall 2011): 201.

68. Uri McMillan, *Embodied Avatars: Genealogies of Black Feminist Art and Performance* (New York: New York University Press, 2016), 39. For examples of studies on Baartman, Chang and Eng, and Sewally/Jones, see Patricia Hill Collins, *Black Sexual Politics: African Americans, Gender, and the New Racism* (New York: Routledge, 2004); Cynthia Wu, *Chang and Eng Reconnected: The Original Siamese Twins in American Culture* (Philadelphia: Temple University Press, 2012); and Tavia Nyong'o, *The Amalgamation Waltz: Race, Performance, and the Ruses of Memory* (Minneapolis: University of Minnesota Press, 2009), respectively.

69. Lowe, *Intimacies of Four Continents,* 19.

70. Stallings, *Funk the Erotic,* 2.

71. Stallings, *Funk the Erotic,* 183.

4. Recovering Addict(ive)

1. Dedra S. Davis, "Press Release: $500 Million SHOULD Hurt!" September 13, 2002, http://o2aa2b1.netsolhost.com/events.html; Jon Caramanica, "Indi Irate," *Entertainment Weekly,* August 16, 2002, https://ew.com/article/2002/08/16/india-irate/.

2. Joe D'Angelo, "Dr. Dre, Interscope Stung with $500 Million Lawsuit over 'Addictive,'" *MTV News Online,* September 19, 2002, http://www.mtv.com/news/articles/1457672/dr-dre-sued-over-addictive.jhtml.

3. D'Angelo, "Dr. Dre."

4. While in no way exhaustive, a list of South Asian–inspired songs that were released after "Addictive" and were arguably recorded to cash in on its popularity include "Toxic," "(I Got That) Boom Boom," "Me against the World (Rishi Rich's Desi Kulcha Remix)," and "My Prerogative" by Britney Spears; "React" by Erick Sermon and Redman; "Get in Touch with Us" and "Shake Ya Bum Bum" by Lil' Kim; "What's

Happenin'" by Method Man; "Rebel Music" by Wyclef Jean; and "Don't Phunk with My Heart" and "My Humps" by the Black Eyed Peas.

5. Joanna Demers, *Steal This Music: How Intellectual Property Law Affects Musical Creativity* (Athens: University of Georgia Press: 2006), 101–2.

6. Wayne Marshall and Jayson Beaster-Jones, "It Takes a Little Lawsuit: The Flowering Garden of Bollywood Exoticism in the Age of Its Technological Reproducibility," *South Asian Popular Culture* 10, no. 3 (2012): 2.

7. Sharma, *Hip Hop Desis*, 225.

8. Roberts, *Resounding Afro Asia*, 168.

9. Roberts, *Resounding Afro Asia*, 157.

10. Roberts, *Resounding Afro Asia*, 157.

11. Jigna Desai, *Beyond Bollywood: The Cultural Politics of South Asian Diasporic Film* (New York: Routledge, 2004).

12. For more on the politics of respectability and the politics of silence, see Evelynn M. Hammonds, "Toward a Genealogy of Black Female Sexuality: The Problematic of Silence," in *Feminist Genealogies, Colonial Legacies, Democratic Futures,* ed. M. Jacqui Alexander and Chandra Talpade Mohanty (New York: Routledge, 1997), 170–82; Evelynn M. Hammonds, "Black (W)holes and the Geometry of Black Female Sexuality," *Differences* 6, nos. 2–3 (1994): 126–45; Evelyn Brooks Higginbotham, *Righteous Discontent: The Women's Movement in the Black Baptist Church, 1880–1990* (Cambridge, Mass.: Harvard University Press, 1993); Darlene Clark Hine, "Rape and the Inner Lives of Black Women in the Middle West: Preliminary Thoughts on the Culture of Dissemblance," *Signs* 14, no. 4 (Summer 1989): 912–20; Brittney Cooper, *Beyond Respectability: The Intellectual Thought of Race Women* (Urbana: University of Illinois Press, 2017); Treva B. Lindsey, *Colored No More: Reinventing Black Womanhood in Washington, D.C.* (Urbana: University of Illinois Press, 2017); and Joan Morgan, "Why We Got Off: Moving Towards a Black Feminist Politics of Pleasure," *The Black Scholar* 45, no. 4 (2015): 36–46.

13. Roberts, *Resounding Afro Asia*, 165.

14. D'Angelo, "Dr. Dre."

15. Marshall and Beaster-Jones, "It Takes a Little Lawsuit," 2.

16. Marshall and Beaster-Jones, "It Takes a Little Lawsuit," 2.

17. Regula Qureshi, "How Does Music Mean? Embodied Memories and the Politics of Affect in the Indian 'Sarangi,' " *American Ethnologist* 27 (2000): 813.

18. Marshall and Beaster-Jones, "It Takes a Little Lawsuit," 3.

19. Truth Hurts, interview with the author, September 24, 2013.

20. Hurts interview.

21. Bryan Brock, e-mail interview with the author, June 5, 2013.

22. Moya Bailey and Trudy, "On Misogynoir: Citation, Erasure, and Plagiarism," *Feminist Media Studies* 18, no. 4 (2018): 1–7.

23. Patricia Hill Collins, *Black Feminist Thought: Knowledge, Consciousness, and the Politics of Empowerment* (New York: Routledge, 1991).

24. Richard Zumkhawala-Cook, "Bollywood Gets Funky: American Hip-Hop, Basement Bhangra, and the Racial Politics of Music," in *Global Bollywood: Travels of Hindi Song and Dance,* edited by Sangita Gopal and Sujata Moorti (Minneapolis: University of Minnesota Press, 2008), 315–16.

25. Roberts, *Resounding Afro Asia,* 159.

26. See Lisa Duggan, Nan D. Hunter, and Carole S. Vance, "False Promises: Feminist Antipornography Legislation," in *Sex Wars: Sexual Dissent and Political Culture* (1985; repr., New York: Routledge, 2006), 43–64; Pat Califia, "Anti-Anti-Porn," *Off Our Backs,* October 1980, 25; and Amber Hollibaugh and Cherrie Moraga, "What We're Rollin' around in Bed With: Sexual Silences in Feminism," *Heresies* 12 (1981): 58–62.

27. Amber Jamilla Musser, *Sensational Flesh: Race, Power, and Masochism* (New York: New York University Press, 2014), 34.

28. Ariane Cruz, *The Color of Kink: Black Women, BDSM, and Pornography* (New York: New York University Press, 2016), 11; Joan Morgan "Why We Get Off: Moving towards a Black Feminist Politics of Pleasure," *The Black Scholar* 45, no. 4 (2015): 40.

29. Vijay Mishra, *Bollywood Cinema: Temples of Desire* (New York: Routledge, 2002), 104; Sanjay Srivastava, "Voice, Gender, and Space in Time of Five-Year Plans: The Idea of Lata Mangeshkar," *Economic and Political Weekly,* May 14, 2004, 2022.

30. Pavitra Sundar, "Meri Awaaz Suno: Women, Vocality, and Nation in Hindi Cinema," *Meridians: Feminism, Race, Transnationalism* 8 (2007): 149.

31. And, in the spirit of the Mary Jane Girls' song "In My House," Truth Hurts's reference to a male partner taking care of "home" might also refer to a vagina.

32. Nabeel Zuberi, "Sampling South Asian Music," in *South Asian Technospaces,* ed. Radhika Gajjala and Venkataramana Gajjala (New York: Peter Lang, 2008), 59.

33. For more on the analysis on the blending temporalities and bodies that occur in sampling, see Elliott H. Powell, "The Ghosts Got You: Hip-Hop, Sampling, and the Future of Intellectual Property," in *The Oxford Handbook of Hip Hop Music,* ed. Justin D. Burton and Jason Lee Oakes (Oxford, UK: Oxford University Press, 2018), https://www.doi.org/10.1093/oxfordhb/9780190281090.013.29.

34. Roberts, *Resounding Afro Asia,* 166.

35. Juana María Rodríguez, "Queer Sociality and Other Sexual Fantasies," *GLQ* 17, nos. 2–3 (2011): 331–48.

36. Gayatri Gopinath, "Bollywood Spectacles: Queer Diasporic Critique in the Aftermath of 9/11," *Social Text* 23, nos. 3–4 (Fall–Winter 2005): 157.

37. Hurts interview.

38. Corey Takahashi, "Musical Masala," *Vibe,* February 2003, 96.

39. Hurts interview.

40. See the Black Eyed Peas, *Monkey Business,* recorded 2004, Interscope Records, B00096S3RC, 2005, compact disc.

5. Do(ing) Something Different

1. It should be noted that Timbaland also produced a song for her debut as well.

2. Bill Pettaway, telephone interview with the author, March 18, 2008.

3. It's also possible that Saregama's lawsuit against "Addictive" played a part in motivating Timbaland to "do something different." Timbaland was already involved in a lawsuit concerning Jay-Z's hit "Big Pimpin', which Timbaland produced and which sampled an Egyptian recording. And so Timbaland might have been concerned that, in light of the "Addictive" and "Big Pimpin'" lawsuits, his continued use of South Asian and Middle Eastern songs would open himself up to further copyright infringement litigation.

4. Sasha Frere-Jones, "Hip-Hop Is a Guest at the Indian Wedding," *New York Times*, August 3, 2003, 2.23.

5. Karl Marx, *Capital: A Critique of Political Economy, Volume One*, trans. Ben Fowkes (London: Penguin Books, 1990); Fred Moten, *In the Break: The Aesthetics of the Black Radical Tradition* (Minneapolis: University of Minnesota Press, 2003).

6. Chronologically, Shwari's first appearance on a song tied to Timbaland was Slum Village's "Disco" remix, which features Timbaland and Shwari in the music video. However, Timbaland's associate Brian Kidd actually produced the song, and Timbaland was not involved in its creation.

7. *The Blueprint* is one of Jay-Z's most critically acclaimed and commercially successful albums. It is notable for its theme of introspection as well as the music's production, which focuses on samples of soul music that are often sped up and pitched; this style, much like South Asian samples, soon led to a number of rappers releasing music with a similar aesthetic.

8. Jay-Z references Osama Bin Laden because *The Blueprint* was released on September 11, 2001; despite the attacks, the album sold extremely well during its first week. "Hov" is one of Jay-Z's nicknames.

9. Monika Mehta, "What's behind Film Censorship: The *Khalnayak* Debates," *Jouvert* 5 (2001), https://legacy.chass.ncsu.edu/jouvert/v5i3/mehta.htm.

10. Gopinath, *Impossible Desires*, 111.

11. Jason King, "Any Love: Silence, Theft, and Rumor in the Work of Luther Vandross," *Callaloo* 23, no. 1 (Winter 2000): 426.

12. Jason Stanyek and Benjamin Piekut, "Deadness: Technologies of the Intermundane," *TDR: The Drama Review* 54, no. 1 (201): 14.

13. Stanyek and Piekut, "Deadness," 20.

14. Carolyn Dinshaw, Lee Edelman, Roderick A. Ferguson, Carla Freccero, Elizabeth Freeman, Judith Halberstam, Annamarie Jagose, Christopher Nealon, and Nguyen Tan Hoang, "Theorizing Queer Temporalities: A Roundtable Discussion," *GLQ* 13 (2007): 159.

15. Joseph G. Schloss, *Making Beats: The Art of Sample-Based Hip-Hop* (Middletown, Conn.: Wesleyan University Press, 2004), 1. For more information on "schizophonia," see Steven Feld, "From Schizophonia to Schismogenesis: On the Discourses and Commodification Practices of World Music," in *Music Grooves: Essays and Dialogues*, ed. Charles Keil and Steven Feld (Chicago: University of Chicago Press), 257–90. Stanyek and Piekut are notably cautious of the schizophonia, which they find to be "itself a problematic, tautological term that seems to describe an exception (sound

severed from source) to some impossible, full presence (sound as identical with its source . . .). Indeed, schizophonia describes sound itself. All sounds are severed from their sources—that's what makes sound sound. Rhizophonia is our term for taking account both of sound's extensity and the impossibility of a perfect identity between sound and source." Stanyek and Piekut, "Deadness," 19.

16. Molly McGarry. *Ghosts of Futures Past: Spiritualism and the Cultural Politics of Nineteenth-Century America* (Berkeley: University of California Press, 2008), 2.

17. For a deeper history into the ways fashion and gender intersect within Black male masculinity, see Monica Miller, *Slaves to Fashion: Black Dandyism and the Styling of Black Diasporic Identity* (Durham, N.C.: Duke University Press, 2009). Moreover, this queer way of reading/listening to "The Bounce" is particularly apt for the ways in which male rappers routinely utilize queer and transphobic language toward other male rappers (mostly using the language of "lifting/pulling up/down skirts") to shore up masculinity and patriarchal norms. See, for example, Audio Two's classic 1987 hip-hop record "Top Billin' ," which Kanye West interpolates on "The Bounce."

18. Elizabeth Wood, "Sapphonics," in *Queering the Pitch: The New Gay and Lesbian Musicology,* ed. Philip Brett, Elizabeth Wood, and Gary C. Thomas (New York: Routledge, 1994), 27.

19. Wood, "Sapphonics," 32.

20. Wood, "Sapphonics," 33.

21. Quoted in Indus at University of California Berkeley, *Andaaz* 1 (August 2003): 15.

22. Zuberi, "Sampling South Asian Music," 64.

23. Hannon Lane, interview with the author, May 16, 2013.

24. Jimmy Douglass, interview with the author, July 2, 2019.

25. Frere-Jones, "Hip-Hop Is a Guest," 2.23.

26. Sharma, *Hip Hop Desis,* 262.

27. Zuberi, "Sampling South Asian Music," 64.

28. Reddy and Sudhakar, "Introduction." Reddy and Suhakar also extend this analysis to include Afro-Asian "bromances" (e.g. Du Bois and Lala Lajpat Rai).

29. Stuart Hall, "Race, Articulation, and Societies Structured in Dominance," in *Sociological Theories: Race and Colonialism* (Paris: UNESCO, 1980), 305–45.

30. Pettaway interview.

31. While it might look the same, this is notably different from the "Addictive" video because, as Beaster-Jones and Marshall explain, "Addictive" highlighted the use of North African dance traditions, like belly dancing, in certain Bollywood cinema.

32. Lane interview.

33. See Murray Forman, *The 'Hood Comes First: Race, Space, and Place in Rap and Hip-Hop* (Middletown, Conn.: Wesleyan University Press, 2002).

Epilogue

1. Rebecca Kumar, "'Let Yo Booty Do That Yoga': Black Goddess Politics," *Scholar & Feminist Online* 14, no. 3 (2018), http://sfonline.barnard.edu/feminist-and-queer -afro-asian-formations/let-yo-booty-do-that-yoga-black-goddess-politics/.

2. Kumar, "Let Yo Booty."

3. See, for example, Carolyn Cooper, *Noises in the Blood: Orality, Gender, and the "Vulgar" Body in Jamaican Popular Culture* (Durham, N.C.: Duke University Press, 1995).

4. Daphne A. Brooks, "'All That You Can't Leave Behind': Black Female Soul Singing and the Politics of Surrogation in the Age of Catastrophe," *Meridians: Feminism, Race, Transnationalism* 8, no. 1 (2008): 180–204.

5. Bald, *Bengali Harlem*.

6. Kumar, "Let Yo Booty."

7. Adrija Bose, "Coldplay Takes Its Love for India All the Way to Their Super Bowl Performance," *Huffington Post India,* February 8, 2016, https://www.huffington post.in/2016/02/08/coldplay-superbowl_n_9184596.html.

8. Mars's set paid homage to Oakland native MC Hammer.

9. For more on the Black queer thematics in "Formation" (including Black queer and trans people critiquing and filing a lawsuit against Beyoncé for copyright infringement), see Marquis Bey, "Beyoncé's Black (Ab)Normal: Baaad Insurgency and the Queerness of Slaying," *Black Camera* 9, no. 1 (2017): 164–78; and Lauron Kehrer, "Who Slays? Queer Resonances in Beyoncé's *Lemonade,*" *Popular Music and Society* 42, no. 1 (2019): 82–98.

Index

12–13, 70, 132, 145; and "Get Ur Freak
On," 100–101; and Rick James, 70, 73,
78, 81, 84; and OutKast, 70, 96,
98–99; performance, 3; and Rajé
Shwari, 124, 126, 134, 136, 138–40;
studies, 6–7, 11–12, 138; and Truth
Hurts, 107–8, 111–12, 116, 119–21
Aftermath Records, 105, 121
Ahmadiyya Islam, 31, 38
AIDS, 9, 69–70, 81–84, 88, 145; and
activism, 82–83
"Alabama" (Coltrane), 33–34, 37
alap, 36–37, 81
aliens, 68–70, 88–89, 93–97, 100
alliances, 7–9, 17, 69; Afro–South Asian,
54, 83, 96, 98, 107, 136
Amar, 140
America. *See* United States
anarchism, 78, 82
Anderson, Vicki, 46, 166n18
André 3000, 15, 65–70, 86–99, 145,
168n5, 171n40; as Bin Hamin, 68,
93–94, 96, 98–99; and Jamaica,
67–68
anthems, 85, 101
anti-Blackness, 3, 6, 34, 42, 87, 92
anti-imperial politics, 6–7, 15–16, 23
anti-racist activism, 6–7, 15, 21, 23, 79
antiwar politics, 74, 83–85
appropriation: and Beyoncé/Coldplay
song, 143; and Black musicians,
10–12, 106–7, 133; and white musicians, 3, 73
Arabic, 68, 93–94
Ascension (Coltrane), 22, 39
Asia, 6, 31, 91, 99–100; South Asia, 16,
91, 106–7, 109, 112, 134. *See also* Asian
Americans; Asian diaspora
Asian Americans, 6, 43, 96–98; and
"model minority" trope, 9, 53, 98.
See also South Asian Americans
Asian diaspora, 6–7, 107, 138
Atlanta, Georgia, 15, 85–90, 170n23

ATLiens (OutKast), 15, 67–70, 86, 88–
90, 92–99; liner notes for, 68, 89, 94

"Baby Boy" (Beyoncé), 142–43, 145
Bailey, Marlon, 45
Bailey, Ruben "Big Rube," 86
Balakrishna, Khalil, 43, 55, 164n3
Bald, Vivek, 91–92, 143
Baldwin, James, 14, 20–27, 35, 38–39, 60,
85–86
Bandung conference, 6, 83–84
Bayoumi, Moustafa, 30–31
Beaster-Jones, Jayson, 106, 109, 111
Beatles, the, 1–3, 72, 157n1
belly dancing, 109, 139, 176n31
Benjamin, André "André 3000," 15,
65–70, 86–99, 145, 168n5, 171n40; as
Bin Hamin, 68, 93–94, 96, 98–99; and
Jamaica, 67–68
Beyoncé, 4, 141–43, 145, 150, 177n9; and
"Baby Boy," 142–43, 145; "Formation,"
141, 143–45; and "Hymn for the
Weekend," 143–44; *Lemonade,* 141
Bhabha, Homi, 11–12
Bhosle, Asha, 136–37
Big Boi, 65–68, 70, 87–90, 93–94, 96–99
Big Reese, 90–91
Bin Hamin (character), 68, 93–94, 96,
98–99
Bitches Brew (Davis), 42, 47, 62
Black aesthetics, 69, 74
Black alterity, 53
Black anality, 75
Black Arts Movement, 20, 59
Black Caribbean culture, 68, 73, 142
Black consciousness movement, 62
Black feminism, 16, 144
Black freedom struggles, 20, 66
Black geographies, 45
Black masculinity, 14–15, 24, 74, 90–93
Black nationalism, 43
Blackness, 4–5, 14–15, 106; anti, 3, 6, 34,
42, 87, 92; and Miles Davis, 45, 50–51,

ELLIOTT H. POWELL is associate professor of American studies at the University of Minnesota.

CPSIA information can be obtained
at www.ICGtesting.com
Printed in the USA
JSHW030916280123
36810JS00004B/185

9 781517 910044